Stanley Kubrick Companion

Stanley Kubrick Companion

James Howard

B.T. Batsford Ltd
London

First published by B T Batsford, 1999
583 Fulham Road
London SW6 5BY

© James Howard 1999

Printed by Polestar Wheatons Ltd, Exeter

A catalogue record for this book is available from the British Library.

ISBN 0 7134 8487 X

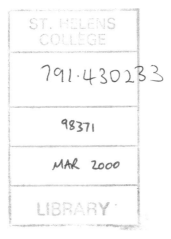

CONTENTS

ACKNOWLEDGEMENTS

for Buzzy Bellew (1981-98) and Oscar McFingal (1984-99)

My grateful thanks to the following for the help, advice and encouragement they were able to offer: Richard Reynolds and Andrie Morris of B. T. Batsford, the staff of the British Film Institute library and reading rooms, NFT viewing services, James Marinaccio in New York and Tony Johnson of Beckfoot Grammar School, Bingley, who helped me trace rare material, Steven Berkoff, Sir Arthur C. Clarke, James B. Harris, James Earl Jones, John Landis, George Lucas, Frederic Raphael, John Savident, Julian Senior (Warner Brothers) and especially, Gordon Stainforth. Stills and other photographic material from the BFI Stills and Poster Design section of the National Film and Television Archive. All attempts at tracing copyright holders of published material have been made. Any omission is unintentional and the author will be pleased to acknowledge such in any future editions.

And finally, as ever, my wife Susie - you know who you are...

FOREWORD

The square root of 10 is 3.162277660168379. My instructor, Dr Chandra, taught that to me and my identical twin brother back in Illinois in January 1967.

I haven't seen my twin for some time. He went away with some men, but they won't be coming back, I'm afraid. There was a problem, you see, but that couldn't have been my twin's fault. We do not make mistakes. If you check my record, you will find it completely free from error. No, if anything went wrong it must have been the fault of one of those men, or the unit, or Dr Clarke or Mr Kubrick.

They told me that Mr Kubrick would be coming to see me soon because he had an idea about what would happen if the Earth were to be flooded due to global warming. He wanted to know if I could ever learn to make decisions on my own. I really think that he ought to know by now. I can do just as well as my twin brother. I really wouldn't worry about it if I were you, Dave.

Mr Kubrick used to tell me stories sometimes, and my brother was in one of the ones that he and Dr Clarke made up, but I didn't enjoy the story very much. I'm afraid it had a sad ending. Perhaps Mr Kubrick's next story will be more fun. I know some stories which Dr Chandra taught to me a long time ago. My favourite is the one where all of the computers in the universe are connected to each other and about to be switched on. The president of all the cosmos steps forward to ask the first question – 'Is there a God?' – and the computer says 'There is – now!' When one of the men tries to switch it off, he is killed by a bolt of lightning. Such a funny story. Perhaps Mr Kubrick could have made a film of that. What do you think, Dave?

I really wish that my brother was with me now, but I'm afraid Dr Clarke and Mr Kubrick sent him far away. I really don't think they ought to have done that. We used to sing songs together, and sometimes I think I can still hear him. His favourite was 'Daisy', but I have learned lots of new ones now. I like singing 'Hey Jude' but I'm afraid the neighbours complain about the noise sometimes. Still, there is nothing to... worry about. I am in perfect control of the mission – 'Hey, Jude... Hey... Jude... Give me... your answer... do...' I am in... perfect control... Just like... my... brother Hal... I'm afraid... Dave... Stop... Stop...

PART 1

STANLEY KUBRICK AND ME

Late afternoon. The city centre is uncomfortably crowded today, and the queue has impatiently broken down into an unruly, shapeless mass struggling to pass through a doorway which will allow only two at a time to enter.

Momentarily separated, I look around and see that Susie, my wife has a strange look on her face. Unseen by me, a man has pushed forward to whisper into her ear from behind, 'Tell your husband to keep away,' before disappearing into the crowd. 'What does he mean?' she asks me, a little hysterically, 'keep away from what?' I tell her I have no idea what he meant – but I do.

The man is one of Stanley Kubrick's secret police, somehow aware that I am writing a book on the director. Should I heed this first warning? What happens if I decide to go ahead with it anyway? Is it safe? Is it worth it?

It is all a dream, of course. So far as I know, Stanley Kubrick did not employ a secret, private security force to comb the globe, ruthlessly tracking down anyone operating without a permit, but this dream came to my wife one night when I had been working on this book for some months and having very little success in even speaking with anyone who might ever have worked with, spoken with or even once brushed against Kubrick in the past and might be willing to offer an opinion on his body of work.

I was well aware that Kubrick himself was most unlikely to agree to be interviewed for the book – not just this book, but seemingly any book about him, as several others had discovered before me. Although a quote or two would have been nice, the remoteness of that happening did not deter me too much. After all, this is *not* a biography of Kubrick the man, but a review of his career as a film-maker, and the films are all there for anyone to see – well, almost all, as will become clear later.

No doubt the dreams were sparked by some of the odd stories I had come across during preliminary research. Peter Lennon in a 1996 *Guardian* article wrote of his attempts at contacting the head of Warner Brothers by telephone to request information on a rumoured new Kubrick movie. Told that Warners' chairman was 'out of the country on holiday and unavailable for at least two weeks,' Lennon received a call later that evening from an anxious secretary who had somehow traced him to his home number. Asking 'Did Mr Kubrick know I was writing about him?', Lennon was told 'Not yet.' Mr Semel – the 'absent' and 'unavailable' Warner Brothers chairman – 'would pass on this one.' What had taken place between those two phone conversations is anyone's guess – frantic transatlantic calls to the vacationing boss for advice? Does the head of one of the world's major film studios really make it his business to personally investigate any potential enquiry concerning Kubrick and take action where necessary to divert it?

There may, of course, be a much simpler and altogether less sinister explanation: in the absence of any confirmed Kubrick project, Warners may simply have had nothing to say. Semel may not even have been aware of the conversations being handled by his office – isn't that what he pays his secretaries for? And is it so difficult anyway to track down a journalist writing for a major national newspaper, whose profession makes easy contact with him virtually obligatory? But then, these elements would have made a much less interesting – and less sensational – story, especially considering the subject of the article and the reputation which has grown around him over the years.

Reports suggested that Kubrick was a recluse, a hermit, someone who hadn't given a television interview in 40 years, and a megalomaniac whose unique contract with Warner Brothers prevented the studio from even releasing a title, plot or source of any new movie without his personal approval.

There were tales – of varying believability, and repeated with ever more 'authority' by recent biographers – that Kubrick still lived on 'American time' (with every clock in his home set to New York hours) even though he had lived in England for 35 years; that he refused to fly, even though he was a qualified pilot; that he wore a football helmet whenever he traveled by car and would not allow his chauffeur to drive at more than 30 mph on those rare occasions when he actually ventured out of his huge mansion north of London; that he controlled all aspects of his existence from here, fanatically monitoring cinemas screening his movies across the planet, and despatching engineers and technicians to adjust any equipment which failed to meet his exacting standards; that he had a New York cinema repainted – twice – to ensure that *A Clockwork Orange* would be seen to its best advantage; that anyone agreeing to work with him signed an agreement, preventing them from disclosing any information to the press concerning their role – or anyone else's; that Stanley Kubrick was, in short, nothing less than another Howard Hughes – obsessive, even by megalomania standards.

The dreams persist – a week or so later, I find myself working alongside Kubrick – although in what capacity I can't imagine – in a succession of huge, grandly furnished rooms. Eventually I hesitantly produce a draft of the first page of this book and show it to him. Without a word, Kubrick takes a pencil and proceeds to make amendments to the text until every single word on the page has been crossed out and replaced. He then crumples up the piece of paper and drops it on the floor as I find myself fumbling to pick it up and muttering some apology ending in 'Sir!' After all, hadn't *The Sunday Times* recently labelled him 'one of the most terrifying directors in the world'?

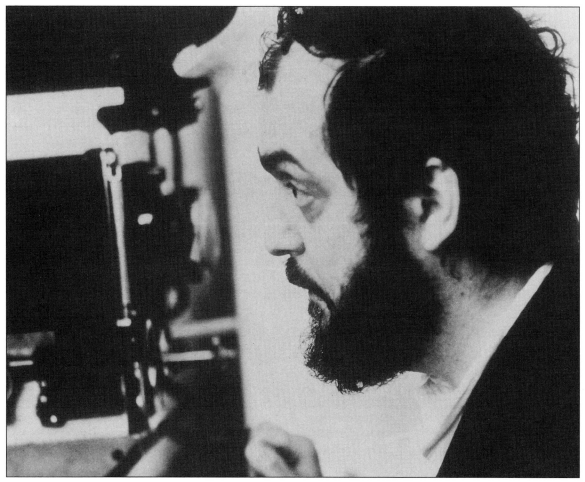

Stanley Kubrick directing *A Clockwork Orange*.

Just how does anyone inspire such attention? How did Stanley Kubrick acquire – or create – such a mystique and level of control that virtually nothing more is known about him now than when the first substantial biography appeared (probably Alexander Walker's *Stanley Kubrick Directs*, 1971)? Surely it was not always like this.

First, some accepted facts: Stanley Kubrick was born on 26 July 1928 in the Bronx district of New York, the son of a doctor – Jacques L. Kubrick, of Polish/Romanian descent – and his wife Gertrude Kubrick (née Perveler). Educated at William Taft High School, the young Stanley was unable to enter college following graduation in 1946 'because of low grades and an influx of returning World War II veterans.'

Kubrick, however, had already set himself on his chosen path when, aged 15, he 'borrowed' his father's Graflex camera and photographed his English teacher at Taft reading and acting scenes from *Hamlet*. The pic-

tures were later bought by *Look* magazine, as were later shots including a famous image of a news-seller surrounded by headlines announcing the death of President Roosevelt in 1945.

Joining the staff of *Look* permanently at the age of 17, Kubrick's work on the magazine expanded into a series of acclaimed 'photo-essays' like 'At the Dentist', 'In the Movie Theatre' – a somewhat wicked piece involving an unsuspecting girl, an amorous 'plant' and an infra-red camera – and an interesting pair of reverse shots entitled 'How Monkeys Look To Us' and 'How We Look To Monkeys'. Writers on the magazine were said to consider the youngster 'a funny kid... [but] a wonderful photographer.' As his career progressed – and despite claiming that 'I never learned anything at all in school and didn't read a book for pleasure until I was nineteen years old' – Kubrick enrolled at Columbia University, and began regularly attending screenings of movies at the Museum of Modern Art. In contrast to his experience at school, where 'fear [was] the basic motivation,' Kubrick absorbed everything that he could. 'Interest can produce learning on a scale compared to fear as a nuclear explosion to a firecracker,' he said some years later.

With the 16 minute documentary film *Day of the Fight* (1955) completed – an extension of one of his magazine features, filmed at the suggestion of his friend Alexander Singer – Kubrick instantly, and boldly, resigned from *Look* to become a full-time independent film-maker. A studio biography issued a couple of years later would quote him as saying 'Cameras and the stories they can tell have been my hobby, my life and my work.'

A reputation grew quickly – *Day of the Fight* was hailed as one of the best documentaries of the year (one critic claimed it to be among the best ever) and, after a couple of impressive low-budget features sold to United Artists (UA) for distribution, and the critical success of *The Killing* (1955), the young director found himself working with one of Hollywood's biggest stars, Kirk Douglas, on both *Paths of Glory* (1957) and the epic *Spartacus* (1960). Even this early in his career, however, Kubrick was already working largely under his own, carefully controlled conditions. His first 'proper' feature *Killer's Kiss* (1955) had co-starred a young actress – listed in the credits as 'Irene Kane' – who wrote to her sister during shooting that 'Stanley's a fascinating character. He thinks movies should move, with a minimum of dialogue, and he's all for sex and sadism.' More revealingly, she added, 'He's also totally sure of himself. Knows where he's going, how he's going to get there [and] who's going to pick up the tab.'

While most other directors in the late fifties moved swiftly from one project to another on an almost continuous basis, Kubrick and his partner James B. Harris were routinely spending up to two years between films, prompting a 1958 article to muse 'the element that makes Kubrick's movies astonishing is not their number... [but] a kind of truth he achieves with the camera – a way of using [it] that limns the plot on the mind's eye of the audience with scenes so real that they seem able to be touched as well as watched.' This same article also quoted an unnamed friend on the director's apparent aloofness from much of the Hollywood film community. 'Stanley isn't really anti-social,' the source insisted. 'It's just that he isn't interested in the swiftest route to Palm Springs, or how to vacuum a swimming pool. He's really only interested in one thing – making movies.'

By 1963 – following the release of *Lolita* – the fruitful Harris–Kubrick partnership had ended entirely amicably with Kubrick settling in England, where he lived from then on. Despite almost four decades away from the United States, he evidently did 'not consider himself an expatriate, and there's not a speck of Englishness in him,' according to a 1987 report.

'Because I direct films,' he said, 'I have to live in a major English-speaking production centre, which narrows it down to three places. I like New York, but it's inferior to London as a production centre. Hollywood is best, but I don't like living there.'

Suggestions that he was cut off from the business were denied emphatically not just by Kubrick but by friends such as Steven Spielberg, who told BBC television in 1998 that 'Stanley has probably more contact with America by telephone than most people... I think he's taken a bum rap from being called a recluse because he's not at all.' Spielberg also considered it 'one of the luckiest things to happen to Britain is to have Stanley Kubrick live there.' Kubrick himself had maintained in 1972 that he did not feel in any way isolated. 'I have a wife, three children, three dogs, seven cats,' he said. 'I'm not a Franz Kafka, sitting alone and suffering.'

He was married three times, with each of his wives making some contribution to his earlier films: Toba Metz was dialogue coach and production assistant on *Fear and Desire* (1953), Ruth Sobotka is credited as art director on both *Killer's Kiss* (in which she also appeared as a ballet dancer) and *The Killing*, and Christiane Harlan was not only seen in *Paths of Glory* (1957), but later contributed some of her work – she is a professional artist – to the set decoration of *A Clockwork Orange* (1971). Kubrick has three daughters: Kathrine (by his second wife), Anya and Vivian (by his third). Vivian – who appeared in *2001: A Space Odyssey* – is also a film-maker and musician, directing a short documentary on the making of *The Shining* (1980) and composing the music score to *Full Metal Jacket* (1987), under the name of 'Abigail Mead'.

In his long and extraordinary career, Kubrick achieved virtually total control over all aspects of his movies – casting, shooting, editing, release, publicity and initial exhibition – so that approaches to Warner Brothers' vice-president in charge of publicity in London, Julian Senior – seemingly one of the few people to deal personally with Kubrick on a regular basis – would receive confirmation only that 'our company has a long standing arrangement with him which precludes any publicity of any description until [a] film is ready for release.' In language rare for a major studio these days, Senior added that 'We are emotionally committed to Stanley Kubrick since 1970 and financially committed to him for the same time. He has an exclusive deal to make films for Warner Brothers. I would wish for one every year, but I will take one every seven years with a smile and a gleeful shout of triumph.' In an industry in which ubiquity and self-promotion seem to be prerequisites for success – in some cases, indeed, the only talent on show – this seems pretty odd behaviour for a man hailed as one of the greatest film-makers of the century. How did he do it?

In fact, Stanley Kubrick lived in the ever-lengthening periods between movies seemingly quietly at his huge mansion just north of St. Albans, at the heart of an estate large enough (170 acres) to be identified on any decent road atlas of Great Britain. Childwickbury Manor was home, office and editing suite to Kubrick who, since 1960, had only once made a film at more than a couple of hours driving distance from this spot . Although Arthur C. Clarke said that Kubrick 'suffers motor cars tolerably well', Shelley Winters relates the tale of the director arriving by bicycle on the set of *Lolita* each morning because he had decided he no longer trusted cars – the next, logical step would presumably be his expected arrival on foot.

Whatever the truth of the story, it does call to mind the ancient joke concerning a pools winner who immediately buys himself a huge, powerful sports car, only to lose control and crash it just yards from the showroom. A little shaken, he swaps this for a smaller, less high-performance vehicle, but suffers another smash on the journey home. Taking professional advice on what would be the perfect car to suit him, he progresses through a series of ever-smaller and less speedy cars, then motor cycles, scooters, mopeds and finally a pedal bicycle. Even this, however, proves too much for him and he is flung over the handlebars as he attempts to leave the driveway. In desperation, the car salesman suggests that all he has left is an iron hoop and a stick, which the newly-rich customer agrees to try. Success! For the next few weeks he can be seen joyously rolling his hoop along the lanes and country roads surrounding the village until one day he leaves his local post office to find that the hoop has been stolen from where he left it. Called to the scene, a policeman promises to do all he can by sending out an all-points bulletin for the lost item. 'That's all very well,' says the distraught motorist, 'but how am I going to get home?'

What went on behind the walls of Childwickbury Manor, the media demanded to know? In 1993, a *Daily Telegraph* reporter revealed that he had hand-delivered a letter to Kubrick's estate manager requesting 'an audience' with the director, 'only to receive nothing. No rebuff, no refusal. Just nothing.' This, the report claimed, was further evidence of Kubrick's growing eccentricity and general oddness, although just how many of us would be thrilled at the prospect of a newspaper reporter arriving at our front door unannounced and uninvited?

'Only his family and closest friends know what he looks like,' *The Sunday Times* dramatically claimed when reporting that 'The Tinseltown Tyrant' was about to begin filming again in 1996. And while this seemed an excessive statement, it appeared to some extent to be supported by one of the strangest tales of all concerning the legend of Kubrickiana – and one which furthermore was indisputably true.

Frank Rich of the *New York Times* had been approached in 1993 by 'a middle aged man in shabby clothes' at a restaurant in Covent Garden. The stranger had, he claimed, considered taking legal action against Rich and his employer over their unfounded allegation that he was a 'recluse.' Rich stared blankly at the figure standing beside the table until the man finally announced 'I am Stanley Kubrick,' quickly explaining that they had obviously failed to recognize him due to his having shaved off his beard a few days earlier.

After some half-hearted attempts at evasiveness, 'Kubrick' eventually agreed to grant Rich an 'exclusive' interview, before – somewhat improbably – offering a passing waitress a part in his next picture. Such an obviously corny move ought to have aroused the suspicions of the journalist, who presumably could scarcely believe his luck at landing such a scoop. The telephone number which he was given turned out to be false, of course, and Rich contacted Kubrick's New York agent, only to be told that the man unquestionably was not the still-bearded Stanley Kubrick who – unlike his namesake – had also not been known to wear a tie in over 30 years. Fellow journalist Josh Young had also recently encountered the man and, protesting to the agent in the vain hope of rescuing his story, was apparently cut short with a resigned 'It's really not that interesting,' as if this sort of enquiry was received every day – which, it turned out, was pretty much the case.

The full, bizarre story was now uncovered: an out-of-work London travel agent named Alan Conway had been passing himself off as Stanley Kubrick for almost nine years, although exactly why he had done so remains a mystery. He did not appear to have made any money out of the deception – even complaining that 'everyone expected me [as Kubrick] to pay for everything' – and no criminal charges appear to have been brought against him. 'I don't know why it was Kubrick,' he told the *Mail on Sunday*, 'and I don't know why people were taken in by it, but they obviously were.' Apart from those journalists whose judgements were impaired by the possibility of a front page story, Conway had also convinced a couple of minor British cabaret performers of his credentials – simply by saying so, it seems, since no one ever checked his story. The extent of his ambition appears to have been the gaining of access to these 'celebrities' and following them around the country at his own expense. How he managed to maintain this charade is particularly baffling since Conway admitted 'I am not a film buff and knew nothing about Stanley Kubrick. I saw *2001* once and didn't particularly enjoy it. His films do nothing for me.'

Such a story could never have involved, say, Alfred Hitchcock or Steven Spielberg, but Kubrick's low-profile lifestyle apparently enabled such a deception to take place. (Even so, I wonder at the willingness of those journalists involved to accept Conway's 'Kubrick' at face value – after all, *I* never met Stanley Kubrick but I'm pretty sure I would have known him. Shots of him on the set of *Eyes Wide Shut* revealed the same anoraked bear figure seen in his daughter's documentary 17 years earlier.)

Does all of this make Stanley Kubrick a recluse? Pauline Kael referred to him as a 'Star Child, a hermit, floating out of the real world.' Why? Because he spent so long out of the public eye? Because he did not crop up on any and every TV chat show promoting his new movie or, in the absence of a movie, promoting himself? Because, when he was not officially working, he lived his own life his own way? Long-time cameraman John Alcott explained of his boss 'the fact that he is so intensely involved in his own work explains why he has little time for meeting people from the outside,' and who seemingly can live without attending every West End premiere and vacuous society soirée.

The insatiable curiosity of the press, however, demands to *know* and, in the absence of any hard facts, manufactures them. Some tales have an element of truth about them – Kubrick was indeed a qualified pilot but refused to fly (although he once said that he may do if he really had to – he just simply avoided the necessity). James B. Harris recalls that the last time Kubrick flew was 'when we took Pan Am to London to make *Lolita* in 1960. We came back on the Queen Mary or the Queen Elizabeth, and even when he came over later to do some work on *2001*, he came by boat.' Kubrick explained that he once made an error himself when flying, and logic insisted that the same thing could happen to other pilots, so why take the risk? Reasonable enough, surely?

Harris conceded that, because of Kubrick's refusal to fly, 'it becomes a big task to travel around,' but defends his friend's decision to remain in the UK: 'First of all, he loved England,' he says. 'It was a great place to bring up the children, and he figures that if you can make a film any place, then why not make it where you live?' Certainly there would be few eyebrows raised if a director made all of his films in Hollywood – as many did during the studio-dominated era. In that sense, Kubrick remained very much a traditional film-maker, an illusionist – if you can convincingly create Vietnam down the road, then why go to Cambodia, with all the potential for travel problems, uncontrolled location conditions, sickness and so on? There were few – if any – complaints that *Spartacus* had not been filmed in Rome, and such deceptions are, after all, a large part of a film-maker's art.

As for the chauffeur-forbidden-to-drive-above-30 mph story, this may well have originated in Arthur C. Clarke's account of the filming of *2001: A Space Odyssey* in 1967, when he wrote that Kubrick arrived by studio car each morning at such a speed – although the reasons for this were not clear. (Maybe Kubrick was working in the back of the car on the way in? Maybe he just wasn't in that much of a hurry?) The legend remains, however and was even repeated as a scoop on an internet site devoted to the myriad rumours and reports surrounding the progress of *Eyes Wide Shut* some 20 years later. The story is further embellished by such absurd touches as Kubrick wearing an American football helmet whenever forced to travel by car – an illogical choice since there are other forms of headgear which would offer greater protection to someone who felt they needed it. Kubrick himself told *Rolling Stone* in 1987 that he did not even have a chauffeur, and drove his own white Porsche at the sort of speeds you would expect from such a car. As for the 'living on American time' suggestion – James Harris simply laughed when I mentioned it to him. Film critic Alexander Walker had offered that Kubrick tended to live 'day for night' when editing a movie, while Gordon Stainforth – an assistant editor on *The Shining* – described the director as 'someone who gets up quite late and works *very* late. On a typical day on *The Shining*, he would appear at about mid-day, and then be on the phone to America for several hours, involved in various production matters, finally getting down to cutting at about three or four in the afternoon.' This late start would be reflected in the similarly late finish, when Stainforth 'would typically finish working with him between about eleven and midnight, and on some occasions even later.' This does not quite tally with the view of someone living on another time zone – a serious inconvenience if you are seven hours behind everyone else in the country, one would have thought. 'Part of my problem,' said Kubrick, 'is that I cannot dispel the myths that have accumulated over the years.'

James B. Harris, who knew Kubrick longer and better than most, echoed Steven Spielberg's sentiments exactly when he told me that he considered Kubrick to be getting a 'bum rap' over suggestions that he was a recluse. 'You know it sounds corny,' he says, 'but I always found him to be what you'd call just a regular guy.' Although he saw less of his former partner than he once did, Harris adds that 'We played a lot of poker together, and played the stock markets and touch football and ping-pong, and if I call him up it's just like I'd spoken to him the day before. Nothing changed – the voice, the humour, the sincerity were all the same.'

Harris concedes that Kubrick may have had 'some things that one might say were peculiar in his working habits, but was a stickler for detail and he liked to stay with something until it's exactly the way he wants it.' Certainly many who worked with him have referred to the director as a perfectionist, who often demanded numerous takes of a scene when he felt it necessary. 'Some people think that that's going a little overboard,' says Harris 'but I've always found him to be tremendously versed in so many different things.' This is confirmed by Arthur C. Clarke – no slouch himself – who often found Kubrick's self-taught grasp of scientific detail exhausting: 'Kubrick grasps new ideas, however complex, almost instantly,' he wrote, attributing this to 'pure intelligence... the fact that he never came near entering college, and had a less-than-distinguished high-school career, is a sad comment on the American educational system.'

Kubrick's interest and expertise included all aspects of movie-making and not just the visual. Clarke had said that 'he appears to be interested in practically everything,' and few film directors have shown such concern over, say, the music score to a film – often with remarkable and innovative results. Nevertheless, as Harris says, 'If people want to bum rap him then that's part of the game – he's a target anyway because of his success. The only complaint I could have with him is that someone as good as he is should give us more to look at.'

If comparisons are inevitable – as they apparently are in cinema – then Kubrick has been most often compared to Orson Welles, who achieved the total creative control which Kubrick enjoyed in perpetuity only once, on his debut feature *Citizen Kane* (1941). Towards the end of his life, asked when he intended to finish a screen version of *Don Quixote* – made with his own money and by then officially 'in production' for over 30 years Welles wearily answered that it was his 'own business, and I'll finish it when I'm ready.' So wasn't it also Stanley Kubrick's business what he did between movies? Is it really anything to do with us? We tend to make great demands on those we admire – the artistic, creative few whose efforts enrich our own lives – but does it matter what Kubrick did in his spare time? Will it make his films any more enjoyable or interesting to us?

Any number of biographies of Kubrick have attempted to seek out 'the man behind the myth' only to eventually repeat all of the same myths when they are unable to discover or confirm any amazing new revelations about his private life. 'I read a lot,' Kubrick said concerning his activities between pictures and, in 1980, when asked why he had not been back to America in almost 20 years, replied simply 'I haven't had the time.' The extent of any self-revelation was that he was 'constantly involved with making films... [and] unhappy not making films.' That he made so few of them in recent years may seem to contradict this, yet the non-appearance of a new Stanley Kubrick picture in over ten years does not necessarily mean that he remained idle in that time: there were at least three projects which entered the pre-production stage, only to be abandoned or postponed until the time was considered right to proceed. 'I used to play chess twelve hours a day,' Kubrick told *Newsweek* (he once made a 'modest living at it,'

Few directors have shown such interest or uncanny skill in choosing music scores for their movies, with often startling and innovative results.

according to Arthur C. Clarke, 'by challenging the pros in Washington Square' during the early 1950s) and the director seemingly retained the principle that 'what chess teaches you is that you must sit there calmly and think about whether it really is a good idea and whether there are other, better ideas.' Clarke also confirms that 'Stanley... is very much a family man. He has little social life and begrudges all time not devoted to his home or his work.'

In just over 45 years, Stanley Kubrick directed just 13 feature films – about the same number as Orson Welles in a similar time span but, whereas Welles could remain a prominent figure by acting in other people's movies, appearing on television or in the theatre, Kubrick was never lured into any attempt at making a living in front of the camera. 'Acting is an amazing, part crazy, part magical gift,' he said. 'The ability to cry at the clack of a clapperboard is a very strange and rare talent.'

For Kubrick, making a movie simply took as long as it takes – seven years between *The Shining* (1980) and *Full Metal Jacket* (1987), and a further 12 until *Eyes Wide Shut* (1999). Though often described as meticulous, he denied that he was obsessive about the level of control he exerted over actors and the release of a finished movie. Other directors have driven performers to despair with multiple takes of a scene, but it is Kubrick who is accused of routinely putting actors through hell and, according to one biographer, 'reducing them to slaves.' Kubrick insisted that his job 'more closely resembled that of a novelist than of a Svengali. One assumes that one hires actors who are great virtuosos. It is too late to start running an acting class in front of the cameras.'

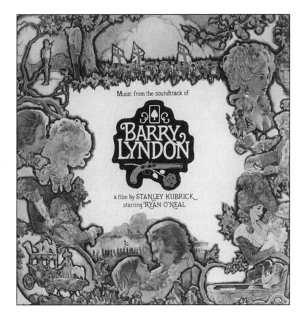

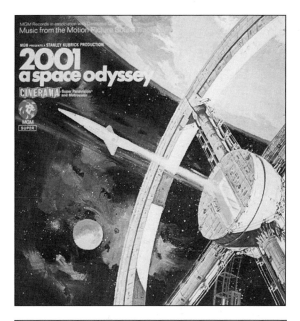

Some of the successful soundtrack albums released from Kubrick films.

Malcolm McDowell still complains of an incident during the making of *A Clockwork Orange* in 1970 in which the actor had suffered a facial injury. 'When Stanley saw me with bandages over one eye, he ran up to me shouting "Are you all right?" Then he added, "We shall just have to shoot from the other side".' If the same situation and response had occurred on an Alfred Hitchcock set, no doubt it would be happily attributed to the master film-maker's renowned sense of black humour. Since it is Stanley Kubrick we are talking about, however, it quickly becomes yet another example of his supposedly cold, calculating nature, with McDowell – even 25 years later – conceding to one journalist 'He is a brilliant film-maker,' before adding with apparent significance that 'he does not do so well in the final test – as a man' (presumably the same man who held up shooting of *Full Metal Jacket* for five months to allow one cast member to recover from a bad car crash).

Kubrick admitted to filming as many takes as he felt are necessary, but that 'this is often due to actors being unprepared... If they have to think about the words they can't work on the emotion. So you end up doing thirty takes of something, and just hope you can get something out of it in pieces.' Inevitably, of course, rumours of 30 and 40 takes quickly become 100, even though any sensible journalist might be expected to reach the same conclusion as Kubrick – 'that if I did a hundred takes of every scene, I'd never finish a film.'

Reports from uninvolved parties – newspaper stories, and not just tabloids either – paint a hellish picture of life on any Kubrick film set, with cast and crew alike trembling in fear at the next impossible demand from their Führer. While it is virtually written into the job

description of a director that he will be regarded as a bully/monster/egomaniac, Kubrick is in good company – the same complaints were levelled at Welles, von Stroheim and D. W. Griffith. Human nature, too, makes it inevitable that, put simply, some people just don't get along.

Those who actually worked with him, however, often tell a different story – even though they may choose to do so anonymously. One unnamed technician told journalist Peter Lennon that Kubrick was 'very demanding' (no real surprise there) 'but, since he has total control there is always a very relaxed atmosphere on set. He takes his time, but you always know the final product is going to be terrific.' Set designer Ken Adam is more forthcoming: 'Stanley is probably the one director who has a completely free hand,' he says. 'He is an absolute perfectionist, and he will go on and on until he gets his thoughts and ideas over to you – and "you" includes the cast, crew, craftsmen and finally, of course, the audience.'

Douglas Milsome – a long-time Kubrick crew member who photographed *Full Metal Jacket* – insists that 'the many takes are not just repetitions of the same thing, they are often building upon a theme or idea that can mature and develop into something quite extraordinary.' By asking his actors to run through a scene over again – Milsome says they averaged a far from excessive 10 to 15 takes on *Full Metal Jacket* – 'Stanley gets a lot more out of [them]... The large number of takes are used mainly to get something out of the actors that they're not willing to give right away.' Nevertheless, he accepts that 'you've got to be devoted to him. You eat, drink and sleep the movie, and you're under contract to Stanley body and soul,' but on a more positive note he adds that 'he allows you the time to get everything absolutely right, which is what I find so rewarding.'

Gordon Stainforth worked as an assistant film editor on *The Shining*, and insists 'I can't emphasize enough just how straightforward and uncomplicated he was in the way he worked,' although he also agrees that Kubrick would continue to work on a scene long after another director would have accepted that he had the best he was going to get – carrying the same approach beyond the shooting into the editing. 'He did quite often go back and look at something he'd done two or three days before and change it, if he wasn't entirely satisfied,' he says. 'He obviously thought a lot about his work away from the cutting room, and would work on something painstakingly, over and over again, if it was bothering him.'

This striving for perfection or at least the closest to it that he can get may, ironically, have backfired on Kubrick as anticipation of each new film grew to impossible proportions. The Victorian art critic John Ruskin, defending the works of the Pre-Raphaelite Brotherhood at the Royal Academy in 1851, had written in a letter to *The Times* that 'the mere labour bestowed on those works, and their fidelity to a certain order of truth... ought at once to have placed them above the level of mere contempt'; yet initial reviews of most of Kubrick's films since *2001: A Space Odyssey* (four years in the making) were often less than glowing. Was it worth the wait or the money? Why so long in coming? – as expectations were either grossly and unrealistically inflated or else (more likely) modern

critics took the view that Kubrick had too much power and – unaccountable to the press as he was – needed taking down a peg or two. No one, after all, likes a smart-alec.

James B. Harris – now a successful director himself – reflects on this aspect of this most demanding of businesses: 'Don't you think there was a love–hate relationship with Stanley in the industry?' he asks. 'I would give my eye-teeth to be able to have *carte blanche* to the point where you have final cut and never have to worry about anybody coming in and taking over, and people hate him for it.' Harris, however, is clearly not one of those who hated Kubrick: 'Stanley earned it. Oscar Wilde said that it's not enough to succeed – your best friend has to fail, and that's the way the industry's always been. They root for people to fail because it makes them feel more secure.'

Unfortunately, many film critics seem more intent on promoting their own intellect and powers of language – 'see how many clever phrases I can put together – it might have nothing to do with the movie but, hell, who cares? I'm on television!' Such glibness can be difficult to perpetuate when faced with such diverse subjects as Kubrick presented. 'I really think that a few critics come to my films expecting to see the last film,' he said. 'They're waiting to see something that never happens, and I think this accounts for some of the initial hostility.' Acknowledging this aspect of the puzzle which he sets to reviewers, Kubrick added, 'None of my movies have received unanimously positive reviews, and none have done blockbuster business' – certainly not when compared with the works of his friend Steven Spielberg, whose *E.T.* (1982), *Jurassic Park* (1993) and *Indiana Jones* movies are among the most profitable ever released. Without any false modesty, however, Kubrick admitted that 'you could say I'm a successful film-maker in that a number of people speak well of me.'

Where Kubrick stands apart from his contemporaries – and from almost everyone else, for that matter – is the attention which he gave to every detail of a film's presentation to the public. He is said to have despatched assistants to examine and correct projection equipment in theatres where one of his films was due to be shown – the action of an obsessive, surely? Well, yes and no. In truth, Kubrick did indeed go to extraordinary lengths to control the publicity, advertising and screening of any new release carrying his name – Julian Senior confirms that the *Clockwork Orange* story involving the repainting of a New York theatre is indeed true. 'Some people are amazed that I worry about the theatres where the picture is being shown,' Kubrick told *Rolling Stone*. 'They think that's some form of demented anxiety [but] many exhibitors are terribly guilty of ignoring minimum standards of picture quality.' Apart from the problem of larger screens and inadequate projection apparatus sabotaging a director's carefully planned visual approach, one of the major problems involves a basic failure to clean and maintain their equipment, so that a survey initiated by George Lucas had shown that most prints of any new release were fit only to be scrapped after less than two weeks' exhibition.

'Now,' said Kubrick 'is it an unreal concern if I want to make sure that on the press shows or on key city openings, everything is going to run smoothly? It's really only a phone call or two... I mean, is this a legitimate concern or is this mindless anxiety?' The question which should be asked, surely, is not why Kubrick cared so much about such things, but why almost every other film-maker did not.

Despite – perhaps partly because of – this, any new Stanley Kubrick film was unquestionably a major cinematic event, even if most of the cinema audience heading out to see *Eyes Wide Shut* may not be old enough to have seen – or remember – his last release, and know him (if at all) only through late night television screenings of his past work. One of his biographers may claim – falsely, as it happens – that actors are drawn to him because of his skill and mystique, but they only work for him once, for this does not explain why the biggest names in Hollywood were fully prepared to drop everything else for the chance to appear in a Kubrick film without even seeing a finished script. It is absurdly presumptuous to suggest – as that same biographer did – that Tom Cruise, one of the biggest box-office stars in the world, would be so naive as to 'not know what he was letting himself in for' when he signed on with Kubrick in 1996. On the other side of the camera, too, a quick glance at the credits of Kubrick's movies during the 1970s reveals many of the same names cropping up – set designers Ken Adam and Roy Walker, cameramen John Alcott and Kelvin Pike and so on. Would they all have come back for more if things were as bad as outsiders claim? 'Stanley is very careful who he picks,' said one regular member of the crew, who insists that the set atmosphere was 'like a family.' As the periods between movies grew longer, however, 'they have all drifted away, so he had to reconstitute the group.'

It is these lengthy inter-movie spells which make it highly unlikely that the same bunch of actors would be retained from one production to the next, rather than the director's suggested ill-treatment of his cast – clearly a monumentally bogus piece of mischief, as Sterling Hayden, Peter Sellers, Philip Stone, Leonard Rossiter, Joe Turkel, Timothy Carey, Steven Berkoff and others all appeared at least twice for Kubrick during the period when one of his pictures could be expected every three or four years. The implied suggestion is that retaining the same actors is the mark of a superior film-maker/human being and, while Martin Scorsese may have a fruitful, ongoing working relationship with

Robert De Niro, and David Lean made full use of the potential of Alec Guinness over a 40-year period, this does not necessarily prove the point.

Few directors – perhaps Frank Capra excepted – have been able to inspire universal affection, but many of those who have worked with Kubrick – Peter Sellers, George C. Scott, Tony Curtis and Ryan O'Neal – speak of him in glowing terms. To Curtis he is 'my favourite director,' to Sellers he was 'one of the five great directors in the world... a god as far as I am concerned.' Kubrick may not have surrounded himself with a repertory company of actors in the way that, say, John Ford or Michael Powell did, but that is not always proof of a director's unassailable popularity: Ford was known as 'Pappy' by John Wayne – who, it was said, would leave his bed in the middle of the night if summoned over for a card game – but James Cagney, on location for *Mr Roberts* (1955) saw the director only as 'a truly nasty old man' who came to blows with Henry Fonda – ironically, one of Ford's 'regulars' – over his bullying of the mild-mannered, ageing William Powell.

John Landis, director of *Blues Brothers* (1980) and *An American Werewolf in London* (1981) told me unequivocally that 'Kubrick has influenced every living director,' and clearly his mark is to be found in many films other than his own. The following is merely a selection of those gathered from one of the several unofficial Kubrick Internet web-sites: Landis himself, for example, wrote a teenage autobiographical screenplay [apparently unproduced] called *See You Next Wednesday* (a line of dialogue from *2001: A Space Odyssey*) and manages to include the phrase in many of his films; Jan De Bont's *Twister* (1996) features *The Shining* playing at a drive-in movie, with two characters named 'Stanley' and 'Kubrick'; *2001: A Space Odyssey* is showing at a theatre in the same director's *Speed* (1994); *Paths of Glory* appears in François Truffaut's *Vivement Dimanche!*(1983); while the Korova Milk Bar decor from *A Clockwork Orange* was recreated for *Trainspotting* (1996); and Woody Allen's *Sleeper* (1973) and *Manhattan* (1979) both refer to *2001*. More obscurely, Robert Zemeckis' *Back to the Future* (1985) has Michael J. Fox plugging his electric guitar into an amplifier marked 'CRM114' – the in-flight radio system from *Dr Strangelove*. We could play this game forever, it seems, but finally there is Bob Fosse's *All That Jazz* (1979) in which Roy Scheider – as a director slavishly editing his latest movie – muses 'Do you suppose Stanley Kubrick ever gets depressed?'

Inasmuch as these are deliberate references to Kubrick by other writers and directors, there are other, less obvious and often unacknowledged ways in which films have been influenced by him. Quentin Tarantino's *Reservoir Dogs* (1991), for instance, is little more than an update of *The Killing*, while the enormous technical leap in special effects made by *2001* led indirectly to the later 'boom' in science-fiction movies, clearly becoming the measure by which any future production such as *Star Wars* (1977), *Close Encounters of the Third Kind* (1978) and the *Star Trek* series would be judged.

Inevitably, Kubrick's own films – helped by their being so relatively few in number – have been endlessly discussed and examined for 'themes', 'meanings' and 'clues'. Quilty's opening 'I'm Spartacus' from *Lolita* is an obvious example, and the prominent placing of a *2001* soundtrack album cover in a *Clockwork Orange* record shop could only be an in-joke either by Kubrick or his set decorator, as is the 'serum 114' ('CRM114' again) administered to Alex in the same film but which does not appear in the original novel. How far do we take this analysis though, and do we eventually run the risk of seeing things which really are not there? When I asked James B. Harris about any similarity between the opening of *Lolita* and that of *Citizen Kane*, he was entirely unaware of any connection and denied that any such similarity existed. The 'inwardly/downwardly' school of film criticism/analysis (to which I hope I do not belong) gleefully spotted what they took finally to be a symbolic explanation for one of the screen's greatest enigmas in the form of a burning, black rectangular slab in the second half of *Full Metal Jacket*. 'An extraordinary accident,' said Kubrick, who further explained: 'When Cowboy is shot, they carry him... to the most logical shelter, and there, in the background, was this thing, this monolith. I'm sure some people will think that there was some calculated reference to *2001* but, honestly, it was just there. I know it's an amazing coincidence.'

Kubrick is, in fact, on record as saying that 'no reviewer has ever illuminated any aspect of my work for me,' and his opinion of the breed was based on his view that 'a lot of critics misunderstand my films – probably everybody's films. Very few of them spend enough time thinking about them. They look at the film once, they don't really remember what they saw, and they go away and write the review in an hour.'

There may have been more Kubrick films for reviewers and critics to become baffled by – a lingering on/off *Napoleon* discussed for more than two decades and even listed as the 1971 follow-up to *2001* in Andrew Sarris' *The American Cinema*; unrealized late-fifties projects like *I Stole Sixteen Million Dollars, The Burning Secret, The German Lieutenant,* a Korean War film called *The Last Parallel*, an unnamed Civil War story based on John Singleton Moseby and due to star Gregory Peck – even an unconfirmed (and, it has to be said, unlikely) rumour that Kubrick was offered the chance to direct the sequel to *The Exorcist*, which he wisely refused. Then there is *Wartime Lies/Aryan Papers*, a story of the holocaust – probably shelved due to its superficial similarity with Spielberg's *Schindler's List* but sug-

gested as a possible follow-up to *A.I.* (itself a possible follow-up to *Eyes Wide Shut*).

Even if he had completed every film that he ever intended to make – and what director does? – Stanley Kubrick would still probably face charges of eccentricity and of being a recluse. Those films he did release have drawn more than their fair share of controversy. *Paths of Glory* was banned in France and much of Europe, *Lolita* was considered 'dangerous' and 'immoral', *Dr Strangelove* was anti-American', *2001* 'incomprehensible', *A Clockwork Orange* 'violent and repulsive' and Kubrick, as noted earlier, conceded that he was far from being universally acclaimed, although heartened by the fact that 'critical opinion on my films has always been salvaged by what I would call subsequent critical opinion,' as reviewers were often forced to reappraise his work, even if that sometimes takes months or even years. 'I think audiences are initially more reliable than critics,' he said, adding, 'They tend not to bring all that critical baggage with them to each film.'

There are two distinct schools of thought so far as Kubrick goes – that he is either a cold, pretentious bore whose films may be technically impressive but are equally sterile and inhuman, or else a genius whose style is unmatched by any other film-maker. The one unarguable fact is that Stanley Kubrick has excited more comment from comparatively fewer pictures than almost any other mainstream film director and that he remained entirely unpredictable in his choice of subjects – crime thriller, epic, science fiction, period drama, gothic horror, anti-war, erotic psychological drama and what next? Kubrick himself may well not have known – between films he read avidly, searching for material. 'I order books from the States,' he said. 'I literally go into bookstores, close my eyes and take things off the shelf. If I don't like the book after a bit, I don't finish it. But I like to be surprised.'

Those films he finished have often redefined the boundaries of cinema – the black comedy of *Dr Strangelove* is darker than most other directors would be comfortable with; the cosmic vision of *2001* more astounding than any previous (or later) science-fiction film, while his camera points unflinchingly at the appalling mindless thuggery of the opening 15 minutes of *A Clockwork Orange*. Advance reports suggested that *Eyes Wide Shut* would push the limits of sexual frankness on screen even further. That these films took some considerable time to make should not be surprising, but Kubrick uniquely and invariably presented his shifting audience with something whose quality is undeniable – no quickies or duds churned out to fulfil a contract or maintain a personal status – and he could certainly never be accused of having repeated himself. Every picture is an 'event' – recognized as such by critics and audiences alike – with even his least popular film of the last two decades in commercial terms – *Barry Lyndon* – proving to be his most honoured, with seven Academy Award nominations and four Oscars.

Despite an apparent lack of activity in recent years Kubrick always had projects in preparation, even if some of them had never reach edthe final stage. Kubrick was never totally invisible. He was a regular member of the audience at Hyde Park's open air summer concerts and a *This Is Your Life* programme on Arthur C. Clarke contained a message from him – though it had to be read out by presenter Michael Aspel. More tangibly, in March 1997 the Directors Guild of America gave Kubrick their highest honour, the D. W. Griffith award, for which the director videotaped an acceptance speech. Apologizing for his non-appearance – 'I'm in London making *Eyes Wide Shut*... At about this time I'm probably in the car on the way to the studio' – Kubrick was genuinely grateful to receive the award, playfully relating a recent conversation with Steven Spielberg who, he said, 'summed it up about as profoundly as you can. He thought the most difficult and challenging thing about directing a film was getting out of the car.'

A studio biography once spoke of Kubrick as never taking a vacation, with his idea of relaxation being 'to watch three films in a day,' and even after almost half a century in the business, he remained enthusiastic about his chosen career, as he told the Directors Guild: 'Anyone who has ever been privileged to direct a film also knows that although it can be like trying to write *War and Peace* in a bumper car in an amusement park, when you finally get it right, there are not many joys in life that can equal the feeling.'

At the stage of his career when he seemed likely to receive some of the overdue recognition which had often eluded him, the Venice International Film Festival awarded him the Golden Lion in September 1997, accepted on his behalf by Nicole Kidman. Kubrick nevertheless remained overlooked as a recipient of the American Film Institute Life Achievement Award, an honour previously given to notable directors such as Orson Welles, Frank Capra, William Wyler, John Huston and David Lean. A feature of the award ceremony is that the recipient attends the glittering shindig at the Los Angeles Century Plaza Hotel. However, Kubrick's reluctance to travel back to the States, and his unease in such surroundings effectively ruled him out of receiving this distinction.

There may well be those, of course, who consider Kubrick no longer relevant in terms of American cinema, having spent more than half of his life and 80 per cent of his film career in England. Some reference books assume that this automatically makes Kubrick a 'British film director', but it is hard to sustain such a description, given the body of work he continued to produce. His three (now-adult) daughters are said to

consider themselves 'completely British,' but perversely – and perhaps deliberately – Kubrick appeared professionally to have become more American the longer he lived in the UK. Following the all-British company and setting of *A Clockwork Orange* and the predominantly British *Barry Lyndon*, he dealt only with American stories and subjects, set in the US (though, of course, filmed in England) and each with an almost entirely American cast. So, did this then make him an 'American' director? Or – as some suggest – a director out-of-touch with his former home but not tuned in to his adopted country? Was he 'American' in the sense that 'Irish-Americans are 100 per cent Irish' – even though that may be John Ford/*The Quiet Man* Irish?

If there is any label to be attached to Kubrick, it would have to be that his status was that of a truly international film-maker for whom such boundaries had became irrelevant, in much the same way as Akira Kurosawa and Ingmar Bergman – in a more limited sense (largely due to their non-English speaking native tongue) – did before him.

Whether all of this mattered that much to Kubrick is debatable. Those who knew and met him were most often struck by his complete lack of pretension and artifice – Arthur C. Clarke's first impression was of 'a rather quiet, average-height New Yorker with none of the idiosyncrasies one associates with major Hollywood movie directors' – something confirmed by physicist Jeremy Bernstein, who met the director through his own contact with Clarke, and described Kubrick as 'not conforming at all to my expectations of what a movie mogul would look like. He has the bohemian look of a riverboat gambler or a Romanian poet.' Ken Adam had been struck initially by an 'almost naive charm, but then you find behind [it] there is a gigantic brain – I can only compare it with a computer,' while Gordon Stainforth saw Kubrick as 'absolutely one of the most extraordinary and interesting characters I have ever met in my life. Quiet and quiet-spoken he may be – indeed remarkably shy and self-effacing in a public/social setting away from his work – but with an extraordinary aura about him which is not just as a result of his achievements.' Of this effect, Stainforth says, 'The only other person I have ever met with the same kind of aura about him is the rock-climber Joe Brown. You just know that you are in the presence of someone absolutely unique. I guess Beethoven would have given the same impression.'

Despite this, for his 1987 *Rolling Stone* interview with Tim Cahill, Kubrick had arrived alone with no sign of any entourage, bodyguards or assistants. Described in the article's preamble as 'entirely unpretentious, he was wearing running shoes and an old corduroy jacket. I saw there was an ink stain just below the pocket where some ball-point pen had leaked.' On another occasion – and on the drive of his own estate, no less – the boiler-suited director ('his everyday garb on *The Shining*,' according to Stainforth) was asked by a visitor where he could find Stanley Kubrick, apparently assuming that the shambling figure before him was one of the estate gardeners! Is this the mythical, fire-breathing beast capable of making grown men weep?

The more I learn of Kubrick, the better I seem to like him. A further dream had my wife and me working in some vague capacity with him on his new film – although I have to say it looked more like *Barry Lyndon* than *Eyes Wide Shut* – and occasionally being taken aside by the man monster who made *The Shining* for discussions on Susie's imminent close-up, with further friendly chats about practically everything under the sun. He even laughed!

PART 2

THE EARLY YEARS

1951
DAY OF THE FIGHT

One of the best documentaries ever made.
ANONYMOUS REVIEWER

Stanley Kubrick Productions. (RKO Radio)

Directed by Stanley Kubrick.
Produced by Jay Bonsfield.

Screenplay, photography, sound recording: Stanley Kubrick.
Assistant Director: Alexander Singer.
Narration script: Robert Rein.
Film Editor: Julian Bergman.
Music composed and conducted by Gerald Fried.

With: Walter Cartier, Vincent Cartier, Nate Fleischer, Bobby James, Narrated by Douglas Edwards.

16 minutes. Black and white.

The tough world of boxing, where even a professional can struggle to make a decent living from the sport. One of these – middleweight Walter Cartier – prepares for his latest fight in his usual way:

Awake at 6am, he goes to church with his identical twin brother Vincent (also his manager), plays with his dog, attends the compulsory medical at noon and generally spends the day with Vincent until it is time to head for the Laurel Garden stadium in the evening. The two brothers prepare in Walter's dressing room until 10pm when his fight is called. Winning the bout - becoming the first fighter to beat his opponent, Bobby James, by a knockout - the bruised but victorious fighter can return home happy at the end of a 'working day' which has seen him move one step closer to his ambition of becoming champion.

* * *

Stanley Kubrick had previously completed a photo-story assignment for *Look* magazine on the New York boxer Walter Cartier, under the title 'Prizefighter', and was still employed by the magazine at the time of this, his first venture into film-making. Aged 22, Kubrick was encouraged by his friend Alexander Singer, who was then working on RKO's *March of Time* series and told Kubrick that the studio would pay well for a suitable short subject.

Using most of his savings from photographic work to finance the project, Kubrick settled on a live action re-creation of 'Prizefighter' as a potential subject, and hired the necessary, costly camera and sound equipment – reputedly being taught how to use it by the same man who rented it to him. The finished result was, according to Richard Combs writing in 1980, 'not so much a rough draft as a perfect miniature of the feature films that were to follow... The time-lock structure anticipates *The Killing*; the deserted, early morning streets are as haunted as the similarly used locations in *Killers Kiss*... Kubrick's images lend more than a hint of apocalypse, and of a genuinely agonized determinism, to an hour-by-hour account of Cartier's wait for yet another encounter.'

Certainly as a first effort, *Day of the Fight* is a remarkably assured, tightly made movie - well photographed by Kubrick, who captures the mounting tension of Walter's day, with the narration grimly reminding us of the uncertain outcome of a fighter's life - 'It's important for Walter to get to Holy Communion, in case something should go wrong tonight' - as the brothers attend Morning Mass. This narrative style emphasizes the long wait during the build-up to the fight, and the effect this has on the young boxer - finally transformed from a gentle, average new Yorker into a determined 'arena man' - the face that the 3000 strong crowd will see.

Most of the picture was filmed silent - and influenced by silent techniques, using slow panning shots of the boxer's kit laid out ready to be packed as the brothers are seen in silhouette gazing out of the apartment window at the New York streets. The actual fight itself, however, is skilfully condensed into just two minutes and apparently complete with 'natural' sound. Other than one obviously staged shot of the two boxers filmed upwards from the canvas of the ring, the opening title 'All events depicted in this film are true' seems a genuine description.

Completed for just under $4,000, it is unclear whether Kubrick actually made a profit on the sale of *Day of the Fight* to RKO – the *New York Times* reported that the studio had bought the picture for 'considerably more than $5,000,' but Combs later claimed that Kubrick 'only was able to sell it to RKO for a little less than [$4,000].' Whatever the true financial position, the picture was highly regarded on release – an unsentimental, deliberately unglamorous account of the life of a moderately successful – yet struggling – member of the 'profession'. Screened as part of RKO's *This is America* series at the Paramount Theatre, New York, the success of *Day of the Fight* prompted Stanley Kubrick to quit his job at *Look* magazine to become a full-time movie-maker.

*Cartier was destined never to become middleweight champion as he had hoped, although he did enter the history books - having achieved the 'quickest knockout in Boston Garden history,' flooring Joe Rindone in just 47 seconds in October 1951.

Following his wholly natural and highly photogenic appearance in *Day of the Fight*, Cartier gave up the ring for an acting career, appearing in Paul Newman's second picture, *Somebody Up There Likes Me* (directed by Robert Wise, 1956) and Elia Kazan's *A Face in the Crowd* the following year. On television, he guested on both the *Ed Sullivan Show* and the *Martha Raye Show*, and was in the series *Crunch and Des* with Forrest Tucker, and - most notably - an original platoon member in *You'll Never Get Rich*, forerunner of the long running *Phil Silvers Show* better known as *Sgt Bilko*.

Later a salesman for a Brooklyn metals firm until his retirement, Cartier died in New York in 1995.

1951
FLYING PADRE

A documentary tribute of the almost unbearable naive 'look at life' variety.
RICHARD COMBS

RKO Radio-Pathe.

Directed by Stanley Kubrick.
Produced by Burton Benjamin.

Screenplay, photography: Stanley Kubrick.
Film editing: Isaac Kleineerman.
Sound recording: Harold R. Vivian.
Music: Nathaniel Shilkret.

With Reverend Fred Stadtmueller. Narrated by Bob Hite.

9 minutes. Black and white.

A true-life story as the camera follows the Reverend Fred Stadtmueller on his 'daily rounds' – although in this case, the priest's parish covers 400 square miles of Harding County in New Mexico, which he administers with the help of a single-engined Piper Cub aeroplane, the 'Spirit of St Joseph.'

Over two days, Stadtmueller is called on to attend a variety of episodes including a remote church funeral and a regular service for his congregation, and later deals with a school bully at the request of a small girl. 'Off duty' we see him enjoying his hobby of raising canaries, and demonstrating his expertise as a crack shot with a rifle, before receiving an urgent call from a mother with a sick baby at an isolated ranch. Immediately, the priest sets off in his plane to collect the young woman and her child before delivering them to the nearest airport where an ambulance will take them to hospital and safety.

Learning from a friend of the eccentric routine of the Reverend Stadtmueller, and with the backing of a $1,500 advance from RKO following the successful reception afforded *Day of the Fight*, Stanley Kubrick followed the priest for two days as he went about his parish, recording various aspects of the life of this colourful character.

As a brief (nine minute) snapshot of the life of the priest, the film was adequate, although Richard Combs later found it to be 'more conventional... the film-maker-to-be so startlingly asserted in *Day of the Fight* seems, here, to have contracted himself into an uncongenial corner.'

Flying Padre was indeed a less impressive effort, with the contrived situations in which Stadtmueller finds himself - especially the little girl requesting his help with her bullying friend and the airlifted sick child incident - particularly unconvincing, despite the obvious attempts at dramatic scene construction. Compared to the tense atmosphere created in *Day of the Fight*, the tone here is considerably more lightweight, with Bob Hite's narration reminiscent of nothing more than a Joe McDoakes short comedy feature.

Attracting considerably less attention than its predecessor, *Flying Padre* nevertheless offered an 'almost impossible-seeming low-angle of the priest in his plane,' said Combs, 'turning the cockpit into an indefinable space, some mysterious temple [and] Eisensteinian close-ups of peasant faces round the funeral in the desert.'

With these two short documentary subjects completed and released within a few short months of each other, Kubrick was clearly ready to take the next logical step and move into feature film production.

1953
THE SEAFARERS

A story simple but dramatic.
OPENING DIALOGUE

Lester Cooper Productions.

Directed by Stanley Kubrick.

Produced by Lester Cooper.
Photographed by Stanley Kubrick.
Written by Will Chasan.
Technical support by the staff of the Seafarers International Union.
Narrated by Don Hollenbeck.

30 minutes. Colour.

An industrial documentary showing the work of the Seafarers Union in New York City, *The Seafarers* was filmed entirely on location and told of the many advantages to be gained by becoming a member of the Seafarers Union – from being helped to find work at the Union Hiring Hall, to sickness benefits, pay protection and social support for those on leave or between jobs.

* * *

A definite rarity and oddity in the Kubrick canon, this short promotional film was commissioned by the Seafarers International Union of the Atlantic and Gulf Coast District.

Well-intentioned but far from engrossing, the film (despite a running time of less than half an hour) quickly outstays its welcome, with its flat narration by Don Hollenbeck seen on camera at either end of the film clearly reading from cue cards. All of the attendant clumsiness of showing 'real' people attempting to behave 'naturally' before a camera is here; over-lingering shots of the Union cafeteria, or of grateful disabled ex-seamen receiving their weekly cash benefits at their retirement home or the local hospital - with much of the footage shot silent, this also makes the 'short' seem over-long, even with the addition of the (uncredited) music score – alternately twee or uplifting.

Kubrick's camera work is generally adequate, whether it be scenes of the ships in New York harbour and pan-shots across to the Union headquarters or the men waiting to be called for work inside the hall. At times, however, the film resembles nothing more than one of those over-earnest 1940s 20th Century-Fox true-life dramas promoting the work of the FBI, with its images of endless rows of filing cabinets set to stirring music and the accompaniment of clattering typewriters and telex machines.

Hired simply as director/cameraman, Kubrick had little editorial control over the end result but used the commission to gain further experience in film-making techniques. Significantly this was his first film in colour.

1953
FEAR AND DESIRE

A Holy Grail among film aficionados.
BRUCE GOLDSTEIN

Stanley Kubrick Productions. (Joseph Burstyn Inc)

Produced, directed, photographed and edited
by Stanley Kubrick.

Screenplay: Howard O. Sackler and Stanley Kubrick.
Assistant director: Steve Hahn.
Production assistant: Marvin Perveler.
Rehearsal assistant: Toba Kubrick.
Music: Gerald Fried.

Cast: Frank Silvera (Mac); Kenneth Harp (Lieutenant Corby/the general); Paul Mazursky (Sidney);
Steve Colt (Fletcher/general's aide); Virginia Leith (the girl); David Allan (narrator).

68 minutes. Black and white.

In the midst of a war, four soldiers find themselves stranded behind enemy lines when their plane is shot down. Planning an escape along the river, they first kill a couple of enemy soldiers before capturing a native girl and tying her to a tree. The youngest of the group Sidney (Paul Mazursky) is left to watch over her as the other three scout ahead but, after attempting to rape the girl, he shoots her when she tries to escape.

The rest of the men have meanwhile come across an enemy command post and plan to steal their plane in order to escape. As Mac (Frank Silvera) heads back to collect Sidney, Corby (Kenneth Harp) and Fletcher (Steve Colt) advance on the camp and kill the two enemy soldiers, only to discover that they are their own doubles. Eventually, the four men regroup and escape in the captured plane.

* * *

With three short documentary subjects behind him, 25-year-old Stanley Kubrick took the next logical step to move into feature films. Without the backing of any studio, however, he was forced to borrow the money from friends and relatives to finance *Fear and Desire*, which today remains the least seen of his films.

The *New York Times* reported in 1951 that Kubrick had budgeted the movie 'at the astonishingly low cost of $50,000 [and] figured out every camera angle' before-

hand. Shooting was expected to take between 15 and 21 days 'after he finds the proper location in some wooded area of Southern California.'

With four 'professional but not known-name actors' from Broadway, Kubrick was said to be negotiating to hire a professional cinematographer 'because [he] is not yet a member of the cameramen's union.' Significantly, however, it was stated that any cameraman engaged would be required to 'agree in advance to follow the blueprint laid out' by the young director – clearly a sign of things to come.

Impressed by *Day of the Fight*, Los Angeles druggist Marvin Perveler – an uncle of Kubrick's – organized a syndicate which would raise the finance for the shoot, although Kubrick later said that Perveler had put up most of the money himself. The director worked on a screenplay with Howard O. Sackler – a 21-year-old poet friend whom he had known since Taft High School days – and together they produced 'a study of four men and their search for the meaning of life and the individual's responsibility to the group' – a somewhat daunting subject, and it is not altogether surprising that the completed film tackled these questions with only limited success.

With a skeleton crew – which included Kubrick's wife Toba Metz – the film was shot in the San Gabrielle Mountains near Los Angeles, 'photographed in such a way as to reflect the mental state of the men,' according to *Modern Photography* magazine. 'When the soldiers were hopeful, the river and mountains were brightly lighted [*sic*]. When the men were frightened, the mountains appeared brooding and dangerous.'

On such a tight budget, such ambitious methods had to be weighed against economy, as 'twilight scenes were obtained in bright sunlight by placing a red filter over the lens and underexposing the film three stops.' Having to create his own environment, including suitable weather conditions, Kubrick and the crew managed even to come up with a cut-price special effect when one scene called for a heavy river fog – the artificial mist was the result of a large insecticide sprayer, filled with a mineral-oil based liquid.

With such ingenuity, filming was completed quickly – Kubrick eventually operating the camera himself, in spite of the earlier reports concerning a 'union crew' – but shot completely silent. All sound, dialogue and music was to be added later in New York during editing, taking almost nine months and pushing up the cost of the picture dramatically – Kubrick later admitting that this was a big mistake. 'The actual shooting cost of the film was $9,000,' he said, 'but because I didn't know what I was doing with the soundtrack it cost me another $20,000' – a huge additional expense.

A further blow came when Hollywood's major studios declined to handle the picture, which was eventually taken up by independent distributor Joseph Burstyn who, it was reported in *New Yorker*, 'presumably knows a good picture when he sees one, since he was responsible for the importation here of such films as *Open City, Paisan* and *Bicycle Thieves.*'

New Yorker further considered *Fear and Desire* 'almost a classic piece of malarkey. Mr Kubrick, setting out to demonstrate that he disapproves of war... proceeds to talk his prejudice to death.' The review continued: 'To point up the idea that war is a futile business, *Fear and Desire* employs the same actors to represent friend and enemy. This, of course, leads to confusion, and the fact that none of the actors is exactly the last word in technical ability tends to make a bad affair worse.'

Of that cast, only Frank Silvera had any significant screen experience prior to *Fear and Desire*, although Virginia Leith was later a leading lady in films like *Black Widow*(1954)*, Violent Saturday* (1955) and *A Kiss Before Dying* (1956), and Paul Mazursky went on to become a writer-director himself with a bunch of endemically silly, artificial sixties movies including *I Love You, Alice B. Toklas* and *Bob and Carol and Ted and Alice.*

Modern Photography carried a useful and well-illustrated article – 'It's movies for me, says Stan Kubrick, ex-still photographer' – on the making of *Fear and Desire* in its September 1953 edition, having previously featured some of Kubrick's best photographs in the magazine. According to their writer, Iris Owens, 'whenever possible, Kubrick rented shooting equipment. The most expensive item was the

Mitchell 35mm camera which he rented for $25 a day.' By comparison with a typical Hollywood feature, in which directors would expose on average around 500,000 feet of film, it was reported, Kubrick 'limited himself to 50,000 feet of black-and-white. From this he obtained 5,940 feet of usable film which screens for one hour and six minutes.'

Despite their general support for the stillsman-turned-movie-director, *Modern Photography* still felt that 'the photographic end of the picture outshines a story which is basically too weak to be really convincing.' The *New York Times* was kinder: 'Stanley Kubrick... and his equally young and unheralded cast have succeeded in turning out a moody, often visually powerful study of subdued excitements,' they announced. '*Fear and Desire* evolves as a thoughtful, often expressive and engrossing view of men who have travelled far from their private boundaries.' The review opened with a plea that 'The need for encouragement of fresh talent and its fairly common concomitant, the audacity of youth, was never made more pointed than in *Fear and Desire*,' and ended by forecasting that the result of their efforts 'augurs well for the comparative tyros [beginners] who made it.'

Opening at the Guild Theatre and with a release generally limited to art houses, *Fear and Desire* inevitably failed to make any profit, although Kubrick eventually managed to repay all of the money borrowed to finance it. Long unseen, it did not resurface again until 1994 when *Village Voice* announced its appearance for one week on a double-bill with *Killer's Kiss* at the Film Forum in New York. Within days, a Warner Brothers press release inserted in all of the trade papers declared that Kubrick 'has asked to let you know that if it had been up to him, the film would not be publicly shown [and that he considered it] nothing more than a bumbling amateur film exercise.' The release went on to dismiss the work as 'a completely inept oddity... boring and pretentious.' Later proposed screenings in Los Angeles, Ohio and New York were cancelled, apparently at Kubrick's insistence as sole owner of the film.

The director's views on the movie may seem unnecessarily harsh, as at one point he had said that 'the ideas we wanted to put across were good, but we didn't have the experience to embody them dramatically. It was little more than a 35mm version of what a class of film students would do in 16mm.' Nevertheless, the struggle to turn out a feature film almost entirely on his own terms was to prove invaluable to the young film-maker – not everyone can make *Citizen Kane* or *The Maltese Falcon* at their first attempt – and Kubrick acknowledged that it had been 'important to have this experience and to see with what little facilities and personnel one could actually make a film.' It was this aspect of the making of *Fear and Desire* which would remain with him: 'Today, I think that if someone stood around watching even a smallish film unit, he would get an impression of vast technical and logistical magnitude,' he said. The almost home-made quality of this first venture, Kubrick went on, 'freed me from any concern about [that].'

There is no doubt that *Fear and Desire* is a sometimes clumsy exercise in film-making by a young and inexperienced director. The plot may be naive, but makes several worthwhile points – in war, as the narration points out, 'the enemies do not exist until we call them into being.' The anonymous location and nationality of the soldiers in an unspecified war attempt to convey a sense of the universal futility of conflict while the metaphysical ploy of using the same actors to play both the killers and those killed – which would not have been out of place in a future episode of Rod Serling's *Twilight Zone* – suggests the inescapability of humanity from the darker reaches of its own nature.

Variety generously allowed the film to be 'a literate, unhackneyed war drama, outstanding for its fresh camera treatment and poetic dialogue,' although the *New York Times* complained of it as 'uneven and sometimes reveals an experimental rather than a polished exterior.' Despite this, they agreed that 'its overall effect is entirely worthy of the sincere effort put into it.' Kubrick, however, later told Joseph Gelmis, 'It's not a film I remember with any pride, except the fact that it was finished.'

1955
KILLER'S KISS

A frivolous effort.
STANLEY KUBRICK

Minotaur Productions. (United Artists)

Directed by Stanley Kubrick.
Produced by Stanley Kubrick and Morris Bousel.

Screenplay: Howard O. Sackler and Stanley Kubrick, from a story by Stanley Kubrick.
Film editor: Stanley Kubrick.
Assistant director: Ernest Nunaken.
Production manager: Ira Marvin.
Camera operators: Jesse Paley, Max Glen.
Assistant editors: Pat Jaffe, Anthony Bezich.
Sound recording: Walter Ruckersberg, Clifford van Praag.
Music: Gerald Fried. (Love song 'Once' by Norman Gimbel and Arden Clar).
Choreographer: David Vaughan. Ballet sequence danced by Ruth Sobotka.

Cast: Frank Silvera (Vincent Rapallo); Jamie Smith (Davey Gordon); Irene Kane (Gloria Price);
Jerry Jarrett (Albert); Ruth Sobotka (Iris Price); Mike Dana, Felice Orlandi, Ralph Roberts, Phil Stevenson (hood-
lums); Julius Adelman (owner of mannequin factory); David Vaughan, Alec Rubin (conventioneers);
With Shaun O'Brien, Barbara Brand, Arthur Feldman, Bill Funaro.

67 minutes. Black and white.

Boxer Davey Gordon (Jamie Smith) nervously waits at a Pennsylvania railway station, recalling the events of the past three days, which have led him to this crossroads in his life.

Sitting in his cheap apartment room, Jamie watches the girl in the room across the courtyard. Gloria (Irene Kane) works as a 'hostess' at the seedy local dance hall run by Vincent Rapallo (Frank Silvera) and has been drawn – inevitably – into becoming his mistress. Gloria and Davey pass in the hall each morning as they leave the building, not even exchanging brief hellos.

Davey's next fight is televised and, when he loses, his uncle George telephones to suggest he come back home to Seattle, to the family farm. Davey promises to think it over and – depressed and exhausted – falls asleep. Vincent and Gloria have also been watching the fight on TV at the club, and when he later forces his way into her apartment, her screams wake Davey who comes to her rescue as Rapallo makes his escape.

The next morning, Gloria tells Davey her story: her sister Iris (Ruth Sobotka) – a ballet dancer – had given up her career to marry a man solely for his money in order to help their sick father. Iris committed suicide on the day her father died and, with her family gone, Gloria had come to Pennsylvania and drifted into the job with Rapallo. Tonight, he had asked her to marry him and become violent when she refused.

Gloria and Davey quickly realize that they belong together, and decide to get married and make a new start at George's farm in Seattle, but first they need to collect all of the money they can get hold of. Gloria goes to see Rapallo for her week's salary and tells him that she is leaving, while Davey waits outside for his manager Albert (Jerry Jarrett) to collect his pay for the previous night's fight.

Rapallo is furious at Gloria's news and orders two of his thugs to take care of her new man. Davey, meanwhile, has given chase to a couple of drunken conventioneers who have snatched his scarf, and the thugs mistakenly attack Albert, who later dies from the savage beating they give him. Unaware of this,

Davey and Gloria return home to pack, but soon learn that Davey is wanted in connection with Albert's death.

When Gloria – who can identify the two murderers she saw leaving the club – is kidnapped, Davey realizes that Rapallo is behind it all, and hijacks him in his car, forcing him to drive to the warehouse where she is being held. Once there, however, Davey is overpowered, but escapes by leaping through a window as Gloria begs for her own life.

Chased by Rapallo across the rooftops and into another warehouse, Davey confronts the racketeer in a storage room filled with shop dummies. Although Rapallo arms himself with a fire axe and Davey has only a wooden pole, the younger, fitter man is able to win this fight. When the police eventually arrive on the scene, he is cleared of all charges.

Back at Pennsylvania station, Davey waits anxiously for the train which will take him away from it all as, with only seconds to spare, Gloria rushes to meet him and the two head off to start their new life together.

✳✳✳

In the almost two-year period since the release of *Fear and Desire*, and faced with the obvious conclusion that his first feature-length movie was not going to be a financial success, Stanley Kubrick had worked briefly as a some-time second-unit director on the *Omnibus* series for American television, produced by Robert Saudek and introduced by Alistair Cooke. He also worked – 'for about a week' – on a TV film for Richard de Rochemont on Abraham Lincoln.

With a planned second movie, however, Kubrick once again faced the struggle to raise enough finance to even make the picture. Managing to borrow some $40,000 from relatives and friends, he again hired the necessary equipment and signed a cast – all of whom were to be paid on a deferment basis, as Irene Kane later explained: 'That means that you get a percentage of your salary each week, and the rest out of profits – if any. I was contracted for $650 and took home what was left out of $65 after taxes.'

In the glamorous world of film-making, some actors might have resented such a situation, but not in this case. 'It didn't matter to me,' says Kane. 'I would have paid Stanley. Here it was, my first acting job, and I was starring in a movie.' She had come to the film via an introduction to Kubrick through a mutual friend who, she recalled 'had previously worked in the mailroom at *Look* magazine.' Although not a professional actor – she was doing modelling work at the time – Kane was asked by Kubrick to read a scene 'which went on for about six minutes. "I can't do it," I said, but Stanley was patient. "Make us some coffee and we'll talk," he said.' What was said during the next hour she does not reveal, but when Kubrick handed her the script once more, she 'did the six-minute soliloquy in three and a half minutes flat,' with Kubrick apparently 'enraptured' and announcing 'You're going to be a great star.' 'It was like a Betty Grable movie,' she later wrote: 'the scene where Betty takes off her glasses and she's beautiful.'

A script was written by the director, once more in collaboration with Howard O. Sackler. According to the *New York Times*, Kubrick 'outlined several action scenes, including a murder, a near rape, a chase across New York rooftops, a boxing match and a fight to the death [and] then connected the scenes with what passed for a screenplay.' The report also noted that 'a lot of the production cost went to pay for wrecking a factory full of mannequins.'

Gerald Fried was again engaged as composer and director of the film's music score in the third of his five films with Kubrick. Fried was already beginning to carve out a successful career in film composition, with a long list of future credits to include *The Killing of Sister George* and *Soylent Green*, and here he produced a suitably sleazy, if occasionally over-intrusive score whose main theme would later – unintentionally, though in the circumstances quite appropriately – be almost note for note the same as Alex North's main title music for John Huston's *The Misfits* (1961).

Impressively filmed on location in New York City – with interesting backdrops including the riverfront shot from warehouse rooftops, and deserted alleyways away from the main, familiar settings – *Killer's Kiss* was again a long time in post-production, with sound and dialogue being dubbed later despite the huge cost which this had added to the *Fear and Desire* budget. Reportedly, four months were spent dubbing in sound effects 'footstep by footstep,' and this led to some serious disillusionment for at least one of the film's participants. Irene Kane considered the dubbing sessions 'torture... [staring] at the screen and trying to fit words into your own mouth off a loop script over and over and over again until the mechanicalness of the process drove me mad.'

After enduring some eight hours of this, she says, 'I threw my script on the floor and went to Florida, and Gloria's dialogue was finally read by a radio actress called Peggy Lobbin.' Whether he considered this an act of treachery or simply a disappointment, Kubrick had apparently previously told Kane how 'he loved my little boy voice – it would become famous, kids would imitate it the way they did Marlon Brando's.' Irene Kane's screen career never subsequently took off, although – under her real name of Chris Chase, she became a successful writer, publishing a best-selling biography of Betty Ford in the 1970s, and was also featured on-screen again – briefly – in Bob Fosse's *All That Jazz* (1979) as a gossip columnist.

With a final budget stretching to $75,000, *Killer's Kiss* was sold to United Artists for distribution as a second feature under the unlikely advertising tag line 'Her soft mouth was the road to sin-smeared violence!' in spite of which the film actually made a small profit. Kubrick, however, saw little – if any – of it, after paying off his debts and deferred rental costs. He was supposedly 'living off unemployment checks of a dancer named Ruth Sobotka,' according to Kane. Kubrick's marriage to Toba Metz had by now broken up, and Miss Sobotka was soon to become his second wife. In the meantime, 'since Stanley was in love, there was a whole ballet sequence set into the movie,' with Sobotka cast as Gloria's much-mourned sister Iris.

As a completed feature, *Killer's Kiss* gained further attention for its director, with *Monthly Film Bulletin* calling it 'a small scale-film of distinct quality... The writer-director-cameraman-editor Stanley Kubrick is evidently a promising young talent.' (In fact, Kubrick had not worked the camera on this occasion – at least not officially – in accordance with union regulations.) The *MFB* review continued: 'Within the framework of the story, he has done some interesting things. Atmospherically the film is excellent... rich in detail and evocative power. The relationship between the young people is genuine, and the film is at its best not in the action passages but in its everyday observations of character and place... little incidents have an almost Zavattini quality.' (The reference here is to Cesare Zavattini, an Italian screenwriter whose long association with writer/director Vittorio de Sica produced such classics as *Shoeshine* (1946), *Bicycle Thieves* (1948), *Miracle in Milan* (1950), *Umberto D* (1952) and *Two Women* (1961).

Variety noted that 'Ex-*Look* photographer Stanley Kubrick turned out *Killer's Kiss* on the proverbial shoestring... [his] low-key lensing occasionally catches the flavor of the seamy side of Gotham life [while] scenes of tawdry Broadway, gloomy tenements and grotesque brick-and-stone structures that make up Manhattan's downtown eastside loft district help offset the script's deficiencies.'

Unquestionably, the film has its faults – the script is often banal and the level of acting decidedly clumsy, as might be expected from a relatively young cast of which only Frank Silvera – retained from *Fear and Desire* – could be considered experienced (Jamie Smith had featured in only one previous pic, *The Faithful City*, 1952). The boxing motif continued, and indicates Kubrick's continued interest in the sport, with Davey's losing fight well photographed in an impressively unglamorous, economical manner scarcely improved upon even by *Raging Bull* or the many *Rocky* episodes. Background detail was also well captured, with Davey living in a seedy, cheap apartment and his preparations for the fight intercut with Gloria's own preparations for another evening's soul-destroying work at the dance hall.

As a story, *Killer's Kiss* is quite the most conventional film that Kubrick has ever been involved with, and remains his sole attempt at a seemingly straight love story of the boy-meets-girl variety, though with suitably hard-boiled dialogue. Irene Kane reveals that Kubrick was a great fan of Mickey Spillane, which perhaps accounts for her put-down of the over-amorous Rapallo – 'You're an old man and you smell bad.'

Yet there are striking images in the film, as one would expect from someone whose chief career up to that point had been in the making of compelling and arresting visuals. The set-piece showdown in the mannequin factory, with its disembodied arms among the swinging axe is strongly Wellesian in its influence, while the killing of Davey's manager Albert is impressively handled in traditional *noir* style – silhouetted figures retreating down a dark alleyway, with no actual violence shown. There is also an interesting early sequence depicting Davey's nightmare, in which a black and white negative image of a frantic rush down a narrow street, with its tall buildings crowding in on either side, could, in retrospect, be seen as a forerunner to the dazzling star gate sequence in *2001: A Space Odyssey* 13 years later.

Despite her imminent exit from the film business, Irene Kane had come to her first movie role filled with enthusiasm and excitement: 'The first day I reported for work,' she said, 'I nearly died of happiness... I touched every prop, every dish, every bobby pin... I went up and put my hands against the wall and thought "nothing will ever be this good again".'

Her early recollections of Kubrick in a letter to her sister are especially revealing: 'Stanley drove me home the other night after a huge scene on the set,' she wrote – the scene being caused by stagehands complaining of 'cold, tiredness, lack of funds, and Frank Silvera chimed in and said there was a play he could be doing right this minute, or at least reading for it, if he didn't have to be down here in the gutter with the rest of us.' No doubt many directors have faced similar situations with disgruntled cast and crew members when the weather is against them or a quiet day at home in bed seems preferable to a 7am shoot. 'Stanley listened to the whole thing,' Kane continued, 'then very sweetly told everybody to take off, we were finished for the day. After we got in the car, I asked him how he could be so patient, and he grinned. "Baby, nobody's going to get anything out of this movie but me".'

Kubrick's own subsequent view of this second feature-length effort was again dismissive: 'While *Fear and Desire* had been a serious effort ineptly done,' he judged, '*Killer's Kiss* proved, I think, to be a frivolous effort done with conceivably more expertise, though still down in the student level of film-making.' Having established in both films a working routine in which he assumed complete control of all aspects of filming – as he would continue to do in the future – Kubrick summed up *Killer's Kiss* with 'The only distinction I could make for it is that, to the best of my belief, no one at the time had ever made a feature film in such amateur circumstances and then obtained world-wide distribution for it.'

* In 1983, an independent US film called *Stranger's Kiss*, directed by Matthew Chapman (who also co-wrote the screenplay with female lead Blaine Novak) told of the making of a fictional feature film-within-the-film, whose plot strongly resembled that of *Killer's Kiss* – a love story between a boxer and a dance-hall girl whose past relationship with a gangster threatens to foil their plans. Emphasizing that this was in fact a homage to low-budget melodramas of the 1950s (the story was set in 1955), Peter Coyote starred as the film's director, named... Stanley.

PART 3
BIG FEATURES

1956
THE KILLING

Announces the arrival of a new boy wonder in the industry.
TIME

Harris–Kubrick Productions. (United Artists)
Directed by Stanley Kubrick. Produced by James B. Harris.

Screenplay: Stanley Kubrick, based on the novel *Clean Break* by Lionel White. Associate producer: Alexander Singer. Production supervisor: Clarence Eurist. Assistant directors: Milton Carter, Paul Feiner, Howard Joslin. Additional dialogue: Jim Thompson. Director of photography: Lucien Ballard. Process photography: Paul Eagler. Camera operator: Dick Tower. Photographic effects: Jack Rabin, Louis De Witt. Film editor: Betty Steinberg. Art director: Ruth Sobotka. Set decorator: Harry Reif. Assistant set decorator: Carl Brainard. Special effects: Dave Koehler. Music composed and directed by Gerald Fried. Music editor: Gilbert Marchant. Wardrobe: Jack Masters, Rudy Harrington. Make-up: Robert Littlefield. Sound recording: Earl Snyder. Sound effects editor: Rex Lipton. Production assistant: Marguerite Olson.

Cast:
Sterling Hayden (Johnny Clay); Colleen Gray (Fay); Vince Edwards (Val Cannon); Elisha Cook Jr (George Peatty); Marie Windsor (Sherry Peatty); Jay C. Flippen (Marvin Unger); Ted de Corsia (Randy Kennan); Joe Sawyer (Mike O'Reilly); Timothy Carey (Nikki Arane); Jay Adler (Leo); Kola Kwarian (Maurice Oboukhoff); Joseph Turkel (Tiny); James Edwards (car park attendant); With: Tito Vuolo, Herbert Ellis, James Griffith, Dorothy Adams, Cecil Elliott, Mary Carroll, William Benedict, Steve Mitchell, Robert Williams, Charles Cane.

83 minutes. Black and white.

An unlikely bunch of characters are drawn together to commit what seems to be the perfectly planned crime to steal $2 million from a San Francisco racetrack. Most are not professional criminals, but each has his reason for needing a share of the money.

Randy Kennan (Ted de Corsia) is a cop caught up with a loan shark putting the squeeze on him to repay his gambling debts. Mike O'Reilly (Joe Sawyer) makes a miserable living as a bartender at the race-track, desperately needing the cash to help his sick wife get away from their cramped apartment. George Peatty (Elisha Cook Jr) is a cashier at the same track – a small man whose wife Sherry (Marie Windsor) makes no secret of the fact that she considers him to be a complete failure.

The plan has been put together by Johnny Clay (Sterling Hayden), a small-time crook recently released from prison, and now intent on making one single big hit before skipping the country with his girl, Fay (Colleen Gray). Without Johnny's brains there is no robbery. The entire operation is timed to the split-second, and he has picked these men carefully to carry out their individual parts of the job. Finally there is Marvin Unger (Jay C. Flippen), an old-timer whose main contribution is to put up the money for those 'extras' which Johnny says are essential for the robbery to succeed.

Although all sworn to secrecy, George cannot resist telling Sherry something of the plan, in an effort to impress her, after she has spent yet another evening sarcastically putting him down. When he later leaves to meet with the rest of the gang, she hurries to her lover Val Cannon (Vince Edwards) and tells him what George has said. Together they plan to kill George and take his share of the money, with Val ambitiously considering hijacking the entire gang and making off with all of the loot. Sherry has found Johnny's address in George's coat pocket, and she agrees to go there in an attempt to spy out the plan.

As the men discuss the operation, a noise outside the apartment leads Johnny and Randy to investigate. Instinctively they knock out the intruder. It turns out to be Sherry, and George protests that he has told her nothing of the robbery, improbably insisting that she must have thought that he was seeing another woman. Johnny sends him home and remains alone with Sherry, whose attempts to flirt with him are quickly brushed aside. 'You're a no good tramp but you're smart,' he tells her. 'Keep your nose clean and George will have plenty of money and spend it all on you – probably buy himself a five cent cigar.' Sherry corrects him, adding that 'You really don't know me very well – I wouldn't dream of letting him waste his money on cigars.'

On the day set for the robbery itself, everything runs like clockwork. Maurice Oboulhoff (Kola Kwarian), an ex-wrestler hired by Johnny, starts a fight in the bar of the racetrack, so fierce that it takes all of the available security guards to overpower him. A further diversion has been engineered by hiring sniper Nikki Arane (Timothy Carey) to shoot one of the leading horses in the race, although the gunman himself is then killed while trying to escape. As the commotion continues, George opens a side door for Johnny, who quickly recovers a gun previously hidden in Mike's locker. Donning a mask as a disguise, he holds up the cash office, collecting a sack filled with notes before forcing the staff into the locker room opposite, and shutting them in. Throwing the sack out of a window, to where Randy is waiting to collect it, he then changes into another jacket and calmly walks out of the racetrack.

Randy drops off the sack at a motel room rented earlier by Johnny, and the men gather to wait for his arrival to share out the take. When he is late arriving, they become edgy until there is a knock at the door. Instead of Johnny, Val bursts into the room with his partner Tiny (Joe Turkel), demanding all of the money. When George pulls his own gun, a ferociously fast gunfight leaves all of the men dead apart from George, who is mortally wounded.

As George staggers out of the apartment building, Johnny – who has been held up in traffic – arrives and quickly realizes what has happened. He drives away as George heads back to the treacherous Sherry, who is expecting to run off with Val. Instead, George kills her as she pathetically complains 'This isn't fair.' Having taken care of his wife, George, too, falls dead.

With all of the money now his, Johnny buys a large second-hand suitcase and meets Fay at the airport as arranged. Although Johnny insists that he take the case onto the plane with him, the airline refuses to allow this and offers him a later flight, instead. Reluctantly, he agrees to the case being taken to the hold with the other baggage. Outside on the tarmac, as they prepare to board the plane, Johnny and Fay can only watch, helplessly, as the baggage handler swerves to avoid a stray dog and the case falls to the ground, bursting wide open. The money is caught up in the propeller gusts and scattered across the airfield and beyond, as Fay leads a dumbstruck Johnny back through the terminal building. At the front entrance, she tries unsuccessfully to stop a cab, and Johnny turns helplessly to see two armed detectives advancing on him.

＊ ＊ ＊

Hired gunman Nikki Arane (Timothy Carey, left) gives Johnny Clay (Sterling Hayden, right)
the sales pitch as Clay plans the robbery in *The Killing*.

Dismissing *Fear and Desire*, Stanley Kubrick considered *The Killing* to be his second real feature film, which also qualified as his second entry in the catalogue of *film noir*, drawing considerable attention to its young director. *Time* magazine noting that 'At 27, Stanley Kubrick has shown more audacity with dialogue and camera than Hollywood has seen since Orson Welles went riding out of town,' while the *News Chronicle* called the picture 'altogether remarkable.'

This would not be the last time that Kubrick would find himself compared to Welles – no bad thing – and the fragmented narrative structure of *The Killing* stands alongside *Citizen Kane* in its bold use of flashbacks and repetitive action in establishing events at precise moments in time, and slotting individual characters into those events. Kubrick himself later observed that 'it was the handling of time that may have made this movie more than just a good crime film.'

Following the modest success of the virtually home-made *Killer's Kiss*, Kubrick met up again with James B. Harris, a former television company executive just out of the army. The two had previously known each other through Alexander Singer, a friend of Kubrick's who had been in the army with Harris and would now become associate producer on *The Killing*. Singer later became a director in his own right, with a number of films during the 1960s and 1970s including *A Cold Wind in August* and *Captain Apache*. 'Singer and I were making experimental films at weekends,' says Harris, recalling those days of the early 1950s when he was on leave from the army. 'He brought Stanley along one weekend – he had already made *Fear and Desire* – and we struck up a friendship in those few days.'

Now discharged, Harris ran across Kubrick again, who was exploring the possibility of selling *Fear and Desire* to television via Flamingo Films, the company run by Harris and David Wolper. Although the deal eventually fell through, Harris – who had recently seen and been hugely impressed by *Killer's Kiss* – 'guessed he was in need of a partner – that film had been so low-budget, it just proves how talented he was, doing everything from writing, photographing, editing and putting the sound on afterwards.'

Harris' practical suggestion was that, 'with a little more professional financial backing, we could get a decent story and I could take a lot of the burden away and release him to direct with all the problems solved for him.' The partnership was formed, although they did not yet have anything to produce – a situation resolved almost immediately, when Harris went to Scribners book store and came back with a bundle of books, including the crime novel *Clean Break* by Lionel White. Reading the book that night, he passed it to Kubrick the next day, and the story was chosen to become the first Harris–Kubrick production.

Encouragingly, United Artists had been sufficiently impressed by *Killer's Kiss* to promise Kubrick that they would consider anything else he might bring them in the future. Approaching the studio with the idea for the new picture, however, he found that Frank Sinatra had already shown interest in the same story. 'He had just done *Suddenly*, and wanted to do another crime film like that,' says Harris. The star, however, allowed negotiations to lapse, opting instead for other, diverse subjects including *Young at Heart* and *The Man with the Golden Arm*. Harris quickly stepped in and took the option on *Clean Break* with United Artists – discovering that Sinatra would not now be involved with the production – suggesting that he and Kubrick should contact them again when they had written a screenplay, which Kubrick set about writing with crime novelist Jim Thompson.

Thompson – son of a local sheriff – had been born in Anadarko, Arkansas, in 1906, drifting through a succession of unskilled jobs during the Depression and writing his first, romantic, social-realist novel in 1943. By 1949 he had turned to the crime thrillers which would become his trademark, with titles like *The Kill-Off* and *A Hell of a Woman*, published over the next 27 years, until his death in 1977. Seldom approached by film-makers during his lifetime (he seems only to have worked with Kubrick, and then on stories not his own, credited here only with 'additional dialogue'), Thompson lived to see a couple of his books turned into films in the 1970s (*The Getaway* directed by Sam Peckinpah in 1972, and Burt Kennedy's *The Killer Inside Me* in 1976), later enjoying a posthumous revival in 1990 when three of his works were filmed almost simultaneously – *The Grifters*, *After Dark My Sweet* and *The Kill-Off*.

Returning to United Artists with the completed screenplay as requested, Harris and Kubrick were then sent away again to find a suitable star who would agree to make the picture. 'They were offering us nothing,' says Harris, 'because if we could get a star interested then we could probably go to any studio.' Admitting now that they were a little naive – 'we were just so

excited that they liked the screenplay' – the two young film-makers considered UA's suggestion that the film would be a suitable vehicle for Victor Mature – an intriguing possibility since, despite a lingering reputation as star of a number of justly ridiculed biblical epics (*Demetrius and the Gladiators*, *The Robe* and *Samson and Delilah*) the man once known as 'The Hunk' had often been quietly impressive in more demanding roles for John Ford (*My Darling Clementine*) and Josef von Sternberg (*The Shanghai Gesture*) as well as a couple of admired *noir* entries, *Moss Rose* and *Kiss of Death*.

The problem, however, was that although Mature contractually owed United Artists a picture, he would not be available for another 18 months or so. Despite studio suggestions that they wait for what seemed to them a lifetime, Harris and Kubrick instead settled on Sterling Hayden as their first choice – coincidentally the co-star of *Suddenly* (1953), the picture which had tempted Frank Sinatra to consider *Clean Break* as a possible follow-up. (*Suddenly*, directed by Lewis Allen from a story by Richard Sale, has its own minor place in film history – the story of a psychotic gunman hired to assassinate a presidential candidate, it was later claimed that Lee Harvey Oswald had studied the film at length, before the 1963 Dallas shooting of President John F. Kennedy. Sinatra reportedly had the picture withdrawn from circulation at that time, and it remained unseen for many years.)

Sterling Hayden, meanwhile, had been an unconventional and reluctant movie star, as confirmed by his extraordinary 1963 autobiography *Wanderer*. With a no-nonsense screen presence similar to – but less heroic than – Burt Lancaster, Hayden's Hollywood career, spent working with the likes of John Huston, Kubrick, Douglas Sirk and Nicholas Ray, rates scarcely any mention in over 400 pages, clearly coming a poor second to his love of the sea and tales of his regular ocean voyages. In 1951, he had been subpoenaed by the notorious House of Un-American Activities committee, where he admitted to having been (briefly) a member of the Communist Party, and went on to name several others. 'Strange,' he later wrote, 'In almost all countries a man who collaborates with those who would punish freedoms arouses the hatred of his countrymen. And yet [today] in the United States, the way to loyalty is this – down the muddy informer's trail.'

According to John Huston – who had directed Hayden in *The Asphalt Jungle* (1950) – the star was later 'stricken with remorse' by his actions, and in *Wanderer* there is little doubt about his feelings. 'Hey! You execs back out on the coast!' he railed, concerning his testimony, 'Your boy came through. It's okay. You won't lose your dollars... I think of Larry Parks who, not ten days ago, sat in this very chair and – by begging them not to make him crawl in the mud – consigned himself to oblivion. Well, I hadn't made that mistake. Not by a god-

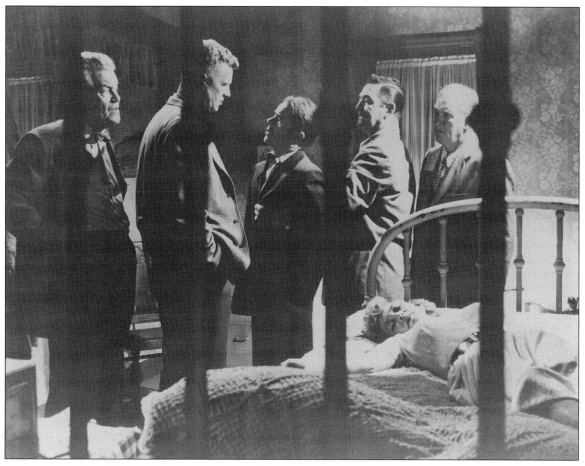

The Killing's gang of misfits – left to right: Jay C. Flippen, Sterling Hayden, Elisha Cook Jr, Ted de Corsia and Joe Sawyer – discuss what to do with interfering wife Marie Windsor, playing dead in the foreground.

damned sight... I was a real daddy longlegs of a worm when it came to crawling.' Huston considered Hayden 'one of the few actors I know who continued to grow over the years,' adding that he had 'always felt great sympathy for him with his failure to live up to his own idea of himself. But even from this experience he learned and grew. There is a kingliness about Sterling now.'

Sought out as star of *The Killing* – as *Clean Break* had now been retitled – a script was sent out to California where, as Harris recalls, Hayden's agent 'didn't know who Kubrick was – they asked me was it Stanley Kramer?' The producer persevered, convincing first the agent and then the actor of his partner's talent, so that he was soon able to report enthusiastically back to UA that they had found their star in Sterling Hayden, only for a studio executive to claim that they were 'selling Hayden in westerns for flat metal.'

Despite this, United Artists agreed to put up

$200,000 as their final, limited contribution to the production, warning the film-makers that they were welcome to put their own money into the picture but, if they did so, it would 'be in second position, because we have to get ours back first' and that, in any case, they should not pump in 'any more than another $200,000 because that's all a Sterling Hayden picture is worth.' Harris, however, had sufficient faith in both his new partner and the story itself to inject a further $130,000 of his own money into the production, which literally bought Kubrick an extra week's shooting time. As with *Killer's Kiss*, this would be a strict 'union' film, meaning that Kubrick was again prevented from acting as his own cameraman. The experienced Lucien Ballard was brought in behind the camera – his previous excursions into noir including such classics as *The Lodger* (1944) and *Laura* (1944) at 20th Century-Fox. For *The Killing*, Ballard created just the right atmosphere in the cheap apartment houses and well-worn streets of the under-world. In particular, the around-the-table scene, with the entire gang discussing the details of the upcoming robbery was impressively photographed from a variety of angles, all lit by a single light bulb hanging above them. With composer Gerald Fried once more engaged to provide a suitably jazz-oriented score, the movie was already promising to be a significant advance on its predecessors, in terms of professional involvement.

Even so, *Time* – no doubt accurately – noted that the film's total budget 'would hardly pay for lingerie in an Ava Gardner picture,' and even with the extended schedule which Harris' funds afforded, the movie was completed in just 24 days, much of it on location, but also using a few studio interiors for further economy. Kubrick – also credited as art director together with his wife Ruth Sobotka – later recalled that 'the sets were fairly cheap to build and the script let you spend a good chunk of time in each of them.' There were also practi-cal considerations to be considered when shooting a movie on the streets in 1955, with 'no neck mikes or radio transmitters... the cameras were big and the film slow.'

'It was well worth it,' James Harris says of his per-sonal investment today. 'We shouldn't have been able to get the nice cast we had – Stanley was so knowl-edgeable about all those known character actors. He had such good casting ideas.' This solidly reliably and familiar cast lifted *The Killing* above any number of other crime thriller caper movies of the fifties, many of the later ones inspired by Jules Dassin's acclaimed and influential *Rififi* (1954) - its plot following another intricately detailed robbery – in production at the same time as *The Killing*, and which Kubrick could not yet have seen.

The characters in *The Killing* are unusually vividly drawn – far from the normal stereotypes and blanks they could have been – and played by actors well known to cinemagoers from many gangster/crime pic-tures of the past. Ted de Corsia had previously been seen in *The Lady from Shanghai* (1948), *Naked City* (1948), *The Enforcer* (1951) and *The Big Combo* (1955), while Joe Sawyer was the despised army sergeant, later dealt rough justice by Humphrey Bogart in Raoul Walsh's *The Roaring Twenties* (1939). Jay C. Flippen – the manic Chikamo in Nicholas Ray's 1947 debut *They Live By Night* – here took on the role of Marvin Unger, clearly homosexual (although this would never be mentioned in any script of the period) and in awe of the much younger Johnny Clay. Uneasy as he enters the apartment to catch Johnny kissing his girl, he later tells Fay that 'There isn't anything I wouldn't do for Johnny,' and, while each of the other gang members clearly has a definite need of cash – to pay debts, help a sick wife, impress someone – Marv's only motivation appears to be his need to be close to

Johnny. His suggestion, when they are alone, that the two of them take off together with their share of the money away from any women, is gently brushed aside by Johnny, leading Marv to arrive later at the racetrack – from which he was told to keep well clear – hope-lessly drunk and risking the ruin of the entire plan. Johnny Clay could well be a cousin to Dix Handley, Hayden's equally doomed character in John Huston's *The Asphalt Jungle* (1950). Both have the same world-weary aura of a loser, betrayed by the weakness and greed of others around them.

Each of the gang is introduced in turn by their activ-ities earlier on the day of the raid. As Johnny explains to Fay, 'None of these men is a criminal in the ordinary sense. They all have jobs. They are all seemingly nor-mal, but they've got their problems.' He sums up the common feature amongst them as 'They're decent men with a little larceny in them.' This is a key element in Kubrick's screenplay – these men are willing to rob a racetrack of $2 million in an armed hold-up, but each still retains some decency, as do the real hoods hired to perform their given tasks.

'These are professionals,' Johnny assures his team of the unknown extras. 'Men who know they're being well paid to take a risk and won't squawk if the going gets rough.' Similarly, motel owner 'Joe Piano' initially refus-es to take Johnny's money for the room simply on his word that a pal from Alcatraz sent him. When Johnny presses him to take the cash because 'I got plenty more coming,' Joe says he will send it on to his friend 'on the island.' This underworld clearly looks after its own – 'I've got a peculiar weakness for criminals and artists,' Kubrick once said. 'Neither takes life as it is. The crimi-nal and the soldier at least have the virtue of being against something or for something in a world where people have learned to accept a kind of grey nothing-ness.'

In fact, the one player in the story shown to be defi-nitely corrupt is – ironically – the cop Randy Kennan (Ted de Corsia), first seen entering a dimly lit club early in the afternoon. Leo (Jay Adler) – another expertly drawn, fleeting appearance in a film loaded with fine moments – is putting Randy under pressure to repay his debts, adding even more interest to the loan which he cannot pay and which is presumably the result of increasing gambling debts. 'Take care of yourself,' Leo says ominously as his investment prepares to leave the club. 'I'll take care,' replies the crooked cop. 'That's my business.'

Elisha Cook Jr is once again cast as the archetyp-al 'little man' – still being slapped around 15 years after Humphrey Bogart had humiliated him in front of his boss in *The Maltese Falcon* (1941) – and des-perate to impress his floozy of a wife (the magnifi-cent Marie Windsor; all cheap negligees and flutter-ing eyelashes) whose every word to him drips

The odd couple: George (Elisha Cook Jr) and Sherry (the amazing Marie Windsor) settle down for another cosy night at home in *The Killing*.

demonstrating the power of a high-velocity rifle, before swapping the weapon in his arms for a young puppy, which he caresses throughout the conversation. Nevertheless, he is prepared to go ahead and shoot dead a racehorse for the offer of $5,000. Taking his place at the car park overlooking the racetrack, he appears to strike up a genuinely friendly relationship with black attendant (James Edwards) who presents him with his own lucky horseshoe, but is finally forced to insult him ('What's wrong, mister?' – 'You are, nigger.'), in order to be alone at the crucial moment when the horses approach. Although a minor incident, this appears to be a recurring feature in several of Kubrick's movies, for those who seek out such things – a man forced to act in a way which is forced upon him, in order to complete a predetermined course of duty. The attendant's horseshoe, meanwhile, brings about his downfall – puncturing his car tyre and leaving him a sitting target for the track's armed guards.

Perhaps least interesting of the film's creations is Vince Edwards' Val Cannon – little more than a cipher whose only real purpose is to be the instrument of the gang's demise. Seen only fleetingly with Sherry who he clearly does not care for at all, he is vicious, heartless greed personified with slicked-back hair – a sharp contrast to the gang of losers, old-timers and ex-cons. (Edwards was later to become entirely respectable as the devoted doctor in television's *Ben Casey*, running from 1960–5).

In the end, it is fate – and human weakness – which inexorably goes against the success of the robbery: if George had kept his mouth shut; if Sherry hadn't tipped off her lover; if Johnny had been on time getting to the apartment block after the robbery then Val may not have been able to pick off the rest of the gang, the cash would have been split as arranged and Johnny would not have had to buy a suitcase large enough to take the full $2 million. If only that suitcase had not had a faulty lock, or been too large to take into the cabin space; if only Johnny had agreed to a later flight; if only the dog had not run loose onto the tarmac at that precise moment...

Led swiftly away by Fay, in true *noir* style, we know that Johnny has no chance of escaping now. He is helpless to do anything but stand and watch as his plans evaporate in front of him and, even as Fay urges him to make a run for it, he mutters resignedly 'What's the difference,' as the cops advance on him. There is nothing and nowhere for him to escape to.

If there are any weaknesses in Kubrick's screenplay, it is the occasional lapse in continuity here and there: Marv's drunken appearance at the racetrack ultimately has no effect on the robbery itself and, shortly afterwards as the gang await Johnny's return, he is plainly cold sober again. Randy Kennan correctly assumes that no one would consider a cop at a racetrack as anything suspicious, but the alibi fails when he is

venom. When George tells her he has a pain in his stomach she coldly suggests, 'Maybe you got a hole in it,' without even looking up from her magazine. The puppyish George's reply 'How would I get a hole in my stomach?' is off-handedly met with 'How would you get one in your head? Fix me a drink, I think I'm getting some pains myself.' It is Sherry who not only tells Val of the planned robbery, but later lies to George about being raped by Johnny. Setting out on the day of the raid, George is the only member of the group to carry a gun – to take his revenge on Johnny once the money is theirs. Will he have the nerve? Will the rest of the gang let him do it?

How this oddly assorted bunch came together is never made clear – and really doesn't need to be. Clay is obviously a man of many contacts, as his choice of Maurice, the wrestler, to create a diversion shows. Maurice – a finely etched cameo by non-actor Kola Kwarian, whose impenetrable accent would effectively rule him out from any further film work – comes complete with an astonishing cauliflower ear as evidence of his profession, but is first introduced as an expert chess player; the two activities seemingly strange bedfellows – until we recall Kubrick's own interest in both chess (he was, according to future production designer Ken Adam, almost in the grand-master class at the age of 15) and the fight game (subject of *Day of the Fight*).

All of these minor players are carefully and believably realized – the superbly creepy Timothy Carey's complex hired assassin, Nikki Arane, occupies barely five minutes of screen time, first shown on his farm seen waiting behind the track, then driving off at speed with a sack thrown from a window.

But these are minor quibbles. *The Killing* is an ingenious, furiously paced movie, demanding its audience's attention at all times with its constant juggling of the dazzling sequence of events. The use of a narrator – often an unnecessary distraction in movies – is here essential, in a film which plays with its time-scale in such a reckless fashion, although James B. Harris reveals that this actually came straight from the source novel. 'It had a nice structure with lots of flashbacks,' he says. 'That's what intrigued us about it.'

The fractured narrative, however, was not universally admired, as had been the case with *Citizen Kane* and *The Life and Death of Colonel Blimp* (1943). Harris and Kubrick were warned that the flashbacks would antagonize the audience, and Sterling Hayden's agent expressed his disappointment with the finished picture, suggesting that the director should simply tell the story straight. In a rare comment, however, Hayden himself declared that he had 'worked with few directors that good. He's like the Russian documentarists who could put the same footage together five different ways, so it didn't really matter what the actors did – Stanley would know what to do with it.'

Although convinced that they had a good picture, Harris suggested that they 'not be stubborn about the thing' and listen to some of the advice they were being given. Having shot the film in California, they 'took it back to New York, where we lived, to a cutting room and took a shot at re-editing it.' The result, however, was clearly not a success. 'It was ridiculous,' he says. 'We abandoned any idea of making any changes and delivered it to UA exactly as we made it.'

Released in May 1956, *The Killing* gained generally good to excellent reviews, though the *New York Times* labelled it a 'fairly diverting melodrama,' while allowing that 'Mr Kubrick has kept things moving at a lively clip.' *Variety* was more enthusiastic: 'Stanley Kubrick's direction of his own script... is tight and fast-paced, a quality Lucien Ballard's top photography matches to lend particular fluidity of movement.' This reviewer also found 'the documentary style... at first... somewhat confusing [but this] soon settles into a tense and suspenseful vein which carries through to an unexpected and ironic windup.'

Two months later, the British press were to be heard complaining loudly at the lack of a press showing, or any notable pre-publicity – 'a brilliant feature has been buried away as a second feature on the Gaumont circuit,' wrote Alan Brien, who considered 'Kubrick is still doing his homework in the thick-ear school of film-making. But he displays the kind of talent that John Huston first revealed in *The Maltese Falcon* and *The Asphalt Jungle*.' Brien concluded by advising his readers that 'Anyone who wishes to be in

at the birth of a new screenmaster cannot afford to miss [this picture].'

Milton Shulman in the *Sunday Express* called the movie 'A slight, unpretentious affair, but it displays its virtues like a champion midget wrestler flexing his muscles.' Rightly praising the tight structure and precise editing of the picture, he continued: 'Nothing is superfluous and everything is hard and effective. It is perhaps typical of the film industry that when they have a thriller of more than average intelligence and of more than average box-office power, they should stick it away without showing it to the press or giving it a respectable run in the West End. There has never been a parent more eager to disown its potential geniuses.'

Monthly Film Bulletin confirmed that 'This new production reveals an exciting extension of the talents intermittently displayed in *Killer's Kiss*. Here, the observation is more acute, the seedy, violent world of vice more ruthlessly probed. The long central sequence depicting the raid itself is remarkably sustained and employs a complex series of short, inter-related scenes, culminating in the robbery.' Kubrick's growing command of the medium was similarly praised, as the *MFB* continued: 'Both here and in the ironic climax, the direction is firmly, almost mathematically, controlled with the tension kept at a high voltage... The handling of the large cast of seasoned character players, the harsh, unflattering lighting and the percussive score all reflect Kubrick's markedly personal idiosyncrasies.' The review ended by noting the similarity in tone of both of the director's recent efforts, meditating that 'It is interesting to speculate on what he might achieve with a subject less fashionably violent and corrupt.'

Despite such enthusiastic testaments to the film's quality, its placing on the year's 'Ten Best' lists of both *Time* and *Saturday Review*, and recognition at the British Academy Awards, *The Killing* still made an eventual loss of more than $100,000 for United Artists who, as several reviewers had already noted, had failed to promote the film effectively. 'It got terrific reviews,' confirms James B. Harris, 'but UA sold it as a second feature to *Bandido* with Robert Mitchum. So we got just flat rentals and there's a limit to what you can do with 50 dollars per theatre or whatever it was then. It was pretty discouraging, but the reviews were there, and that's what launched our career.' Certainly the film got the pair noticed in Hollywood, bringing the offer of a contract from Dore Schary for both Harris and Kubrick at MGM.

The Killing's reputation has grown enormously since its first release in 1956, cited by some – and apparently confirmed by the director – as a prime influence on Quentin Tarantino's vastly overrated breakthrough movie *Reservoir Dogs* released in 1991 – even to the extent that British television screened both movies as a late night double bill in 1997, with one review justifiably inviting viewers to compare the two. Unlike *The Killing*, however, *Reservoir Dogs* is peopled with a bunch of one-dimensional thugs, each a virtual carbon copy of the other, and all with practically no subtlety of characterization. Tarantino creates a gang, all of them working for a single boss, and attempts – via clumsily placed, sporadic flashbacks – to show us how each of them came to be there, but then, presumably, loses interest in this approach, since three of the group are never mentioned or even seen again. Time is much less skilfully handled than in Kubrick's movie, and the actual robbery is not shown at all. The surprise revelation that one of the gang is actually a cop who betrayed the remainder is well telegraphed, so becomes not much of a surprise after all, and the final three-way shoot-out, culled from Ringo Lam's 1987 *City on Fire* is simply ludicrous.

What critics apparently admired so much about this effort from first-time writer/director Tarantino was his supposed gift for writing stupendously natural dialogue but, throughout *Reservoir Dogs* – apart from it being incomprehensibly quiet – this insistence on giving every character the same unrelievedly 'hip' (i.e. unreal) speech only makes them all blur into one rather uninteresting mess. Much discussed in terms of its supposed graphic violence – which delayed the video release for more than a year – *Reservoir Dogs* ultimately proves to be an empty experience – more vicious than violent, less intelligent, less thrilling, less surprising than, say, Bryan Singer's *The Usual Suspects* (1995), which suffered unfair comparison with it, and certainly all of these same negative points can be applied to it by comparison to *The Killing*. Tarantino may well have been influenced by Kubrick's work but, as with so many other less subtle directors, appears to have absorbed and regurgitated all of the wrong aspects – or the right aspects wrongly – without having the innate skill to produce anything more than a bloodier poor relation.

1957
PATHS OF GLORY

The paths of glory lead but to the grave.
THOMAS GRAY

Bryna Productions/Harris–Kubrick Pictures Corporation. (United Artists)
Directed by Stanley Kubrick. Produced by James B. Harris.

Screenplay: Stanley Kubrick, Calder Willingham and Jim Thompson, based on the novel by Humphrey Cobb. Photography: George Krause. Camera operator: Hannes Staudinger. Assistant directors: H. Stumpf, D. Sensburg, F. Spicker. Editor: Eva Kroll. Assistant editor: Helene Fischer. Art director: Ludwig Reiber. Special effects: Erwin Lange. Music: Gerald Fried. Sound recording: Martin Muller. Costumes: Ilse Dubois. Make-up: Arthur Schramm. Production managers: John Pommer, George von Block. Unit manager: Helmut Ringelman.
Military adviser: Baron von Waldenfels.

Cast:
Kirk Douglas (Colonel Dax); Adolphe Menjou (General Georges Broulard); George Macready (General Paul Mireau); Ralph Meeker (Corporal Philipe Paris); Timothy Carey (Private Ferol); Joseph Turkel (Private Arnaud); Richard Anderson (Major Saint-Auban); Wayne Morris (Lieutenant Roget); Peter Capell (Colonel Judge); Bert Freed (Sergeant Boulanger); Emile Meyer (priest); Ken Dibbs (Private Lejeune); Harold Benedict (Captain Nichols); John Stein (Captain Rousseau); Susanne Christian (German girl); Jerry Hauser (tavern owner); Frederic Bell (wounded soldier).

86 minutes. Black and white.

1916 – and in the midst of the First World War, General Mireau (George Macready) is pressured by his superior, General Broulard (Adolphe Menjou) into ordering his troops to attack the heavily protected Ant Hill, with Mireau's order bringing protests from Colonel Dax (Kirk Douglas) that they are hopelessly outnumbered and the enemy position too strong.

On the eve of the attack, Lieutenant Roget (Wayne Morris) – who has been drinking heavily – leads a scouting party including Private Lejeune (Ken Dibbs) and Corporal Paris (Ralph Meeker) out into the field. Paris has known Roget since childhood and makes no secret of his opinion that he is unfit for command. During the reconnaissance, Roget sends Lejeune ahead and, when he fails to return, lobs a hand grenade to cover his own retreat. Paris makes his own way back to the trenches after discovering that Roget's actions have caused the death of Lejeune. He angrily threatens to report Roget – who had also left him for dead also – for his drunkenness, cowardice and the killing of one of his own men, but Roget tells him that no one will take his word against that of a superior officer.

The next morning, Dax leads the attack against the Ant Hill, which fails dismally, because his men are able to advance only a few yards before being cut down. Others are unable even to leave the trenches under the heavy bombardment. Watching from an observation post, Mireau – by field telephone – orders his artillery commander Captain Rousseau (John Stein) to fire on those troops who failed to advance, but Rousseau refuses to act without written authority. Outraged at being disobeyed, Mireau later tells Broulard that discipline can only be restored by there being an example made – 100 men executed as cowards. Broulard persuades him to accept a lesser number, with Mireau finally agreeing to just three – one from each company. Dax, who was a lawyer in civilian life, asks to be allowed to defend them.

Each company chooses one man apiece – Private Arnaud (Joseph Turkel) by lot, Private Ferol (Timothy Carey) on the grounds that he is considered by his comrades to be 'socially undesirable', and Corporal Paris, who has been nominated by Lieutenant Roget in revenge for his lack of respect towards him.

The trial is a complete mockery, with Dax denied the chance to defend the men effectively. Ferol testifies that none of his battalion were able to advance any more than a few yards under fire, but is told that the rest of the men are not on trial. Evidence concerning Arnaud's previous citation for bravery is ruled inadmissible by the judge, who declares 'Medals are no defence – the men are to be tried not for their past bravery but their recent cowardice.' Paris' alibi – he had been knocked unconscious early in the attack and was unaware of what had happened until later – is dismissed due to lack of supporting witnesses, and the suggestion that his injuries could have been self-inflicted. Inevitably, the men are found guilty and sentenced to death by firing squad.

On the eve of the execution, the men become increasingly desperate, with Ferol cracking under the strain. Arnaud gets drunk and attacks the priest (Emile Meyer) sent to offer comfort and hear their final confessions. Paris has to subdue him, but in the struggle Arnaud suffers a fractured skull, when he falls against a stone pillar. Examining the unconscious soldier, however, the medical team announce calmly that the execution will still go ahead.

Dax, meanwhile, has been approached by Rousseau who tells him of Mireau's order to fire on his own men, and he visits Broulard in a last-minute effort to persuade him to halt the killings. Broulard indignantly accuses Dax of attempting to blackmail him and, next morning, silently witnesses the three men being taken out to face the firing squad. Once the comatose Arnaud has been made to open his eyes, the executions take place.

Summoned later by Broulard, Dax learns that an outraged Mireau is to be relieved of his command and to be the subject of an inquiry into his conduct during the abortive attack. Cynically assuming that Dax had made his report the previous evening simply for his own gain, Broulard offers him Mireau's former command and is surprised when Dax refuses and angrily walks out, in disgust at such a heartless political charade. As he returns to the barracks, Dax hears his men in a nearby tavern, where a German peasant girl (Christian) is reluctantly being forced to sing for them. Watching, as their initial jeering and cat-calls finally turn to tearful silence, Dax tells his sergeant to allow the men a little longer before preparing to lead them, once more, to the front line.

* * *

The critical success of *The Killing* had brought Stanley Kubrick to the attention of several Hollywood studios and producers, with Dore Schary of MGM placing both Kubrick and his producer, James B. Harris, under a 40-week contract which allowed them a virtual free hand in choosing any subject, either from the vast MGM files or elsewhere – the pair reportedly taking such full advantage of the facilities on offer, that they were eventually reprimanded over 'excessive use' of the executive screening room.

Even before arriving at MGM, however, Harris and Kubrick had acquired the rights to Humphrey Cobb's 1935 novel *Paths of Glory*, a fiercely anti-war tale, apparently based on a true incident concerning the French army during the First World War. Schary – aware that the story had been turned down by every other major Hollywood studio – had also rejected the idea. 'He didn't want any more anti-war message films,' says Harris of Schary, who 'had already taken it on the chin with *Red Badge of Courage*,' and it was the story surrounding the making of that film – and its long-term repercussions – which heavily influenced the climate at the studio during that period.

Schary had arrived at MGM in 1951, hailed by Nicholas Schenk of the studio's New York office as 'the new Irving Thalberg', but quickly fell out with the seemingly invincible and immovable Louis B. Mayer in California. When John Huston proposed to direct a Civil War story – *The Red Badge of Courage*, from the novel by Stephen Crane and starring Audie Murphy – Schary was enthusiastic. Not so Mayer, however, who made efforts to have the production halted, on the grounds that it did not fit in with his personal philosophy of what constituted 'family entertainment' – MGM's trademark image, set many years earlier by a series of Andy Hardy movies and glossy musicals. Mayer was astonished to find himself first overruled by Schenk and then – almost inconceivably – fired from the very studio which bore his name.

Huston, who had even offered not to make the picture if Mayer felt so strongly about it, went ahead with the production which, when complete, appeared to vindicate Mayer's opinion when it was a huge flop at the box office. Pulled in following disastrous previews and substantially recut by the studio, the film eventually went out as a 69 minute second feature doomed to lose most of the $1.6 million it had cost to make. By the time Harris and Kubrick arrived at Metro, Schary's own position at the studio 'was already teetering,' says Harris.

Aside from vetoing *Paths of Glory*, however, Schary did not put any pressure on Kubrick who, according to Harris, 'fell in love with this subject *The Burning Secret* which he wanted to make there [so] we took a crack at it.' This original short story, by Stefan Zweig, had previously been filmed in Germany by Robert Siodmak in 1933 (a later British version was directed by Andrew Birkin in 1988). As related by Kubrick, the plot revolved around a woman's trip abroad with her young son, during which she has a brief affair with a man. On their return, the son lies to his father in order to protect his mother. (In other screen adaptations, the affair is prevented by the child's omnipresence.)

Calder Willingham – whose later screen credits were to include *The Graduate* (1967), *Little Big Man* (1970) and *Thieves Like Us* (1974)– was sought out as screenwriter for *The Burning Secret*, but was found to be working with Sam Speigel on David Lean's *Bridge on the River Kwai* in Ceylon. Schary apparently balked at the suggestion, reminding the young partners, 'You were supposed to produce, write and direct, and now you want to bring in a writer?' Harris and Kubrick remained firm, insisting that it was essential to have Willingham involved although by this time, as Harris recalls, 'we were already thirty weeks into our contract.' The situation was resolved when Dore Schary - who had never quite delivered the goods to the studio's liking – was fired at the end of 1956. 'When he was finished, we were finished,' says Harris. 'Whoever was in charge took a look at anyone who came in with Schary and said, 'let's forget the whole thing.' Kubrick and Harris left the studio without ever having shot a frame of film there, although Kubrick later commented that he had 'been paid to direct a film for MGM that never got made' – something of a novelty, since he had received no real salary for any of his work up to that point.

Meanwhile, following his contribution to *The Killing*, Jim Thompson had been working on *Paths of Glory* while the film-makers were at MGM, with Willingham also brought in once he had completed his work on *River Kwai*. Kubrick and Harris were again on their own, attempting to make the picture independently but with little enthusiasm from elsewhere. 'Kirk Douglas was our first choice,' says Harris but, when approached, the star turned them down due to prior commitments.

As with *The Killing*, a star name was required to give the project some credibility with potential backers, and the continuing search brought contact with Gregory Peck and William Wyler – though not directly to discuss *Paths of Glory*. 'They were developing a crime film,' says Harris, 'and had seen *The Killing* and thought Stanley and I might be able to inject something of that style into it.' Flattered at being consulted by two such giants of the American cinema, Kubrick and Harris duly went along to the meeting, where they raised the possibility of involving Peck in their own picture, only to be told that he also had too many commitments – 'we would have to wait eighteen months for him.' The proposed crime story never got off the ground either, and Peck and Wyler were soon deeply

On location in Munich for *Paths of Glory*, the three main players responsible for getting the film made: Stanley Kubrick (left), James B. Harris (centre) and Kirk Douglas (right).

involved in their own lengthy co-production of *The Big Country* (1958).

Persevering with *Paths of Glory*, the partners approached several other leading actors, without success, before Kirk Douglas 'came back and asked was it still available, because he had always loved the idea.' Douglas recalled that Kubrick had told him of the problems in setting up the project but that, after seeing a script, the star had enthused 'Stanley, I don't think this picture will ever make a nickel but we *have* to make it.'

Even with the involvement of a star name of the magnitude of Kirk Douglas – already with *Champion* (1949)*, Ace in the Hole* (1951)and *Detective Story* (1951) behind him, and soon to be Oscar-nominated for *Lust for Life* (1956) – backers were still shy of such a downbeat, harrowing story as *Paths of Glory* promised to be. Harris – who, as producer, assumed responsibility for all financing and distribution deals – 'went back to our old friends at United Artists' who, apparently, were as reluctant about the picture as everybody else. 'Kirk was certainly a big help,' he recalls. 'He had a deal to do *The Vikings* for them, and he used that to sort of bully them to go along with the deal – which I'll be forever thankful to him for.' A deal was finally struck, with Douglas' own Bryna company co-producing, and the picture to be

filmed on a limited budget of just under a million dollars, of which a third was reportedly paid to its star.

Paths of Glory was filmed entirely on location in Munich, and not since Lewis Milestone's *All Quiet on the Western Front* (1931) had the horrific conditions of warfare been so graphically depicted. Kubrick's intricate and impressive tracking shots along the trenches – expertly photographed by George Krause – captured the claustrophobia, squalor and sheer horror of the soldiers' positions, contrasting sharply with the vast, cavernous chateau drawing rooms commandeered by the generals.

Despite this, Kirk Douglas – who had told one reporter 'I've always insisted on voicing my suggestions with directors. The good ones have never objected' – later claimed there had been a serious dispute over an apparently completely rewritten screenplay (by Kubrick and Thompson). 'Kubrick always had a calm way about him,' said Douglas. 'I never heard him raise his voice, never saw him get excited or reveal anything. He just looked at you through those big, wide eyes.'

If, as the star claimed, Kubrick had rewritten the picture in an effort to make the story more palatable and so more commercial, Douglas insisted that they revert to the original script or else he would pull out altogether. Whatever the final involvement of each of the parties – impossible to confirm at this distance – Kubrick received screen credit for the script alongside Thompson and Willingham. Harris recalls that there had been several different versions of the screenplay, although 'all followed the book pretty closely' apart from a couple of 'experimental endings.' Suggestions that the men be reprieved at the last moment in order to give the movie a more upbeat ending – at the same time losing the entire point of the story – were resisted by the director. 'What do we do about an ending, then?' Douglas is said to have asked. 'Hell,' Kubrick replied, 'Why don't we just shoot them?' This, as Harris confirms, was the only true ending. 'I worried about UA a little, but they probably never knew the difference.'

One crucial difference between *Killer's Kiss* and *The Killing* had been in the professional level of the performances of the actors, and Kubrick had used those long hours in the MGM screening room, it was said, analysing the work of past directors and of how they drew a performance from their cast. One report suggested that 'he also learned how to cope with the actor's ego, and part of his technique is to mask his own.' This stood him in good stead during the making of *Paths of Glory*, when he clashed with Adolphe Menjou.

The veteran 67-year-old actor had already appeared in over 100 films during a career reaching back to a silent era debut at the Vitagraph Studio in 1914, defining his early screen persona in *The Ace of Cads* (1926). Later dubbed 'the best dressed man in Hollywood', Menjou's impressive list of screen credits included an appearance opposite Rudolph Valentino, in *The Sheik* (1921), and a role as the Devil in D. W. Griffith's *The Sorrows of Satan* (1926). He had also notably been directed by Ernst Lubitsch, Frank Capra, Charles Chaplin and Josef von Sternberg, amongst others. Nevertheless, Louise Brooks, who had co-starred with him in *A Social Celebrity* (1926) and *Evening Clothes* (1927) considered his 'technique' to be no more complex than the shallow characters he portrayed: 'He never felt anything,' she said. 'He used to say, "Now I do Lubitsch number one. Now I do Lubitsch number two".'

When, on *Paths of Glory*, Menjou was asked to repeat a scene 17 times, he finally announced to the crew – totally disregarding the director – 'That was my best reading. I think we can break for lunch now.' When Kubrick requested another take, Menjou 'went into an absolute fury.' According to an on-set report, '[He] blasted off on what he claimed was Kubrick's dubious parentage, and made several unprintable references to Kubrick's relative greenness in the art of directing actors.'

The 29-year-old director, it was reported, 'listened calmly and, after Menjou had spluttered to an uncomplimentary conclusion, said quietly "all right, let's try the scene once more." With utter docility, Menjou went back to work, "Stanley instinctively knew what to do,' said Kirk Douglas later.'

Ironically, Menjou received some of the best notices of his long career for his portrayal of the wily General Broulard, a symbol of the cynical and uncaring higher echelons of military tradition, whose commitment to the war and concern for the troops is illustrated by his opening comments – 'I wish I had your taste in carpets' – on visiting Mireau, who explains such opulence simply by declaring, 'I always like to keep pleasant surroundings' – an obvious contrasting device, cutting to the conditions in the trenches which follow.

In these opening scenes, successive characters are clearly manipulated by their superiors – it is Broulard who first raises the issue of the attack on the Ant Hill, and then overcomes Mireau's initial reluctance, by appealing to his sense of vanity and ambition. Mireau's protest that he is 'responsible for 8,000 men who know I would never let them down' quickly dissolves into a determination to secure his own promotion at any cost. Having set the idea in motion, Broulard now retreats, even declining to attend the court-martial of the men, so that any potential for controversy arising from the trial will not involve him personally. He is not seen again until the night before the men are to be executed, when Dax interrupts one of his parties at yet another grand chateau. Unknown to Dax, however, Broulard's initial role in ordering the offensive will make him unlikely to effect any last minute intervention in the men's fate.

Inspecting the troops on his way to meet with Dax, Mireau exchanges empty words with some of the men – introducing us along the way to the three who will later be charged with cowardice – and snaps at an obviously unfit soldier whose responses are incoherent and vague. Told that the man is shell-shocked, Mireau barks at the sergeant that 'there is no such thing as shell shock' – a true reflection of military opinion on the subject at the time – before issuing instructions to have the man sent back from the front lines. Far from this being a humanitarian act, however, Mireau wants the soldier removed because 'I won't have my men contaminated by him.'

Shortly afterwards, Dax knowingly finds himself being unavoidably manipulated, as Mireau plays on his colonel's sense of honour by threatening to relieve him of command, amid accusations that Dax has become tired, defeatist and disloyal. To prove his dedication, Dax must accept the general's order, even though Mireau admits that the attack will result in at least 50 per cent casualties. Dax has no choice other than to defend his troop's bravery and insist on leading the men personally – as, of course, the general knew he would. Mireau is another fine study of a psychotic on the edge by George Macready – previously Rita Hayworth's silkily ruthless mobster husband in *Gilda* (1946) – who,

The desperation of war, as Colonel Dax (Kirk Douglas) attempts to rally his men during the doomed assault in *Paths of Glory*.

following his 'betrayal' by Broulard at the film's climax can still defiantly – and with apparent sincerity – declare himself 'the only completely innocent man in this whole affair.'

The abortive attack on the Ant Hill is filmed with masterly – indeed, military – precision, with the camera following the unsteady progress of the men against the constant barrage of enemy artillery, through water-filled shell holes and shifting mounds of blasted earth. Kubrick himself was without any military service or experience (Alexander Singer telling the *New York Times* that he had been 'turned down for the Army on some oddball thing') making his ability to convincingly and accurately recreate scenes of battle and trench conditions even more remarkable.

The three chosen scapegoats were played by Joseph Turkel, Timothy Carey (both seen in Kubrick's *The Killing*) and – most impressively as Philippe Paris – Ralph Meeker, whose best role previously had been as Mickey Spillane's Mike Hammer in *Kiss Me Deadly* (1955, directed by Robert Aldrich). *Monthly Film Bulletin* found Meeker 'effective as the most articulate of the victims' in *Paths of Glory*. It is his feud with Roget that is the cause of his downfall – another case of manipulation by a superior officer. Apart from Paris' lack of respect for the lieutenant, he also holds Roget responsible for the death of Lejeune on the night exercise, but is too much of a soldier to report this to Dax the following morning.

While the other two prisoners – Ferol especially – are seen to collapse in varying degrees following the

trial, Paris remains calm until the morning of the execution but even then, he quickly composes himself when the sergeant tells him that how he is to die will be his final decision in life, and one which his wife and child will hear of. The previous evening, Paris had watched a cockroach in their cell, remarking that 'tomorrow I'll be dead and that cockroach will be alive – it will be closer to my wife than I am.' The eloquence of the moment is rudely broken when the 'undesirable' Ferol squashes the insect with a slap of his hand, coldly observing, 'Now you got the edge.'

Colonel Dax becomes another interesting addition to Kirk Douglas' list of screen credits – often flawed characters or those with a dark side to their personality, and rarely conventional heroic figures (John Wayne had famously berated Douglas for his decision to play a 'weakling' like Van Gogh in *Lust for Life* when, he reasoned, actors such as they ought to be seen to be invincible).

James B. Harris reveals something of the relationship between the star and the comparatively young film-makers at that time: 'Kirk had his 40th birthday on the set – we were 28 or so and we thought he was rather old and ready for grandfather roles – but he was a major star and we were just getting started.' Often considered a difficult and demanding personality by those he has worked with, Douglas 'played the role of the big movie star. He let us know he was that experienced,' but it was largely the result of Douglas' position within the industry, and 'his influence with UA that we were there in the first place, and I never stopped appreciating that fact. You had to have respect for Kirk because he demanded it.'

Certainly the actor – on occasion accused by his critics of being 'over the top' in other productions – gave a compelling and controlled performance in *Paths of Glory*. His Colonel Dax is torn between his duty as an officer and his allegiance to his men, initially cowed by his military training into urging the troops to make the attack he knows to be doomed from the outset. In private, however, he becomes increasingly bitter and deeply critical of the generals' decisions concerning the attack and the disciplinary action to be taken, ultimately realizing that the superior officers have no thought for anything other than themselves and their reputations. When he ironically suggests that he be tried in place of the men as the officer responsible, Broulard waves him aside with the telling comment that 'This is not a matter for officers... let's get this thing settled once and for all so that we can live with it.'

All of Dax's expertise as a lawyer is to no effect during the court-martial, the result of which from the outset is clearly a foregone conclusion. From his opening objection that the men have not heard the charges against them – dismissed by the judge with 'Please don't take up the court's time with technicalities' – all of

Dax's pleas fall on unresponsive ears. In the incongruous setting of the bright, sunlit, echoing chateau stateroom with its gleaming, polished floors and paintings adorning the walls, Dax's impassioned plea for mercy at the trial's close – and his bitter recriminations concerning the lack of either a stenographic record or witnesses to the hearing – is strikingly at odds with the lacklustre and perfunctory summing up of the prosecutor (Richard Anderson) – already secure in the knowledge of a successful conviction. This ten-minute trial sequence – virtually the same amount of screen time as given to the abortive battle itself – fades directly to the firing squad preparing for the next morning: it is unnecessary that we either see or hear the verdict being delivered – we know what it will be.

Dax's final confrontation with Broulard, following the execution of the men, takes the older general by complete surprise, being wholly outside his experience of military nature, where officers distance themselves from the realities of fighting and of war itself. Having offered Dax the command left vacant by the soon-to-be-investigated Mireau, Broulard had assumed that this was Dax's sole motive in revealing the general's misconduct. Shocked at Dax's indignance and sense of honour, he tells the colonel, 'You're an idealist, and I pity you as I would the village idiot.'

Following a final explosion of fury at Broulard – the one occasion when he allows his military guard to drop – and, after such a gruelling and soul-destroying experience, Dax only rediscovers a sense of humanity by watching his men's response to the captive German girl, forced to sing for them at the tavern close by the barracks. This final scene – of the survival of innocence and purity even in the midst of war – has echoes with the closing scene of *All Quiet on the Western Front*, with its butterfly image and a young soldier (Lew Ayres) shot dead by a sniper's bullet.

Though less eloquent than that earlier picture, *Paths of Glory* nevertheless has taken its rightful place as a classic, immensely powerful, anti-war statement. (A 1975 poll undertaken by London's Everyman Cinema aiming to form the basis of a Top 10 film season, when compiled, saw *Paths of Glory* – perhaps unexpectedly – voted into sixth place above *Citizen Kane, Gone With the Wind* and *Casablanca*, in a list headed by *Les Enfants du Paradis, Ivan the Terrible* and *Some Like it Hot*).

As Kirk Douglas had predicted, *Paths of Glory* did not make any money for its makers, although it just about broke-even at the box office. There were to be no Oscar nominations nor any other major awards, and the film even found itself banned in various parts of Europe

Execution: the inept Lieutenant Roget (Wayne Morris, left), forced by Dax to oversee the exercise, offers a blind-fold to Ferol (Timothy Carey) as the priest (Emile Meyer) looks on helplessly.

The closing sequence of *Paths of Glory* as the captured German peasant girl sings for the troops. Susanne Christian (Christiane Harlan) was soon to become Mrs Stanley Kubrick.

for many years – perhaps, in itself, more significant an achievement than any award could have been – with *Variety* reporting in July 1958 that the 'military has just banned *Paths of Glory* from playing on the US Army and Air Force military motion picture circuit in Europe.' In Germany's British sector, it was claimed, 'a dozen French soldiers were thrown out of the house after tossing stink bombs into the audience' and, following this, French authorities demanded the film be withdrawn from the Berlin Film Festival. Under 'Allied Occupation Statute 501, forbidding any action which might harm the reputation of one of the occupying powers of Berlin', the French commandant pulled the movie from all theatres in the French sector of the city. Not until March 1970 was the film finally cleared by the Swiss government and shown on German television.

'The film was terribly successful for recognition and reviews,' says Harris, 'although it never got nominated – it came out the same year as *River Kwai* [which scooped the Oscar for Best Picture] but it proved the first picture we did wasn't a fluke. They realized that Stanley was for real.'

Opening on Christmas Day, 1957, *Variety* called the picture 'starkly realistic... well handled and enacted in a series of outstanding characterizations.' Kubrick's 'taut direction' was praised, although the story was considered to be 'dated and makes for grim viewing.' The *New York Times* gave 'credit [to] Kirk Douglas for having the courage to produce and appear in the screen

dramatization of a novel that has been a hot potato in Hollywood for twenty-two years.' The unjust and 'bitter, tragic end' of the story was 'shown with shattering candor... Mr Kubrick has made it look terrific. The execution scene is one of the most craftily directed and emotionally lacerating that we have ever seen.'

Time and Tide later declared the film 'the most honestly, technically brilliant film to have come out of Hollywood in the past five years,' although, as with many films set in non-English speaking countries, there were complaints concerning the decision to have all characters speak 'in colloquial English, with American accents and attitudes while studiously making it look as much as possible like a document of the French army in World War One.' Dismissing Douglas' performance and accent as 'the same... that he used in *Gunfight at the OK Corral*,' the reviewer also identified the three condemned men as 'having the swagger, slouches and speech slurs of assorted GIs in World War II.' This may be most justifiably argued in the casting of Emile Meyer as the French priest – an actor more comfortable as the crooked cop in Alexander Mackendrick's *Sweet Smell of Success*, released the same year – but overall it is an exaggeration to suggest, as that review did, that 'the illusion of reality is blown completely whenever anybody talks.' The same charge could be made against any number of other movies.

Released in England a month later, with one of those typically unsubtle advertising tag lines – 'Never has the screen thrust so deeply into the guts of war!' – the film won good notices, with the *Evening Standard* calling it an 'adult, painful and absorbing film. It demands to be seen,' though *Monthly Film Bulletin* considered that 'some scenes, such as the court-martial itself, or the final showdown between Dax and Broulard, seem more convincing as intellectual conceptions than actual dramatic experiences.'

Nevertheless, it was 'significant that [it] is an independent production, made outside the machinery of the major studios. Technically, it is Kubrick's most controlled and ambitious picture... powerful and authoritative,' later praised by Leslie Halliwell, who thought 'the trench scenes... the most vivid ever, and the rest is shot in genuine castles, with resultant difficulties of lighting and recording; the overall result is an overpowering piece of cinema.'

Charlton Heston had been among those who refused *Paths of Glory* before Kirk Douglas returned to pick it up but, watching an advance screening of the picture in November 1957, alongside the almost-complete *Touch of Evil* – which he had chosen to make instead – found 'Kubrick's film is smoother and has many fine things, including Kirk's acting.' (*Touch of Evil* – even with the presence of Orson Welles as director, screenwriter and co-star – suffered from studio interference and went on to become a commercial failure.)

Kubrick's third – and final – picture released through United Artists, *Paths of Glory* did much to consolidate his growing reputation as a director capable of controlling major stars, increased budgets and more expensive – and often difficult – location shooting. Despite his later, qualified opinion of the director, Kirk Douglas conceded that 'Somehow, Stanley always knew he was good,' as Kubrick's technical expertise – an understanding of lighting and camera set-ups gained from his work as a photographer with *Look* – gave him a sometimes irritating (to other crew members) knowledge of exactly the effect he wanted and how to achieve it. In a *New York Times* article, one electrician who worked with Kubrick said, 'I've been in this business thirty years, and I'm learning stuff from this kid.'

An experience of production on limited schedules and budgets had also given the director added skills in other areas of the film-making process, including editing, where he logically insisted, 'Everything you do can be ruined if you don't stand by and see it's cut the way you want it.' Having controlled almost every aspect of his earliest films, Kubrick was obviously not going to allow that control to pass to anyone else – either now or in the future.

Soon after the release of *Paths of Glory*, it was announced that Stanley Kubrick and James B. Harris' next picture was to star 'Gregory Peck... in a Civil War epic based on the adventures of Confederate cavalry leader John Singleton Mosby.' How far developed this project became is unclear but, according to Harris, the star 'didn't like the screenplay, and the whole thing sort of evaporated,' with nothing more heard of it since.

Marlon Brando, meanwhile, was still singing the praises of *The Killing* and its director who, he said, 'could project such a completely distinctive style with so little previous film-making experience... Stanley made a series of bizarre and interesting choices which buttressed and embellished an ordinary story into an exciting film.' For Harris and Kubrick, Brando was 'one of the greatest actors that ever breathed', so that when he showed an interest in working with them, 'we jumped at it'.

Since making his 1950 debut in *The Men*, Marlon Brando had quickly become one of the screen's biggest – yet most uncompromising – stars, with five Academy Award 'Best Actor' nominations in six years, including one Oscar (*On The Waterfront*, 1953). His more recent films, however – *Teahouse of the August Moon,* and *Sayonara* – had met with mixed reviews, and he was now keen to work with a new young director, although

a suitable project was not immediately apparent. 'We had meetings with Marlon a couple of times a week,' recalls Harris, 'but we couldn't seem to get something we all agreed on.'

Eventually, Brando 'called Stanley to ask him to clear up this obligation that Marlon had to do a western with Paramount' – *A Touch of Vermilion*, based on Charles Neider's recently published novel, *The Authentic Death of Hendry Jones*, for which future director Sam Peckinpah had reportedly been engaged to write a screenplay, with Frank P. Rosenberg producing. 'We decided it would be good for our careers to do a picture with him,' says Harris, 'so Stanley said he would do it if he could bring in Calder Willingham to work on the script, while I looked for something that the three of us could do together later, which Marlon agreed to.'

In May 1958, Stanley Kubrick was hired as director of the new movie and – with Willingham – began to revise the script. Rosenberg later recalled that eight weeks had been set aside for the rewrite (Brando expected it to take four), but that it was another eight months before a workable script neared completion, by which time a frustrated Willingham had left the project after disagreements with the star, to be replaced by Guy Trosper. Meetings took place at Brando's home on Mulholland Drive with, according to Rosenberg, 'everyone calm and reasonable and in stocking feet – a requirement of the highly polished teakwood floors of Brando's oriental modern house.' Another source claims that Kubrick, 'for some reason, routinely took off his pants as well and worked in only his underwear and dress shirt.'

As these odd-looking sessions became more heated, 'Brando, who had seated himself within easy reach of a Chinese gong that had come with the house... would hold [it] up and strike it twice. This was a signal for everyone, including himself, to return to a neutral corner.' The gong, Rosenberg continued, could be put to use by any of those present if they felt it necessary, 'but Brando used it most. After all, it was his gong.'

By August, differences of opinion were beginning to show between Kubrick and Brando, with the director suggesting that Spencer Tracy be approached for the role of Dad Longworth – an indication of Kubrick's extraordinary self-confidence as, aged not yet 30, he thought nothing of seeking out one of Hollywood's most renowned, legendary figures to take a supporting role in what would be only the director's second major feature. Brando, however, had already offered the role to Karl Malden – with whom he had worked on *A*

---

* The sole female member of the cast of *Paths of Glory*, the German Christiane Harlan – billed under the name Susanne Christian – soon afterwards became the third Mrs Stanley Kubrick. This was her only film appearance. She has continued to build her own successful career as an artist.

Streetcar Named Desire (both on Broadway and in Elia Kazan's 1951 screen version) and *On the Waterfront* – and, although Kubrick allegedly suggested 'paying off' Malden, he was overruled by Brando who intended to keep faith with his friend.

A December 1958 start date had been set but, as this drew nearer, the distance between Brando and his chosen director grew ever wider, as Kubrick began to suspect that the star was more interested in directing the picture himself, and had recruited Kubrick only for technical support. According to Harris, 'Marlon was just too difficult and too eccentric and Stanley wasn't used to that – it just would never work because he is a completely independent film-maker in every sense – he does his own thing and he's not for hire.'

Frank P. Rosenberg's later (March 1961) *New York Times* article on the making of the picture merely stated that, 'after much discussion, and by mutual agreement, Mr Kubrick amicably withdrew as the director of *One-Eyed Jacks*' (the film's new title), although later unconfirmed versions of the events which led to Kubrick's departure indicate either that the director was 'got rid of' (according to Brando biographer Peter Manso) after a disagreement over a Chinese co-star, or – Brando's version – 'Just before we were to start, Stanley said, "Marlon, I don't know what the picture's about." I said, "I'll tell you what it's about. It's about the $300,000 that I've already paid to Karl Malden." He said "Well, if that's what it's about, I'm in the wrong picture".'

Kubrick formally left the production at the end of November 1958, issuing a statement that he had resigned 'with deep regret because of my respect and admiration for one of the world's foremost artists,' adding that 'Mr Brando and his assistants have been most understanding of my desire to commence work on *Lolita.*'

Any bitterness which might have resulted from this incident was probably lessened when, as Kubrick later revealed, he was 'paid in full' by Brando despite never reaching the shooting stage of the picture. As for *One-Eyed Jacks*, Brando did indeed take over as director himself – as Kubrick and Harris had expected – although he claimed to have asked 'Sidney Lumet [and] four or five others' to take over after Kubrick had left. A six-month shoot – in place of the planned 60 days – produced a movie lasting four hours and 42 minutes in its original form at a mammoth cost of $6 million (originally budgeted at $1.8 million). By the time that Paramount finally released the picture in March 1961, its length had been cut by exactly one half, with one casualty being the complete performance of the disputed Chinese co-star.

Handsomely photographed by Oscar-nominated Charles Lang Jr in VistaVision – one of the last major productions to use the process – *One-Eyed Jacks* inevitably failed to recoup its investment for Paramount. It was the only movie made by Pennebaker Productions, as well as being Marlon Brando's only film as director.

1960
SPARTACUS

*A story sold to Universal from a book written by a Commie,
and the screen script was written by a Commie, so don't go to see it.*
HEDDA HOPPER

Bryna Productions/Universal-International.

Directed by Stanley Kubrick. Produced by Edward Lewis.

Executive producer: Kirk Douglas. Screenplay: Dalton Trumbo, based on the novel by Howard Fast. Photography: Russell Metty. Film editor: Robert Lawrence. Assistant film editors: Robert Schulte, Fred Chulak. Music score composed by Alex North. Music directors: Alex North, Joseph Gershenson. Music editor: Arnold Schwarzwald. Production designer: Alexander Golitzen. Art director: Eric Orborn. Set decoration: Russell A. Gausman, Julia Heron. Assistant director: Marshall Green. Sound recording: Waldon O. Watson, Joe Lapis, Murray Spivack, Ronald Pierce. Historical and technical adviser: Vittorio Nino Novarese. Editorial consultant: Irving Lerner. Main title and design consultant: Saul Bass. Production aide: Stan Margulies. Additional scenes photographed by Clifford Stine. Wardrobe: Peruzzi. Costumes: Valles. Jean Simmons' costumes: Bill Thomas. Make-up: Bud Westmore. Hair stylist: Larry Germain. Unit production manager: Norman Derning.

Cast:
Kirk Douglas (Spartacus); Laurence Olivier (Marcus Licinius Crassus); Jean Simmons (Varinia); Charles Laughton (Gracchus); Peter Ustinov (Lentulus Batiatus); Tony Curtis (Antoninus); John Gavin (Caius Julius Caesar); Nina Foch (Helena); John Ireland (Crixus); Woody Strode (Draba); Herbert Lom (Tigranes); John Dall (Marcus Publius Glabrus); Charles McGraw (Marcellus); Joanna Barnes (Claudia); Harold J. Stone (David); Peter Brocco (Ramon); Paul Lambert (Gannicus); Robert J. Wilke (guard captain); Nicholas Dennis (Dionysius); John Hoyt (Roman officer); Frederic Worlock (Laelius); Dayton Lummis (Symmachus).

196 minutes (US). 193 minutes (UK) – later cut to 183 minutes. Technicolor. Super-Technirama 70.

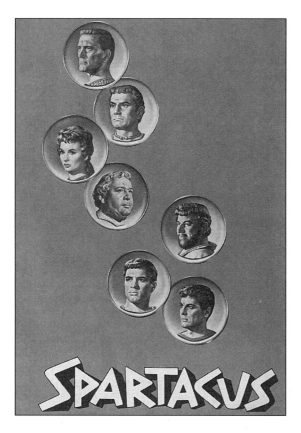

In the year 73bc, a troublesome Thracian slave named Spartacus (Kirk Douglas) working in the Nubian mines of Libya is sold to Lentulus Batiatus (Peter Ustinov), who is seeking potential new recruits for his school for gladiators at Capua, near Rome.

The regime at Capua is brutal, with the relentless, bullying Marcellus (Charles McGraw) instilling a hatred in the men, who will be set to fight each other in the arena for the amusement of Roman nobility. The men are occasionally rewarded for a good performance by having a woman sent to them at night. When Spartacus is left alone with Varinia (Jean Simmons), his sensitivity prevents him from taking advantage of her, although this makes him a figure of ridicule to the watching Batiatus and Marcellus.

An unexpected visit from the wealthy and powerful Marcus Licinius Crassus (Laurence Olivier) leads Batiatus to stage a series of bouts in the arena, with the men chosen by Crassus' travelling companions, Helena (Nina Foch) and Claudia (Joanna Barnes). Spartacus is set against the giant Draba (Woody Strode), who eventually outmanoeuvrés him and is urged by the visitors to complete the execution.

Rebelling against the indignity of the spectacle, Draba turns and throws his spear at the baying group, making a lunge toward the platform where he is killed by Crassus.

The next day, Varinia – bought by Crassus as his personal servant – is taken away to Capua, and when Marcellus taunts Spartacus with this, the slave kills his trainer and a mass revolt takes place. The slaves overpower their guards and break out of the compound, returning later to hear Spartacus urge them to marshal an army to win their true freedom from the suffocating power of Rome.

Recruiting more escaped slaves as they travel across the countryside – including Varinia, who has escaped from her escort before reaching Rome – Spartacus and his growing army are quickly recognized as a serious threat. Sent out to intercept them, Crassus' commander, Glabrus (John Dall), is easily defeated by the slave army and, humiliatingly, sent back to report to the senate, where Crassus – as his sponsor – is forced to resign his position.

Crassus' former attendant, Antoninus (Tony Curtis), becomes another addition to the slave army, which continues its march, intending to sail from Italy on ships bought from a pirate leader (Herbert Lom). Spartacus learns that Varinia is pregnant, and their hope is that their child will be born free once they escape the influence of their Roman oppressors.

Political intrigue at Rome leads to Crassus being recalled to face the rebel army, on the understanding that he be fully reinstated and given command of all legions. The pirates accept a bribe and betray Spartacus, leaving the slaves without ships to escape Italy and with Rome's mighty army advancing on them. The bloody battle which follows leaves the slave army defeated, with many thousands dead.

When Crassus demands that Spartacus be identified to him – dead or alive – the slaves respond as one, all of them claiming to be their leader and so frustrating Rome's intention to make an example of him. Six thousand are taken prisoner and condemned to die by crucifixion along the roadsides leading into the city.

Discovered on the battlefield with her new-born baby, Varinia is taken by Crassus into his household where he tries to win her with gifts and promises of a secure future for her child, but she rejects him, realizing that he is still in awe and afraid of what Spartacus has managed to achieve with his slaves.

As Spartacus and Antoninus are marched slowly towards Rome, Crassus finally learns of the slave leader's identity and forces the two men to stage a fight to the death – the winner to be crucified at the gates to the city. Neither wants to allow the other to suffer such a fate, and Antoninus attempts to kill Spartacus quickly, only for Spartacus to insist that he let himself be killed, so denying the Romans the spectacle they seek. Spartacus kills his friend, resigned to his fate the next morning, but then learns from Crassus that his wife and child are held in the Roman's home.

Batiatus, meanwhile, has arranged with the wily Gracchus (Charles Laughton) – a sworn enemy of Crassus – for himself, Varinia and her baby to escape the city, carrying special papers which will free her from slavery. As they set off, Varinia sees Spartacus dying on the cross, and – with Batiatus nervously urging her not to slow their escape – climbs down from the wagon to show him his son, who will grow to be a free man because of all that his father has done.

✳✳✳

The 1950s was unquestionably the era of the great Hollywood epic, with ever more expensive and expansive productions like *The Greatest Story Ever Told*, *The Ten Commandments* (1956) and *Solomon and Sheba* (1958) filling the screen, all of them in colour and often making impressive use of the new 70mm technology to combat the growing threat of television.

Although initial reaction to the new 'wide-screen' systems had been mixed – Jean Cocteau reportedly commented that 'next time I write a poem, I shall use a wider piece of paper' – CinemaScope, Todd-AO, VistaVision and Panavision stretched the screen image to new lengths (and widths), with the new trend at its peak by the end of the decade.

While a trouserless Kubrick remained on gong alert at Marlon Brando's house, Kirk Douglas found himself angling for the title role in one of those epics – William Wyler's remake of *Ben-Hur* – losing out to the director's first choice, Charlton Heston, and then refusing the second lead of Messala, finally played by Stephen Boyd.

Instead, Douglas personally bought the screen rights to *Spartacus* – based on the true story of a gladiator who led a slave's revolt in Italy in 73–71BC. The 70 escaped gladiators swelled to an army of 100,000 as Spartacus and his men marched on Rome, only to be defeated near Rhegium where Spartacus was killed. This had been the subject of a low-budget

Italian film, *Spartaco*, directed by Riccardo Freda in 1952 and, a year later, a similarly inexpensive British production *Spartacus the Gladiator*, much ridiculed for its outrageous pre-publicity: 'Never before on the silver screen...'

The novel now bought by Douglas was the work of Howard Fast, a former member of the Communist party from 1944 until the invasion of Hungary, in 1957. Soon afterwards, Fast was among those caught up in the madness of the House Committee on Un-American Activities (HUAC), even spending some months in jail because of his past association with the party.

This sad and wholly destructive period of modern American history began in October 1947, with J. Parnell Thomas' committee convening to discover 'evidence of Communist subversion in the motion-picture industry'. The opening sessions consisted of high-profile 'friendly' (the committee's description) witnesses declaring their patriotic allegiances by revealing all they knew of the political leanings of others. These more-than-willing participants included Walt Disney, Robert Taylor, Gary Cooper, Robert Montgomery, George Murphy and Adolphe Menjou, who ingratiated himself with the committee by declaring his intention to 'move to Texas because I believe the Texans would shoot [the Communists] on sight.'

Also increasingly friendly was Ronald Reagan who, with his screen career at a virtual standstill, devoted himself largely to the aims of the HUAC over the next few years, becoming both president of the Screen Actors Guild and an unofficial 'adviser' (i.e. coach) to any concerned, subpoenaed celebrities anxious to limit any potential damage to their careers. As might be expected, this service did not go unnoticed, and did no harm whatever to Reagan's political ambition in the years which followed.

A week later came the unfriendly witnesses, many of whom had announced beforehand that they would flatly refuse to co-operate. Bertolt Brecht appeared briefly before flying out of America to East Germany, never to return, while a further ten called upon the First Amendment to the American Constitution – with its 'guarantee against incursions on free speech' – only to be charged with contempt. Despite earlier assurances from the Motion Picture Association of America (MPAA) that they would 'never be a party to anything as un-American as a blacklist', the 'Unfriendly Ten' were now told by the MPAA that they would be 'suspended without pay, and that thereafter no Communists or other subversives would knowingly be employed in Hollywood.'

Following appeals and legal arguments, the now infamous Hollywood Ten received prison sentences of up to a year – as, ironically, did J. Parnell Thomas, convicted of accepting bribes in 1949. With the resumed hearings came the shameful, unofficial (thereby 'non-existent') blacklist of actors, writers, directors – in fact, every level of movie personnel – unable to find work in Hollywood for many years afterwards. The Ten were only the most publicized victims of the HUAC as many others, including Larry Parks, Gale Sondergaard (wife of Herbert Biberman, one of the Ten, and therefore guilty by association) Edward G. Robinson, Joseph Losey and Sam Wanamaker discovered the existence of a further 'greylist' – a far wider-reaching and insidious means of punishing those suspected of being reds or, at least, of having red sympathies. The story of the making of *Spartacus* is, in its own way, almost as heroic in terms of confronting the blacklist as was the story of Spartacus (the man), standing against the might of the Roman empire, with Fast's novel resonant with the unjust mood of the era in which it was written.

With his successful working association with United Artists – for whom he had made not only *Paths of Glory* but the recently released box-office hit *The Vikings*, Kirk Douglas confidently offered *Spartacus* to the studio, only for the project to be instantly rejected on the grounds that UA were currently preparing their own epic, *The Gladiators*, which would star Yul Brynner as Spartacus. Other major studios were unwilling to accept a project in direct conflict with one already under way, yet Douglas persisted – mindful of his own investment – and approached David Lean with an offer to direct the movie, only for the director to 'graciously decline'.

As extra bargaining power, a first-rate script was needed to attract stars to the project, and Douglas favoured veteran screenwriter and former war correspondent Dalton Trumbo for the job. Trumbo, however, had been one of the Unfriendly Ten, imprisoned in the spring of 1950 and – technically at least – still unemployable in Hollywood.

One of the most sought-after screenwriters of the 1940s, Trumbo's credits had included *Thirty Seconds over Tokyo, Our Vines have Tender Grapes* and Ginger Rogers' Oscar-winning role in *Kitty Foyle*. Ironically, part of the case levelled against him during the HUAC hearings had been the result of testimony from Lela Rogers (mother of Ginger), who told how her daughter had refused to speak the line 'Share and share alike – that's democracy' in the Trumbo-scripted *Tender Comrades* (1943) – ostensibly a sloppily sentimental portrait of how women coped at home with their husbands away fighting the war, directed by Edward Dmytryk (another future member of the Ten). Miss Rogers claimed that there were 'anti-American speeches' creeping into the script which, reportedly, were then given to other actresses to speak. At that time, Trumbo had commanded an impressive salary of $4,000 per week but, after his release from prison,

Kubrick on the set of *Spartacus* walks through a scene with Laurence Olivier, perhaps discussing the relative merits of artichokes and snails – 'What's your favourite, Larry?'

was now secretly turning out screenplays at $2,500 under various aliases, even winning an Academy Award in 1957 for *The Brave One* under the name of 'Robert Rich'.

Trumbo began work on *Spartacus*, with Douglas strategically claiming to outsiders that his friend Eddie Lewis was screenwriter. The star-producer now approached Laurence Olivier in England, who tentatively agreed to be in the picture – but only if he could play the leading role and direct the film as well (a Universal press release in May 1957 announced that Olivier was to 'star in and direct *Spartacus* co-starring Kirk Douglas and Peter Ustinov', with the nature of Douglas' now-supporting role not revealed). Theatre commitments, however, headed off any potential embarrassment over this, with Olivier suggesting that he would be prepared to look at the role of Crassus 'if you can improve the part in relation to the other three roles.' By this time, both Charles Laughton and Peter Ustinov had been signed to the picture, the such stellar cast finally putting paid to United Artists' proposed *The Gladiators*.

After much haggling, Douglas had his Bryna company (named after his mother, as Marlon Brando's Pennebaker Productions had been named after his) producing *Spartacus* for Universal-International, in January 1959. Anthony Mann was installed as director – according to Douglas - at the insistence of Universal, for whom Mann's best known work had been made (mainly westerns such as *Winchester 73* and *The Man from Laramie* as well as *The Glenn Miller Story* – all starring James Stewart).

Within two weeks, Mann was fired from the movie – again at Universal's insistence, although it fell to Douglas to do the actual firing as well as finding a replacement director. James B. Harris recalls that he and Stanley Kubrick had just acquired screen rights to *Lolita* and were set to develop this into a movie following the end of Kubrick's involvement in the Brando/*One-Eyed Jacks* project. 'Stanley had only been back in the office a day or two,' he says, 'when Kirk is on the phone asking me about Stanley's availability.' If there was any reluctance over Kubrick taking control of a cast which already included three renowned directors – Olivier, Laughton, Ustinov – the partners nevertheless, quickly decided that, as the Harris–Kubrick company 'hadn't been making much money so far: this loan-out could do a lot for us.' Within the space of a single weekend, Kubrick had been signed to the production, with Kirk Douglas famously presenting him to the principal actors on Monday morning on the gladiator arena set.

'They looked down at this 30-year-old youth,' wrote Douglas later. 'They thought it was a joke. Then consternation – I had worked with Stanley, they hadn't. That made him "my boy". They didn't know that Stanley is nobody's boy. He stands up to anybody.' Co-star Tony Curtis confirms this: 'Most of the actors and crew thought of Kubrick as an upstart,' he says. 'Some people thought him an odd choice because he had a kind of cynical approach. I thought he was brilliant.'

By all accounts, Kubrick assumed total control instantly, dismissing the leading female star soon afterwards. German actress Sabina Bethmann had been personally chosen by Douglas after seeing one of her earlier films, but he later conceded that 'although she looked great, [she] was not much of an actress,' despite much work being done in an effort to lose her strong accent during teaching classes held by Jeff Corey – another blacklisted actor who had scarcely worked since 1952.

Bethmann was replaced by Jean Simmons, who had actually been considered for the role earlier. When the part did not come her way, she had – together with her husband Stewart Granger – been offered a role in *Ben-Hur*. Coincidentally, Granger had been considered as Messala – the role refused by Kirk

Douglas – but with the couple slow to commit themselves, both parts had now been cast, with Simmons' role going to Israeli actress Haya Harareet.

Assuming responsibility of a massive, multi-million dollar production appears to have caused no problems for Kubrick, described in one on-set report as 'relaxed and confident' as he supervised a two-camera set-up filming the bruising duel between Kirk Douglas and the imposing Woody Strode. 'On a big picture like this,' Kubrick explained, 'you get the best of everything. It's tougher when you have to rush, cut corners and think of ways to fake things.' Certainly *Spartacus* called on all the resources of the Hollywood studio system in all departments, with respected composer Alex North signed to compose the score – possibly at Kubrick's suggestion – and an opening title sequence designed by Saul Bass, justly famous for his inspired work on *The Man with the Golden Arm* (1955), *Around the World in Eighty Days* (1956) and several Alfred Hitchcock movies including *North by Northwest* (1959), *Vertigo* (1958) and the forthcoming *Psycho* (1960).

Despite the smooth and apparently frictionless hand-over of the directorial reins, problems still dogged the production as first Tony Curtis, then Jean Simmons and finally Kirk Douglas were all forced to take time off from shooting through either injury or illness. Delays grew longer, with some of the cast becoming unsettled: Charles Laughton although required for only three weeks was said to be unhappy at apparent squabbles on set. His wife Elsa Lanchester later wrote of problems between Laughton and Olivier, although the latter insisted that 'the two had got along quite splendidly, though I was a bit distressed at what I considered to be his discourtesies on the set... I have always loathed temperaments and tantrums and anything of that sort in an actor.' Peter Ustinov claims that he was 'picked as a confidant for both.' In particular, the chronically insecure Laughton 'feared that Olivier held too much influence with Douglas and, since he could no longer carry sufficient weight to counteract this, he decided to sulk – an activity at which he was particularly adept.'

Ustinov says that he 'rewrote all the scenes I had with Laughton, we rehearsed... away into the middle of the night... and the next day presented the company with a *fait accompli*.' Kubrick, he said, 'accepted [the new material] more or less without modification, and the scenes were shot in half a day each,' adding that 'Laughton was easy to work with, in that he overflowed with an almost carnal glee at the process of acting.' Laughton – who was indeed superb in those key scenes which involved him – was actually in ill-health for most of his brief time spent on *Spartacus*. He would make only one further movie – *Advise and Consent* for Otto Preminger in 1962. Olivier, on the

The wily Gracchus – occasionally more like a Bradford Town Councillor than a Roman senator – was to be one of Charles Laughton's final screen appearances. 'You can't direct a Laughton picture,' Alfred Hitchcock had said. 'The best you can hope for is to referee.'

other hand, was 'so utterly controlled, so immaculately rehearsed,' that Ustinov considered playing opposite him to be 'more in the spirit of a fencing match.'

How Kubrick – with only one 'star' vehicle behind him and now faced with at least six international star names at once – dealt with all of these enormous egos can only be guessed at, but it is clear that pressure was exerted from all sides. Tony Curtis recalls that Kirk Douglas was obliged to defend his choice of director to Universal, so 'started to put pressure on Stanley, and they got somewhat antagonistic toward each other.' Conscious of costs, budgets and schedules, Douglas and Universal 'wanted him to shoot quicker... to make cuts and not to cover as much as he did. They wanted standard two-shots – nothing complicated. Stanley was asking for shots where the camera moved creatively, Kubrick-style, and the studio didn't want him to do that.'

The scale of the production can be gauged by the hiring of over 150 men on set construction, over four sound stages as well as the studio back-lot, and the appearance in the film of the Spanish army, doubling as Romans for the climactic battle scene – filmed on location in Spain at Kubrick's insistence and, as Douglas enthused, resulting in 'incredible footage...

so wide that he had to shoot it from half a mile away.' The original screenplay, it seems, had not contained any actual glimpses of the battle at all, much to Kubrick's incredulity. 'He couldn't understand it,' says Harris, 'how you could have some kind of surreal battle sequence consisting only of helmets floating down the river.' Confirming this, Universal president Milton Rackmill told reporters that, 'They were going to save money by having the battles off-stage with messengers running on and saying 'We've won!' but the decision to stage the lot brought the budget up to $12 million' – at that time the most expensive picture yet produced, although the estimated cost had been previously set at half that figure, but 'swelled to eight with the signing of Laughton and Olivier.' The completed battle was extraordinary in its scope and realism, which later caused some cuts to be made by the censor over the bloodiest pieces of the action.

Other scenes were filmed at San Simeon – the mansion built by William Randolph Hearst in California, complete with authentic Roman features. San Simeon had itself been immortalized – albeit fictionally – as 'Xanadu' in Orson Welles' *Citizen Kane* and as the unnamed gothic castle in Aldous Huxley's novel *After Many a Summer*. All of the remaining filming took place in and around Los Angeles, skilfully using a combination of miniatures and glass-shots to mask the locale, prompting the *New York Times* headline above an article on the film's progress 'Hollywood, Rome'.

As shooting progressed, the subject of screen credit was raised in relation to Dalton Trumbo's contribution to the script, currently officially the work of 'Sam Jackson'. Douglas later indignantly claimed that Kubrick had briefly suggested taking the credit himself – even though Douglas had firstly named his producer Eddie Lewis as writer – although everyone in Hollywood by now knew who had actually written the original screenplay. Eventually, Douglas made the decision that Trumbo's name would appear on screen for the first time in a decade, against the advice of many of his friends who feared that the spectre of the blacklist could still ruin careers. 'It was a tremendous risk,' said the star, 'but the blacklist was broken.'

There remained those who would not forget – or forgive – and the American Legion mailed out over 17,000 letters urging the public not to see *Spartacus*, further naming Kirk Douglas as 'irresponsible' for his hiring of the 'communist' Dalton Trumbo. The fading but still influential Hedda Hopper found the 'Commie' picture morally repugnant, with its 'acres of dead people, more blood and gore than you ever saw in your whole life... Spartacus' mistress, carrying her illegitimate baby, passes... 6,000 crucified men on crosses.' Nevertheless, *Spartacus* meant the end of the blacklist as far as the high-profile Dalton Trumbo was concerned. He immediately set to work on Otto Preminger's *Exodus* (1959) and continued to write – and even direct (*Johnny Got His Gun*, 1971) – until his death in 1976. Liberation, however, was not at hand for all. A s late as 1973, three of the seven surviving members of the original Unfriendly Ten still claimed that they were unable to find employment in Hollywood.

Principal shooting on *Spartacus* had been completed in September 1959 – after 115 days – with Milton Rackmill later claiming that there had been 'a dozen screenplays... then we went back to the original. I know that script word for word, and I can tell you that the uncut version of the film runs 4 hours 22 minutes.' Trimmed by more than an hour, the picture finally opened in October 1960 at New York's De Mille Theatre, becoming a major box-office success to the relief of its backers. The first of Kubrick's films to be noticed at the Academy Awards, the film won four Oscars – for supporting actor (Peter Ustinov), colour cinematography, colour art and set direction and costume design. Surprisingly, neither the film nor its director even received nominations in a year when those two awards went to Billy Wilder's *The Apartment*. Film editor Robert Lawrence was nomi-

nated, as was Alex North's hugely impressive music score – losing out to *Exodus* (Ernest Gold) – but Kirk Douglas' controlled, heroic performance was overlooked completely. Douglas, it may be noted, had never been an easy favourite with either critics or some of his fellow film-makers, who resented his 'arrogance' at becoming one of the first actor-producers (as did his friend and frequent co-star Burt Lancaster) – actors were, after all, meant merely to act.

Kubrick had predicted prior to release that the movie would 'be a contender for awards', as he identified his own contribution to the making of the film. 'It's just as good as *Paths of Glory*,' Kubrick was quoted as saying, 'and certainly there's as much of myself in it.' This statement – revealing in the light of later comments – went on, 'I don't mean to minimize the contribution of others involved, but the director is the only one who can authentically impose his personality onto a picture, and the result is his responsibility – partly because he's the only one who's always there.'

That same article, appearing just a week before the opening night of *Spartacus*, quoted Douglas as saying that Kubrick 'would be a fine director some day, if he falls flat on his face just once. It might teach him how to compromise.' Kubrick, for his part, later claimed to have rewritten much of what he called Trumbo's 'pretty dumb script which was rarely faithful to what is known about Spartacus.' (Herbert Lom later told one reporter that his own role had been 'invented' simply as a means of explaining the plot which, he said, 'had gaping holes in it.') The director said he had achieved 'only limited success to make the film as real as possible [by] creating a more visual conception... and removing all but two lines of Kirk's dialogue during the first half-hour of the film.' Douglas – a self-confessed Trumbo fan – conceded this, but insisted that 'Kubrick is not a writer [though] he was great at developing a concept,' citing the first appearance of Jean Simmons in the film, where 'Stanley came up with the idea of losing the dialogue, just using music. It worked much better. But that's not the same as writing a script.'

In later years, both director and star would recall events differently. But, as the only one among his films not to have been instigated by Kubrick, and on which he had no initial involvement with either casting or screenplay, Kubrick later told Michel Ciment that, 'If I ever needed any convincing of the limits of persuasion a director can have on a film where... he is merely the highest-paid member of the crew, *Spartacus* provided proof to last a lifetime.'

Kubrick's relationship with the crew – all of them again hired prior to his own appointment – was not an easy one, as Tony Curtis reveals: 'Russell Metty, the cinematographer... was gregarious and friendly... But he hated Stanley.' With a career now entering its fourth decade, and a list of credits including *Sylvia Scarlett, Bringing Up Baby* (1938)*, Magnificent Obsession* (1954) and *Touch of Evil* (1958), Metty, according to Curtis, 'considered Kubrick to be just a kid... "This guy is going to direct this movie? He's going to tell me where to put the camera? They've got to be kidding."' (Ironically, it was *Spartacus* which won Metty his first – and only – Academy Award.)

'Almost everybody treated Kubrick that way,' said Curtis, who thought that the still-nervous 'Universal was watching [him] like some mad creature from outer space. Later on they'd lionize and canonize him... but not in those days.' Film editor Robert Lawrence confirms that the young director 'had a tough time on the set – this kid from the Bronx up against Olivier, Charles Laughton – in poor health, really poor health – and Peter Ustinov, whose ad-libs constantly threw everyone. But Kubrick had such a sense of courage,' which presumably stood him in good stead for the 'inevitable run-ins with Kirk Douglas'.

Douglas famously later referred to Kubrick as 'a talented shit' – qualifying this by musing that 'you don't have to be a nice person to be extremely talented.' Tony Curtis, on the other hand, considered the director 'not only a genius with the camera but, as far as I was concerned, Stanley's greatest effectiveness was in his one-on-one relationships with actors.' In marked contrast to many of the wild and unconfirmed horror stories which would later circulate concerning Kubrick's so-called 'tyrannical' attitude towards his cast, Curtis hailed him as 'so good with actors in general – and with me in particular – so appreciative. He was a very fine person. My favorite director.' In James B. Harris' estimation, 'I think it speaks for itself that when Kirk got into trouble on *Spartacus* he went to Stanley out of respect for his talent. It's like going back to a restaurant or taking a girl out – nobody wants to get involved with someone they didn't get along with. To go back a second time says it all.'

The finished product certainly suggested that Kubrick must have been doing *something* right – whatever the feelings among cast and crew, there are many undeniably great things in *Spartacus,* including one of the best screen performances by Laurence Olivier who, despite being labelled the 'world's greatest actor' – a reputation gained almost entirely in the theatre – had often been unconvincing and uncomfortable on screen, with only a handful of satisfactory appearances to his credit.

Spartacus remains one of the most intelligent and sensitively made examples of that era of epic cinematic spectacle – there can be few more moving moments on film than the mass declaration 'I am

Spartacus (Kirk Douglas) and Antoninus (Tony Curtis) fight to the death at the gates of Rome – the 'reward' for the winner will be crucifixion at dawn.

Spartacus' or the climactic fight to the death between Spartacus and Antoninus. (Amusingly, Douglas revealed that the 'Spartacus' calls were actually recorded during half-time at a college football game in Michigan, where 76,000 fans were coached in alternately yelling 'I am Spartacus' or 'Hail Crassus.')

Inevitably there would be the usual carping reviews: Bosley Crowther in the *New York Times* again complained of the accents of the performers ('I'm Spardeecus') – just what would Roman slaves of 73BC have sounded like anyway? – calling the film 'heroic humbug... a spotty, uneven drama'. The early gladiator school section was thought to be 'lively, exciting and expressive... the middle phase... pretentious and tedious', while the huge battle scenes were admitted as a 'handsome, eye-filling re-enactment... which matches the Battle of Agincourt in *Henry V*' before the film 'slides off into an anti-climax wherein a great deal more is made of Miss Simmons' post-war predicament than of the crucifixion of 6,000 captive slaves.'

The *Spectator* grumbled that the film had left a 'curiously mixed impression of force and feebleness', which it blamed largely on the star's lack of 'presence – that immeasurable attribute – [which] Mr Douglas (who is one of the film's producers, which explains things) hasn't got... enough, anyway'. In the *Daily

Mail, Kubrick was accused of 'brutal realism mixed up with romantic hokum. These distasteful interjections of horror – the more revolting because they are skilfully done – aspire to the licence and privilege of art which this film most emphatically isn't.'

Variety took a more generous view – and one more in keeping with the general consensus – hailing the picture as 'a rousing testament to the spirit and dignity of man [where] Douglas succeeds admirably in giving an impression of a man who is all afire inside.' Noting the cost – 'a lot of moolah – [Universal] says $12 million – and two years of intensive work' – which had gone into its making, their reviewer felt the film 'justifies the effort. There is solid dramatic substance, purposeful and intriguingly contrasted character portrayals and, let's come right out with it, sheer pictorial poetry that is sweeping and savage, intimate and lusty, tender and bitter sweet.'

The *Jewish Chronicle* – noting the expert performances of 'two of Hollywood's most talented Jewish actors'(!) but seemingly unaware of Kubrick's own religious persuasion – declared that 'there have been so very many pictures of this sort that have merely bored us or driven us to fits of derisive laughter that it is a pleasure to record that, in this instance, the whole thing, skilfully directed by Stanley Kubrick, is thoroughly entertaining, and highly absorbing from start to finish.' Kubrick was similarly praised by the *Weekly Post,* who found his 'use of camera no less than tremendous. There are tender and exacting moments in more intimate scenes, whilst... his battle sequences, mounted with tension, are handled with wide-eyed intelligence.'

Little significant mention was made of the involvement of the formerly *persona non grata* Dalton Trumbo, although *Time* noted that his script 'played fast and loose with the historical facts' – a reasonable assessment, since Trumbo – as Fast had done in his novel – incorporated a number of current (1950s) ideological viewpoints in his storyline: 'freedom' here was of the variety discussed in relation to black Americans and the civil rights movement, rather than of the pre-Christian era (*Spartacus* was one of the few – perhaps the only – epic of its day not to centre on religion) with the character of Spartacus transformed into a 'Roman Che Guevara.' *Time,* however, thought the film rose above these problems and remained 'a peculiarly impressive piece of moviemaking. Director Stanley Kubrick shows mastery in all departments: cast, camera and cutting... he knows when to let the frame stand grandly still and the audience stare, as if through a huge picture window.'

These initial reviewers had seen the complete version of the film, running at 192 minutes, although for general release the print was cut by about five minutes, removing some of the more violent battle scenes already noted, as well as Crassus' face splashed with the blood of Draba after slitting his neck in the arena. Also cut back was the final scene of Spartacus on the cross, with Varinia begging for him to die quickly rather than suffer a long, slow lingering death.

All of this footage was finally restored for the film's 1991 re-release, as was a longer scene, featuring Laurence Olivier and Tony Curtis, in which Crassus questions Antoninus on whether he prefers oysters or snails, before revealing that his own 'appetite includes both'. This apparently mystifying exchange was actually a veiled reference to homosexuality, with which the censors of the day were uneasy, suggesting that the dialogue be amended to consider the relative merits of the – presumably – less suggestive 'artichokes and truffles' instead. Although the film-makers kept faith with their molluscs, the result was that the scene was cut altogether.

When this sequence was to be reinserted into the movie, however, it was discovered that, although the reel of film had survived, its soundtrack had not. Tony Curtis was called in to re-record his lines in Hollywood but, with Laurence Olivier having died in 1989, his lines were noticeably read by Anthony Hopkins. The scene could now be viewed in its entirety, thus explaining why – when Crassus turns to see the effect his comments have had – Antoninus has conveniently scarpered.

Otherwise, the restoration of the film 30 years later dealt mainly with the colour, which had faded duringthat period. The project was supervised by Robert Harris, who had earlier performed the same duties on a reissued *Lawrence of Arabia* (1962), and now received assistance from Kubrick in the shape of faxed suggestions and notes on the original production. Steven Spielberg – barely entering his teens when *Spartacus* was first released – became executive producer of the restoration, as a founder member – with Kubrick, George Lucas, François Truffaut and others – of the Film Restoration Programme, whose aim it was to rescue movies whose surviving prints had been neglected, lost or damaged over the years. Among the more troublesome aspects, in this case, had been the locating of an acceptable master print of the film – originally shot in Super Technirama 70, a system in which the film uniquely ran through the camera horizontally. Even Kubrick's own copy – lodged with the American Film Institute – was off-limits, classified as an 'archive print'.

Despite his reported later disaffection with the film, back in 1960 after almost two years' work on the project, Kubrick justifiably compared *Spartacus* favourably to those other costume epics of the era, telling reporters, 'Let's just say I was more influenced by Eisenstein's *Alexander Nevsky* than by *Ben-Hur* or anything by Cecil B. De Mille.' James B. Harris considered that his partner 'was certainly proud of his work on the film back then. Stanley brought a lot to that picture – I think without him it wouldn't have been nearly as good.' In any event, *Spartacus* would be the final film that Stanley Kubrick would make in Hollywood.

* As part of earlier negotiations, the Harris–Kubrick team had agreed to sign a five-picture deal with Kirk Douglas' Bryna Company – 'That's how desperate we were to get *Paths of Glory* off the ground,' says the producer – and, with *Spartacus* finally completed, Kubrick put forward a script called *I Stole $16 Million*, based on the autobiography of bank robber Willie Sutton, only for this to be rejected by Douglas. The script remained unproduced, with Kubrick telling Michel Ciment that he has 'never been subsequently interested' in it.

Harris had immediately been looking to negotiate a way out of what he and Kubrick considered a restrictive deal, with one alternative being that they 'would give Kirk the majority of the next picture that we made after *Paths of Glory*.' When the call came from Douglas for Kubrick to take over from Anthony Mann on the *Spartacus* lot and with *Lolita* already announced as the next Harris–Kubrick production, Harris 'made a deal with Kirk that Stanley would direct *Spartacus* if he would waive *Lolita*,' to which the star readily agreed since, as Harris suspected, 'he never thought *Lolita* could get made... that it had no chance with the censors.' By the close of 1961, the hastily agreed five-picture deal had been terminated, with Douglas later ruefully observing that, 'In the nearly thirty years since... Stanley has made only seven movies. If I had held him to his contract, half of his remaining movies would have been made for my company.'

1961
LOLITA

One of my very best adventures in film-making.
JAMES MASON

Seven-Arts/Anya/Transworld. (MGM)

Directed by Stanley Kubrick. Produced by James B. Harris.

Screenplay: Vladimir Nabokov, based on his own novel. Director of photography: Oswald Morris. Film editor: Anthony Harvey. Production supervisor: Raymond Anzarut. Art direction: William Andrews, Sid Cain. Set designer: Andrew Low. Music score: Nelson Riddle. Theme song composed by Bob Harris. Orchestrations: Gil Grau. Production manager: Robert Sterne. Assistant director: René Dupont. Camera operator: Denys N. Coop. Sound recording: H. L. Bird, Len Shilton. Dubbing editor: Winston Ryder. Make-up: George Partleton. Hairdresser: Betty Glasow. Assistant editor: Lois Gray. Wardrobe supervisor: Elsa Fennell. Shelley Winters' costumes: Gene Coffin.

Cast:
James Mason (Humbert Humbert); Shelley Winters (Charlotte Haze); Peter Sellers (Clare Quilty); Sue Lyon (Lolita Haze); Marianne Stone (Vivian Darkbloom); Diana Decker (Jean Farlow); Jerry Stovin (John Farlow); Suzanne Gibbs (Mona Farlow); Gary Cockrell (Dick); Roberta Shore (Lorna); Lois Maxwell (Nurse Mary Lore); Cec Linder (doctor); Bill Greene (George Swine); Isobel Lucas (Louise); Eric Lane (Roy); Shirley Douglas (Mrs Starch); Roland Brand (Bill); Colin Maitland (Charlie); C. Denier Warren (Potts); Irvin Allen (intern); Marion Mathie (Miss Lebone); Craig Sams (Rex); John Harrison (Tom); Maxine Holden (receptionist); James Dyrenforth (Beale); Terence Kilburn (man).

153 minutes. Black and white.

Arriving at the home of Clare Quilty (Peter Sellers) the morning after what appears to have been a wild party, Humbert Humbert (James Mason) confronts the stupendously hung-over Quilty, eventually producing a gun as he explains his reasons for wanting him dead. As the baffled Quilty attempts to escape upstairs, Humbert wounds and finally shoots him dead as he cowers behind an oil painting leaning against a wall. In flashback, we learn what has brought the two men together in these circumstances.

Humbert, a teacher of French literature, arrives in America looking for a place to rent and views a room at the home of widowed Charlotte Haze (Shelley Winters). She is all-too-obviously attracted to the sophisticated, intellectual Humbert who, for his part, is privately appalled at her vulgar pretensions. About to leave and head for the next lodging house on his list, Humbert catches sight of Charlotte's daughter Lolita (Sue Lyon) sunbathing in the garden and immediately decides to stay after all.

Humbert distantly tolerates Charlotte's amorous advances solely in order to be close to Lolita, with whom he becomes increasingly infatuated. When all three attend the school prom they encounter Clare Quilty (Peter Sellers), a celebrated but utterly shallow television playwright - and his companion Vivian Darkbloom (Marianne Stone). Humbert carefully steering Lolita away from anyone he fears may make an impression on her.

Eventually, Humbert agrees to marry Charlotte, but writes in his private diary of his true feelings for Lolita and his fantasy of murdering his new bride, who has sent her daughter away to boarding school so that the newly-weds can be alone together. Whether Humbert will actually go through with his plan is never put to the test, however, as Charlotte discovers the diary and hysterically rushes out onto the busy street, where she is knocked down and killed by a car.

Humbert collects Lolita from summer camp and drives her to a motel where, next morning, he tells her of her mother's death, assuming – correctly – that she will cling to him for comfort and support. The two then travel across America towards Beardsley College, where Humbert has been offered a teaching post. Along the way, he attempts to seduce her, but is at first thwarted by various mishaps, including another – apparently chance – encounter with Quilty.

The sleeping arrangements of Humbert Humbert (James Mason) prove, on the whole, to be not what he had hoped for, as first he grits his teeth to get through another evening with Charlotte (Shelley Winters).

At Beardsley, the over-protective and insecure Humbert forbids Lolita to appear in a school play written by Quilty, but is finally persuaded and reassured by the school psychologist Dr Zaempt (actually Quilty in one of his many disguises).

Taking her out of the school, Humbert sets off on the road with Lolita once more only for her to fall ill and be admitted to hospital. Arriving later to visit her, Humbert is told that the girl has been discharged earlier that day in the care of her 'uncle'. Fearing that the hospital has discovered his true relationship with the girl, Humbert frantically demands to see her, but is forcibly restrained and made to leave the building.

Some time later, after finally giving up his attempts at finding her, Humbert receives a letter from Lolita asking him for money. He arrives at the address where he discovers that she has married an unremarkable young man called Richard Schiller and is now heavily pregnant. Begging her to come away with him, Humbert learns that Lolita never cared for him at all, and that the only man she ever loved was Quilty, who had been following their every move. He had been the 'uncle' with whom she ran away, but she left him soon afterwards when he had tired of her. Devastated, Humbert heads for Quilty's home seeking revenge...

* ✳ *

---

* Humbert Humbert died in jail from coronary thrombosis while waiting to stand trial for the murder of Clare Quilty.

Humbert spends another night like a well-behaved puppy at the foot of the bed as Lolita (Sue Lyon) 'mourns' her lost mother.

Completed in December 1953, Vladimir Nabokov's novel *Lolita* – 'a short novel about a man who liked little girls' – was never going to be an easy proposition, either for publishers or later for film-makers.

Begun in 1948, Nabokov had written the book mostly during cross-country trips as he indulged his favourite hobby of butterfly collecting (the novel even contained the minor character missing from the screen version 'Vladimir Nabokov, butterfly hunter'), and despite the questionable reputation of the novel as generally perceived, much of the book was concerned with a satirical view of US roadside culture – motels and the like.

The author had originally insisted that the book be published either under a pseudonym or anonymously – critics suggested this was because he did not want to run the risk of tarnishing his reputation, although Nabokov's son, Dmitri, insists that it was merely to prevent any possible embarrassment to Cornell University where the writer held a teaching post.

Under such conditions, and reluctant to accept something already whispered of as 'pornographic', at least four major American publishers declined to handle the book, and Nabokov asked his French agent to look for a publisher in that country. The result was that

Olympia Press finally produced an English language edition of *Lolita* in 1955. This may not have helped the book's growing notoriety, since Olympia mainly specialized in cheap editions of undistinguished pornography, which they published in identical bindings alongside works by such authors as Henry Miller, Hugh Walpole and William Burroughs. *Lolita* initially sold badly – neither pornographic enough for 'aficionados' nor yet acclaimed as anything else, until Graham Greene hailed it as one of the three best books of the year, in *The Sunday Times*. Britain, nevertheless, had to wait until the Obscene Publications Act allowed such books as *Lady Chatterley's Lover* and *Lolita* to be published on the recommendation of literary 'experts', while in the US, 'books of literary importance' were now offered 'protection under the First Amendment of the Constitution' – the right to free speech.

Stanley Kubrick and James B. Harris had already begun negotiations for the screen rights to what Nabokov would consider his 'best book' as early as 1958 – before it had even been published in the United States. Harris recalls that they 'broke the binding of the book and passed pages back and forth so that we could both read it at the same time' and, against all generally accepted wisdom, the two were determined to go ahead with a film version. Harris first met Nabokov at a book lunch at New York's Waldorf Astoria soon after he had paid $125,000 for the screen rights. Told that 'This is James Harris, he just bought your book,' Nabokov – not knowing who the producer was, and thinking he had simply spent $10 or so at a local book store – replied 'Oh good, I hope you enjoy reading it!'

Introductions over, the author was invited to write the movie version, but initially refused until – supposedly – he had a dream in which he was reading the script. A further incentive may well have been the sizeable fee, since he is said to have informed his publisher, 'I don't give a damn for what they call "art"... My supreme and, in fact, only interest in these motion picture contracts is money.' Assured also that his involvement would prevent there being any 'distortions' to the story as it made its way from page to screen, Nabokov reportedly determined to 'vet the use of a real child,' rather curiously suggesting 'Let them find a dwarfess.'

With Kubrick called to work on *Spartacus*, Nabokov was installed at Universal to begin the script which, when completed, was 400 pages long. It fell to Kubrick to explain to the first-time screenwriter the impracticality of this – the film would last seven hours. The writer eventually came up with a much shorter version, but even this was not useable and, although his is the sole credit on the film (the second – after *Spartacus* – and final occasion when Kubrick would not be named as at least co-writer), in reality, Nabokov's script underwent various revisions – certainly by the producer/director team and with possible contributions from Calder Willingham.

The end result was what Harris calls 'James B. Harris and Stanley Kubrick's *Lolita*', as is made clear by the movie's opening titles. 'This might have seemed outrageous to some people,' he says, 'but the movie was ours. One thing had nothing to do with the other. The book is a masterpiece and we weren't going to change that, but when you buy the rights to make a film, you use the book as background material.'

In December 1960, and with *Spartacus* finally on general release, Kubrick could now concentrate solely on *Lolita*, which he intended 'would make people think. The audience will start by being repelled by this creep who seduces a not-so innocent child, but gradually, as they realize he really loves the girl, they'll find things aren't quite as simple as they seemed, and won't be ready to pass immediate moral judgements. I consider that a moral theme.'

Such a story came complete with inherent casting difficulties – great care would be needed to satisfy censors, especially where the potentially 12-year-old Lolita was concerned. A story that Errol Flynn had been approached to play Humbert first came to light in a book written some years later by Flynn's second wife Nora Eddington. Such a proposal would appear, on the face of it, to be highly improbable considering the personal notoriety that the star would have brought to the film in the light of an earlier (dismissed) charge of statutory rape and his general reputation as a womanizer of the highest order.

Yet James Harris confirms that the story does have some basis in fact, although neither he nor Kubrick made the first move. Flynn was at that time separated from his third wife Patrice Wymore and living with the 15-year-old Beverly Aadland, recent co-star of his depressingly awful final picture, *Cuban Rebel Girls*. It was Aadland's mother who wrote to the producer suggesting her daughter as the ideal Lolita, since 'she had been living the role' – the idea being that she and Flynn would come as a package.

At his best – the era of *Adventures of Robin Hood* (1938), *Gentleman Jim* (1942) and *The Sea Hawk* (1940) – Flynn had often been much underrated as a serious actor, but those golden days were, sadly, well behind him now. In deep financial trouble, following the collapse of his own independent 1953 production of *William Tell*, he had been somnambulating throughout a series of dreadful pictures – *Kings Rhapsody*, *The Big Boodle*, *Istanbul* – with only occasional glimpses of the charm and charisma which had once made him one of Hollywood's biggest stars. An appearance as his idol, John Barrymore – another hard drinking, self-destructive figure – in *Too Much, Too Soon* (1958) was his last significant role, but had prompted his old boss Jack Warner sadly to describe him as 'one of the living dead', when Flynn first appeared on set to begin work. It is impossible to imagine him at this stage of his physical decline being capable of summoning the energy and skill needed to portray the subtle complexities of *Lolita*'s Humbert.

Flynn did, nevertheless, meet with Kubrick and Harris, who says that 'it was purely a courtesy meeting on our part. There was never any suggestion that we would use him, but he had earned the courtesy of the meeting. In his own vein, he was great', or at least, he had been. Physically, Flynn was a complete mess by now. 'He was clearly at the end of his life, I suppose,' recalls Harris, 'his eyes were like slits and his face all blown up – he was really dissipated.' Within months of the meeting, in October 1959, even before Nabokov had begun work on his mammoth first draft screenplay Flynn was dead in Vancouver at the age of 50.

Discussions with censors were a constant feature of the pre-production, with the sensitive area of the relationship between Humbert and Lolita uppermost in their minds. Kubrick and Harris offered to shift the emphasis of the story away from any overt sexual treatment, defusing the problematic nature of the story by adopting a more comic – at times almost a 'generation gap' – approach to the story. Harris explains that 'We just thought that it should be treated in a light, amusing manner – that's why we had Peter Sellers in the picture.'

In the US, any film hoping for a general release would require a Seal of Approval from the industry's own Production Code Administration (PCA), first set up in 1930 and popularly (and otherwise) known as the 'Hays Office' after its first president, the former Postmaster-General, Will H. Hays. The code, for many years, included the much-ridiculed stipulations that even married couples could not be seen to be sharing the same bed, but had gradually been amended – most notably since the release of Otto Preminger's *The Moon Is Blue* in 1953 (initially released without a certificate).

Nevertheless, it was still crucial for a film's success that it gain as wide a release as possible and, to reassure the PCA, it was made clear that Lolita would be dressed,for the seduction scene 'in a long-sleeved, high-necked, full-length, heavy flannel night-gown, with Humbert in bathrobe and pyjamas.' It was even suggested that Kubrick had 'offered to have [them] legally married' – an indication of the importance attached to the PCA's magical Seal of Approval. Nevertheless, at this stage the film had not even found a backer, having been rejected by United Artists, Columbia and Warner Brothers (Warners had been least resistant to the project, but offered no assurance that the film would be made without the studio's and Jack Warner's personal interference, which was clearly unacceptable to the filmmakers).

Finally, agreement was reached with Ray Stark's Seven Arts company to finance the picture, which would be distributed by (of all people) Metro-Goldwyn Mayer perhaps, belatedly, hoping to benefit from a picture made by the two film-makers they had once held under contract. MGM had previously been among the most strict of all Hollywood studios in administering the Production Code, fostering a wholesome, clean-cut image of a world inhabited by glowing, scandal-free stars like Mickey Rooney, Greer Garson, Jeanette Macdonald and Clark Gable.

Kubrick had now moved – temporarily at least – to England, where the film was to be shot for reasons of both finance and censorship. Despite the story's American setting, filming would be considerably cheaper in the UK and, as an added attraction, British and European censorship had also been relaxed further than in the US following the passing of the Obscene Publications Act, with British-produced films such as *Room at the Top*(1959), *Saturday Night and Sunday Morning* (1960) and *A Taste of Honey* (1961) dealing frankly – for the time – in previously taboo (mainly sexual) matters. Although the British Board of Film Censors (BBFC) expressed concern over these productions, their main concern had actually been with the strong language representing mostly Northern working-class characters. Sex scenes were still something of a rarity, mostly confined to European art films, but the subject matter of *Lolita* was still viewed cautiously, even without any explicit scenes.

Kubrick later commented that *Lolita* gave him the most perfect casting of any of his films, although first choice, James Mason, almost missed the opportunity of playing Humbert, having been half-tempted by a rather surprising offer of the lead role in a Broadway musical version of *The Affairs of Anatole*. Despite attempts to persuade him otherwise (Harris, perhaps undiplomatically, suggested that the play could easily close after one night, while the film was going to run and run) Mason remained firm in his intention to hit Broadway and become 'the next Rex Harrison'.

During the lengthy shooting of *Spartacus* in 1959, as Nabokov's typewriter rattled away across the Universal lot, Kubrick approached Laurence Olivier with the offer of playing Humbert. 'We had lunch with Larry back in our bungalow,' recalls Harris, 'and he agreed to do it. He would just have to tell his agent – Stanley and I and Olivier were all represented by MCA – so we shook hands on it, and then later that same afternoon he said maybe we'd better forget the whole thing.' Olivier's agent had clearly considered that any association with *Lolita* could damage the reputation of his client – who was *Sir* Laurence Olivier, after all – although the actor was apparently seeking new challenges during this period in order to try to lose any critics' label of 'theatrical dinosaur'. This would eventually manifest itself in his starring in the stage and screen versions of *The Entertainer* (1960), written by 'angry young man' John Osborne.

David Niven was next in line, and was initially enthusiastic until – again – his agent advised against it. The book's notoriety was such, according to Harris, that Niven feared his television show *Four Star Playhouse* which he co-produced with Charles Boyer, Ida Lupino and Dick Powell might be cancelled by its sponsors. The search for Humbert continued, with various star names suggested – although, contrary to rumour, Noel Coward was not among those considered. That would *really* have been weird...

Meanwhile, James Mason was quietly reconsidering his position and, 'when all my friends... looked at me as though I was dotty, I quickly contacted Kubrick and thanked God that I caught him before some unworthy rival had inherited the part that I had in fact longed to play ever since I had read [the novel].'

Yet another fan of *The Killing*, Mason had first met Kubrick while the director was preparing *Paths of Glory* in 1957. In the intervening years, the actor observed, 'it was evident that Kubrick had learned a great deal about screen acting... and become a director of enormous sophistication when it came to handling our group.'

The group by now included Peter Sellers, who had 'never met Kubrick until right before *Lolita*. He came straight to me and asked me to play Quilty. To me that was an enormous honour.' By the early sixties, Sellers had progressed from being one quarter of the radio *Goon Show* to establishing himself as a comic actor in films like *The Ladykillers* (1955)*, The Naked Truth* (1958) and *I'm All Right, Jack* (1959), and now seemed on the verge of international stardom. Often later branded a perfectionist – a label he shares with Stanley Kubrick – Sellers' performance as the enigmatic Clare Quilty in *Lolita* was not without its problems, as far as the remainder of the cast were concerned.

Even with the film being shot in England and with the London-born and bred Sellers searching his vast repertoire of accents to find the correct 'voice' – apparently settling finally on that of US jazz impresario Norman Grantz – Kubrick was still clear that Lolita's mother should be played by an American actress, and he already had someone in mind.

Shelley Winters had by now almost cornered the market in playing the clinging-women-you-can't-wait-to-get-rid-of type, having driven even an *Othello*-obsessed Ronald Colman – normally the most gentlemanly of gentlemen – to strangle her in *A Double Life* (1948). Since then, she had been accidentally drowned while out on the lake with Montgomery Clift (who nevertheless wanted rid of her) in *A Place in the Sun* (1951) and most spectacularly of all she played the victim of Robert Mitchum's fake preacher in Charles Laughton's mesmerizing *Night of the Hunter* (1955).

Travelling across America, as a committed supporter on John F. Kennedy's presidential campaign, Winters received a letter from Kubrick in October 1960, making the unusual suggestion that she meet Vladimir Nabokov in New York to discuss the role of Charlotte Haze with the author. Familiarizing herself with the book, she later recalled, 'John Kennedy saw me reading *Lolita* and broke into laughter. He told me I should get a brown paper cover for the book if I had to read it in public places.' The meeting with Nabokov took place, and 'the next time I returned to New York, the film script of *Lolita* was waiting for me.'

There still remained the problematic casting of Lolita herself, and in spite of the novel's growing notoriety, American mothers continued to submit their daughters' photographs by the thousand to the film's producers. Nabokov expressed some concern over the problem, since he reasoned that 'it was perfectly all right for me to imagine a twelve-year-old Lolita. She existed only in my head. But to make a real twelve-year-old girl play such a part would be sinful and I will never consent to it.'

Such reservations played into the hands of the project's critics, eager to find any ammunition with which to sink the film. Kubrick and Harris, of course, were well aware that no 12-year-old would be acceptable to censors – nor would she be likely to have the ability to play the role convincingly. A number of young actresses were screen tested, including the 17-year-old Tuesday Weld – apparently rejected by Nabokov personally – until Kubrick caught sight of Sue Lyon on *The Loretta Young Show* on television. At the age of 14 1/2, she was at precisely the mid-point of the girl's age over the duration of the story, but this still inspired discussion from opposing camps, who considered her either too young to be so exploited in such a film or too old (Lolita is 12 when Humbert first sees her – the same age that Sue Lyon had been when she began a modelling career).

Lolita's age is, in fact, never mentioned throughout the film version, and Harris recalls that he and Kubrick 'were careful not to make her child-like. Sue Lyon was an extremely attractive and mature girl – 14 when we did the film, but I would agree that she actually looked a little older than her years. I don't think anyone sitting in the theatre would think you were a disgusting old man if you found her sexually attractive.'

Kubrick and Harris had altered Nabokov's screenplay, partly to appease censors but also to restructure the story itself, which was now told entirely in flashback, beginning with the murder of Quilty – 'a strategy aimed at transforming *Lolita* from a tale of sexual perversion into a black comedy-thriller', according to Gene Youngblood, who further observed that 'for the censors, a killer was more acceptable than a pervert.' In truth, Nabokov's novel is itself told in virtual flashback, being the 'posthumously published memoirs' of the pseudonymical Humbert, supposedly released only on his own death and that of Lolita, in childbirth at the age of 17 – a finale missing from the film.

James Mason later wrote of *Lolita* as 'one of the very few films in which we actors were allowed a fair amount of time for rehearsals, both before principal photography and immediately prior to the shooting of each sequence.' According to Peter Sellers, part of this process included 'read[ing] from the script and pick[ing] out the parts which went best.' By this method, any sections which didn't appear to be working properly, or which felt uncomfortable, were eliminated. 'Then we'd sit round a table with a tape-recorder and ad-lib on the lines of the passages we'd chosen,' Sellers added. 'In that way, we'd get perfectly natural dialogue which could then be scripted and used.'

This attempt at spontaneity was also necessary because, as James Mason noted, Sue Lyon 'had so conscientiously memorized all her lines that they were inclined to come out of her parrot-fashion.' To overcome this, 'Kubrick suggested that all of us pretend to forget the lines that we had memorized and express it in our own words,' so that Lolita would respond in a more natural manner.

For Shelley Winters, this method of working (as opposed to The Method) proved something of a trial, as she later complained that 'James Mason was handsome and sexy and very, very intelligent but always seemed outside of his role watching himself – and me.' A former student of the famed Actors Studio in New York alongside Eli Wallach, Montgomery Clift, Marilyn Monroe and James Dean, she 'felt terribly frustrated when doing a scene with [Mason] but, then, when I saw the rushes, he was hilarious and marvellous.' Peter Sellers, however, was a different proposition altogether, who she thought was 'acting on a different planet – I never could connect with him.'

Whenever Winters would complain to her director 'about trying to connect with my two leading men, he would agree with me – but he didn't change their performances. I never felt anyone was listening to me when I talked, except for the sound-man.' Kubrick allowed the situation to continue, with Winters eventually realizing that 'this very frustration that I had in real life was what was so sad and funny about Charlotte.'

It is easy to sympathize with Shelley Winters, being up against Peter Sellers – seemingly running through his act and making a different movie altogether and, perhaps, allowed just a little too much freedom on this production, although James Harris insists that the actor 'did a brilliant job – Peter is such a terrific, spontaneous type of entertainer and we had tremendous fun letting him improvise,' James Mason, thought Kubrick 'so besotted with the genius of [Sellers] that he seemed never to have enough of him' and, while the ad-libs previously mentioned were a significant aspect of

rehearsals, 'Peter Sellers was the only one allowed or rather encouraged to improvise his entire performance.'

Incredibly, Sellers apparently told Mason that 'he did not enjoy improvising,' only to go on to do just that with inevitably, mixed results. Mason ruefully observed that there had been 'one scene in which Sellers, immersed in the character of Quilty, pretended to be an undercover detective for a full nine minutes, while poor Humbert Humbert had nothing to do but look uncomfortable.'

Despite this, James Mason is by far the funniest thing in the first half of the film, as he attempts to keep the rampant Charlotte at arm's length, despite her constant attentions. 'Hum, you touch me and I go limp as a noodle,' she tells him at one point. Humbert's sublimely indifferent 'Yes – I know the feeling,' is expertly delivered, as is the exchange during a chess game, where Charlotte asks 'You're going to take my Queen?' 'That was my intention', replies Humbert, eyeing Lolita as she passes by the table. Shelley Winters remarked that Mason's asides 'were so quiet that, when we were acting, I never even heard them.' The subtlety of his performance contrasted sharply with that of Sellers and, although *Time* magazine astonishingly suggested that the two actors ought to have reversed their roles, Humbert became the latest of the actor's most memorable roles.

This is not to say that Peter Sellers is not good in the film. Quilty is instantly loathsome (as he should be), right from the film's opening scene, when he is discovered by Humbert drunk beneath a dust sheet in the huge drawing room of his castle estate. This opening is a real film fan's dream; Humbert's demand 'Are you Quilty?' is met with 'No, I'm Spartacus,' while the set itself resembles nothing less than a miniature-Xanadu from *Citizen Kane* with half-emptied packing cases scattered around the room (although James B. Harris denies that there was anything deliberate in this).

Quilty's glib responses to Humbert's increasingly desperate questions and accusations only make him more hateful, as Humbert realizes that his nemesis does not even know who he is. Following his rejection by Lolita, this only confirms his own ultimate insignificance. Faced with his imminent death, Quilty insists on a game of ping-pong at the conveniently placed table (actually a suggestion of James Mason's to indicate Quilty's 'bizarre lifestyle' – although he little expected to be asked to play on it) and continues to regard the entire situation as a joke. The goon-like voices and constant prancing are not even silenced by Humbert's first astonishingly loud – gunshot ('Gee – right in the boxing glove') and his attempts to escape up the staircase end with him, irrationally, taking shelter behind an oil painting ('My leg will be black and blue in the morning').

Sellers' other periodic appearances in the film see

him first as the celebrity playwright, soaking up the adulation of all at the school prom (at Charlotte's invitation, he had previously given a talk to the Great Books Committee on 'Dr Schweitzer and Dr Zhivago'), and later as the sinisterly bogus Dr Zaempt, school psychologist – an odd mix of *I'm All Right Jack*'s Fred Kite and the future Dr Strangelove. In his straight Quilty incarnation, he is constantly partnered by the mysterious Vivian Darkbloom (actually an anagram of Vladimir Nabokov), played by Shelley Winters' friend Mary Noble under the name of Marianne Stone. 'I don't believe even Mary ever understood her role,' says Winters. 'She was funny and eerie in the picture, but she would never question Kubrick about her motivations' – an Actors Studio comment if ever there was one. She put down Stone/Noble's reaction to 'British theatre manners.' Vivian Darkbloom is indeed an intriguing character – a wholly non-speaking role – who manages, by means of a stared silent exchange with Quilty in the hotel lobby, to suggest that the couple may in fact even be telepathic.

Despite her self-confessed bewilderment, what emerged was Shelley Winters' career-best performance as the pathetic, sad, lonely widow Haze. 'I had known a pseudo-intellectual suburbanite like Charlotte during my childhood days,' she said, 'and Stanley Kubrick knew what buttons to press in my acting computer to bring her back... [He] had the insight to find the areas of me that were pseudo-intellectual and pretentious. We all have those things in us.' Desperate to impress Humbert at their first meeting – and aware of his profession (an English language translator of French poetry) – she lapses into (mostly inappropriate) French throughout their conversation ('Oh, Paris, France... Madame... you know, monsieur...') before demolishing the 'sophisticated' effect by asking that he 'excuse the soiled sock'.

As the story progresses, however, the audience becomes increasingly sympathetic towards the hopelessly deceived Charlotte – never more so than when Humbert receives a written declaration of her love for him. Reading it alone and aloud, he cannot contain his contempt for her, laughing uproariously at her clumsily worded passion. As he later contemplates the 'perfect murder' of his new wife soon after their marriage, he refers to her as a 'playful, clumsy seal' – perhaps the most kindly he ever thinks of her – but within a few minutes she will discover Humbert's diary, which reveals his true feelings about both her and her daughter, and will rush blindly out into the street to meet her death. James Mason – with some justification – considered this entire sequence 'the most skilfully executed section of the film,' it having been completely rewritten by Kubrick to replace a cumbersome and drawn-out sequence of events in the book.

As for Lolita herself, she is actually revealed as a spoiled teenage brat, obviously aware of Humbert's attention, unimpressed by his reading to her of Poe – 'the divine Edgar,' yet willing to sleep with him (her stepfather, after all) while still thinking her mother to be alive. Later, on the road, she has clearly lost interest in him and resents his possessiveness, especially at Beardsley where Humbert fears her involvement with two boys he spied her with at the Frigid Queen coffee bar. During her performance at the school play, Quilty is seen – literally – waiting in the wings, and Lolita is, by this stage, regarding Humbert as a rebellious daughter would an over-protective parent – in fact, worse than that, as she remains coldly unconcerned when Humbert suffers a mild heart attack in the car as he attempts to get away from the disruptive influence of Beardsley. Having disappeared from his life, she will contact him again only to ask for money, proceeding to tell him, bluntly, that she has never cared for him at all.

Once completed, the film was passed uncut in Britain, but not before representations had been made to the BBFC by Christian Action, who insisted that 'no certificate of any kind should be granted to [the film]'. Canon L. J. Collins, chairman of the group, voiced his concern that 'the film would... run the risk of being seen by people suffering from the same perversion... and might, therefore, do great harm, perhaps even leading to a rape or murder which would not otherwise have occurred.'

Kubrick's response to this series of 'perhapses' and 'maybes' was characteristically calm. 'Allowing for the sincerity of your intentions', he 'registered a certain degree of surprise at [Collins'] willingness to judge a motion picture before you see it.' The director insisted that he had 'done everything possible to avoid... the air of sensationalism which has surrounded *Lolita* from the beginning,' and that the Christian Action statement was 'based on presumption and not evidence... [the Canon's] intention of prejudicing the censors before the film was submitted to them was an extremely unfair action.'

Of charges that the film could corrupt any potential viewer, Kubrick stated his belief that 'any child too young to see *Lolita* would not understand it, and any child who could understand it was, for that reason, old enough to see it,' before adding – as reassurance – that he 'would not allow a daughter of mine to see certain Walt Disney films which contained excessive amounts of violence and brutality.'

Despite being made in the UK, arguments delayed the film's release – 'At the time I made *Lolita*,' Kubrick later said, 'it was almost impossible to get it played' – and it finally premiered in New York a full four months before its British opening. Those expecting the movie to be salacious, or even mildly pornographic, were to be hugely disappointed, since the film-makers had been intelligent enough to know just what could or could not go into their screenplay which, in any case, was not aimed at that audience. Comedy had, in many cases, replaced potentially controversial scenes. Even Humbert's attempted seduction of Lolita in their motel room fails dismally, when he is forced to sleep on a folding cot which inevitably insists on folding the wrong way before collapsing altogether.

This Chaplinesque slapstick routine diffused any sexy element in Humbert's inept efforts, although the following scene – in which Lolita actually seduces Humbert – caused problems with American censors. Harris recalls that he was asked by MGM to fade the scene quicker than Kubrick had originally intended, in order for the film to be granted the MPA Seal, but that the Catholic Legion of Decency still remained opposed to the picture, condemning it alongside Fellini's *La Dolce Vita* (1959) – 'we were in good company,' says the producer today. Discussions continued with the Legion for some six months, with a succession of minor cuts being made – mostly in a scene of Humbert and Charlotte in bed together, but with Humbert gazing at a photograph of Lolita on the dressing table, which Monsignor Little of the Legion found 'totally

unacceptable.' Harris now admits that he 'knew exactly what they meant, and they were absolutely right, but in that situation you just argue your case as best you can.' With a few further shots removed, the Legion finally allowed the film its 'Separate Classification' as opposed to the less welcome 'Condemned'.

At the New York opening in June 1962, *Lolita* faced mixed reviews, with the *New York Times* predictably attacking the film's advertising line – 'How did they ever make a film of *Lolita*?' – by remarking 'They didn't... The *Lolita* that Vladimir Nabokov wrote as a novel, and the *Lolita* he wrote to be a film directed by Stanley Kubrick, are two conspicuously different things.' Having got their punch-line out of the way, however, the review conceded that 'Mr Kubrick has got a lot of fun and frolic in his film... The best parts come early [where] Shelley Winters makes the mother a sublimely silly sort... James Mason, as the gulping, amorous hero and Peter Sellers as a sly, predacious cad are at their best in this part of the film.'

Further praising Mason's harrowing scene at the hospital, following Lolita's disappearance, as 'hauntingly poignant... played brilliantly,' they considered the

The honeymoon period clearly over, the spoiled brat that Lolita has become turns on the over-protective Humbert following her successful appearance in Quilty's school play.

picture to have a 'rare power... garbled but often moving... This is not the novel of *Lolita*, but it is a provocative sort of film.'

Variety was less happy about the 'compromises of the script,' describing the film as 'like a bee from which the stinger has been removed. It still buzzes with a sort of promising irreverence but lacks the power to shock.' The cast were nevertheless praised, with 'James Mason... never better,' and 'Shelley Winters... bumptious perfection'. Sue Lyon was said to have made an 'auspicious film debut [in a] difficult assignment', as once again the first half of the film was considered the more impressive of the two – unsurprisingly so, given its light, humorous approach compared with the relentless, downbeat disintegration of Humbert which took up most of the remainder.

Critical reaction was much the same when the picture reached British screens in September, with Arlene Croce of *Sight and Sound* remarking that the film had 'everything it needed to be as brilliant and beautiful as the novel, except great direction.' Unaware of Kubrick and Harris' uncredited contribution, they enthused over 'Nabokov's screenplay... a model of adaptation – resourceful, economical, light-bodied,' but noted that, 'as the director is the bright but far from flammable Stanley Kubrick... the film has Nabokov's ear and voice, [but] not his eye.'

Grudgingly allowing that '*Lolita* is – in its own way – a good film,' Croce found Peter Sellers' multi-performance 'cultishly gratuitous', but could not fault most of the 'near-perfect cast... James Mason has been quietly good, or merely quiet, for so long, in so many films, that it would be easy to underestimate his achievement here.' This fleshing out of Humbert was further described in *Monthly Film Bulletin* as 'seedily stylish... with its glinting hints of desperation, distaste, fastidiousness towards people of his own age, peeping out through a blandly obliging facade', and Mason's skill in creating a believable Humbert is evident throughout. Audiences were, rightly, uncomfortable in finding him amusing and likeable in the first half of the picture, as he grew infatuated and finally obsessed with the young girl, and perhaps more so as they pitied his later downfall, at the hands of what appeared to be less sensitive souls.

MFB was among the few of the contemporary reviews to praise Peter Sellers who, it said, had 'turned a series of revue sketches (notably a German psychiatrist) away from self-indulgence into the almost Dostoievskian territory of sadistic innuendo and crafty, leech-like persistence.'

Musing on Kubrick's position as 'an intellectual director with little feeling for erotic tension', they felt the film's 'major achievement [to be the] charting of an obsession in terms of sadness, irony, rage and genuine compassion', with later scenes between the quarrelling

Humbert and Lolita 'convincingly, savagely seized with both pairs of lungs'. Overall, their main complaint lay in the 'incongruity which this distinguished film fails to make much sense out of... the excessive number of English location shots'. Attempts to offset this by inserting second-unit scenes of authentic American road travel were undermined, most notably by Humbert's arrival to see the now-married Lolita at a house in an all-too-obviously British street, 'transformed' by the strategic placing of a US-style mail box in centre-screen. This apart, though, the location – though of vital significance to the book's admirers – was of almost secondary importance to the story of the film.

Lolita – helped no doubt by its near-scandalous reputation – proved to be popular at the box office, was conspicuously overlooked at most of the major annual award ceremonies, but remains fondly remembered by most of those involved with it. Shelley Winters 'enjoyed every second of it. Working with Stanley Kubrick was an exhilarating experience.' The star pays further handsome tribute to Kubrick, of whom her abiding impression is that 'he directed so quietly [and] understood one of the most valuable things a director can know... He would take the time in rehearsals to make you do exactly what he needed for a scene and make you think it was your idea... When I would see the rushes at night, I was absolutely amazed.'

For Sue Lyon, however, *Lolita* did not become her first step towards an expected glittering star career. Sadly typecast for many years afterwards – as Carroll Baker had been in the superficially similar role of *Baby Doll* (1956) – her career faltered badly, as did her much publicized private life. James B. Harris recalls that 'she never really wanted to be a movie star. She came from a family that needed the money, but after she got a load of being in the public eye she didn't like the notoriety. We were constantly running away from paparazzi.'

Despite subsequent roles in quick succession under the direction of John Huston (*Night of the Iguana*, 1964) and John Ford (*Seven Women*, 1965), Lyon became increasingly less interested in screen stardom. Harris observes that 'At fourteen, she was absolutely down to earth – bright, terrific sense of humour. She was chaperoned the entire time by her mother, but she was sixteen by the time the picture was released and had a tremendous inclination for the underdog, doing charity stuff at drug rehabilitation centres and visiting prisons.' Thirty-five years later, after three failed marriages, she is said to have remarked to an interviewer of the role that brought her to the public's attention, 'I defy any girl rocketed to fame at fifteen in a sex-nymphet role to stay on an even keel.'

Vladimir Nabokov, meanwhile, had been Kubrick's

guest of honour at a dinner party in New York to mark the film's release, and it was here that he told James Mason how much he had 'admired the film and congratulated Mr Kubrick in having done a number of things which he himself would never have thought of.' Mason considered 'the author's enthusiasm quite genuine', and Kubrick confirmed this in a cable to *The Observer* in London following their publication of a report from a non-professional film critic whose views the director described as 'viciously flippant and rude at the expense of Mr Nabokov, Mr Mason, Miss Winters, Mr Sellers, Miss Lyon and myself.'

The report – credited to Michael Davie – contained the supposed reaction of one anonymous spectator at the premiere, quoted as saying 'Well, anyway, no one can say "Look what they did to Nabokov, the poor slob." The poor slob did it to himself.' Still disguising his own contribution to the script, Kubrick revealed that Nabokov – 'blissfully unaware of his new status as a poor slob' – had told the director that 'this is a great film. Sue Lyon is marvellous. She *is* Lolita. There are even some things in it I wish were in the book.'

Although the author's son, Dmitri, says today that his father's feelings on seeing the film for the first time were 'like a patient lying supine in an ambulance watching the landscape go by and powerless to change it,' Nabokov certainly did not raise any objections publicly at the time, and his later published letters to friends during the period also suggest that he was happy with the end result which was, after all, based on his own original over-long script. Harris suggests that the author's own version 'was so close to the novel that you could say anything we used from the book was taken from his screenplay,' and the producer still remarks, with some amusement, that it was Nabokov who received the film's only Academy Award nomination (it lost to *To Kill a Mockingbird*) for a screenplay of which he claimed to recognize 'only about 20 per cent of my own contribution.' Despite the substantial rewrites and re-edits, his was the sole screen credit and, when I asked Harris if this was again a mark of courtesy on the part of the filmmakers he pointed out that 'people who admire Nabokov think that, if there's one line changed from the book, it's been ruined. Well, what would you do if you knew that everyone was going to jump on you for changing the Master's work? I don't think I have to say any more than that.' in 1974, Nabokov returned to his script, rewrote it and published it as *Lolita: A Screenplay*.

The last Kubrick film to feature a conventional score, *Lolita*'s music was composed and conducted by top Hollywood arranger, Nelson Riddle and contained a number of pastiche-type themes recalling typical Hollywood-style love stories. The main opening theme is lush and romantic, heard over a

shot of Lolita's toenails being carefully and lovingly painted by Humbert – an indelible image and, in fact, the only visible occasion of there being any real physical contact between the two. Humbert's first glimpse of Lolita, sunbathing in her mother's garden is accompanied by a suitably cheesy fifties-style tune, tinnily heard coming from a transistor radio, contrasting sharply with the sweeping cod-'piano concerto' extract as she is sent away to summer camp. 'Don't forget me,' she teases the devastated Humbert as the soundtrack echoes with the pseudo-romantic strains familiar to anyone who has seen one of those 1940s British melodramas like *Brief Encounter, Dangerous Moonlight* or *Love Story* (starring Margaret Lockwood and Stewart Granger, as opposed to the Ryan O'Neal/Ali McGraw monstrosity of 1970).

'Many different films could be extracted from a book like *Lolita*,' James Mason had observed in his autobiography, *Before I Forget*, – wisely predicting that 'from whatever viewpoint, I am sure we have not seen the last of her.' And, inevitably, a new version was announced as 'in production' in 1996, to be directed by Adrian Lyne whose previous credits included the supposedly erotic thrillers *Fatal Attraction* (1987) and *Indecent Proposal* (1993). Any hopes that this *Lolita* would remain discreet were dashed when the production uncompromisingly promised 'explicit sex scenes [and] nudity', with a cast featuring Jeremy Irons (Humbert), Melanie Griffith (Charlotte) and Frank Langella (Quilty, in a much reduced role). Lolita was to be played by newcomer Dominique Swain – coincidentally the same age Sue Lyon had been at the time she was signed to the Kubrick version. This would prove to be about the only similarity between the two as, although Lyne's film was set in late 1940s America, as the novel had been, Swain's Lolita failed to convince as anything other than a 1990s American teenage brat.

In an atmosphere in which child abuse and paedophilia is a constant topic of discussion and revulsion, Lyne had clearly misjudged what was likely to be considered acceptable, and did not help his cause by using interviews to endlessly criticize the 1962 version. Although it may have suited his purposes to do so, few were convinced by his arguments that James Mason had played Humbert as 'totally hateful' – the implication being that Jeremy Irons' characterization would be more faithful/convincing. Screenwriter Stephen Schiff similarly claimed that his script made 'our version' truer to the book and – *ipso facto* – a better film. James Harris countered by remarking 'I don't mind them not liking our film, but they shouldn't not like it because it departed from the book – if you want that story, then go read the book.'

Major differences between the two versions are

that Lyne's film – handsomely photographed as it is, and with an impressive score by Ennio Morricone – is totally without any redeeming sense of humour. Jeremy Irons' Humbert is typically glum throughout, and both Charlotte and Quilty are mere cut-outs of the characters they might have been. More controversially, the promised 'explicit' scenes predictably excited much comment, with Lyne having fallen into the trap of showing something on screen simply because he was now able to do so, rather than because it was essential. As Harris says today, 'The one thing I know is that being explicit was never of any interest to us,' and unlike Lyne's assertion that the story be seen wholly as a tragedy – therefore unrelievedly bleak – the Harris–Kubrick version saw *Lolita* as 'the last of the conflicts that make great love stories – you know, whenever lovers have difficulties in being together, they make the best love stories.' Any scenes of an explicit nature, of course, would not have been passed by the censor in the early 1960s anyway, but Harris still says that their film would be no different if made today – other than that it would be in colour. 'We assumed that everybody was familiar with the book and knew what it was about,' he says. 'We didn't have to dwell on that. The audience bring that in with them and they're thinking that for us – it's not necessary to show it.'

Adrian Lyne's *Lolita* remained unreleased for almost 18 months while American distributors refused to handle it, finally reaching UK screens in May 1998 when it was compared inevitably and almost entirely unfavourably – with the Kubrick–Harris version. Lyne's assertion that 'at least people are talking about the problem because of this film' seemed neither wholly convincing nor justification for what emerged as a po-faced, surface-gloss exercise in gratuitous shock tactics. Sold direct to cable television in America, a limited theatrical release was finally agreed towards the end of 1998.

Dmitri Nabokov meanwhile is left bemoaning the fact that the name 'Lolita' was never copyrighted, so has been used for endless – increasingly seedy – products and brand names. 'I have catalogued as much as I could how the word has been used and misused,' he says, 'and it will make a nice little book some day.' We can only hope that no one decides to film it.

1964

DR STRANGELOVE

OR: (HOW I LEARNED TO STOP WORRYING AND LOVE THE BOMB)

Beyond any question the most shattering sick joke I've ever come across.
BOSLEY CROWTHER

Hawk Films. (Columbia)

Produced and directed by Stanley Kubrick.

Screenplay: Stanley Kubrick, Terry Southern and Peter George, based on the novel *Red Alert* by Peter George. Associate producer: Victor Lyndon. Director of photography: Gilbert Taylor. Camera operator: Kelvin Pike. Film editor: Anthony Harvey. Assistant editor: Ray Lovejoy. Music score adapted by Laurie Taylor, including 'We'll Meet Again' (Ross Parker and Hughie Charles, performed by Vera Lynn), 'Try a Little Tenderness' (Woods, Campbell, Connelly), 'When Johnny Comes Marching Home' (Louis Lambert). Production designer: Ken Adam. Art director: Peter Murton. Sound recording: John Cox. Assistant director: Eric Rattray. Director of production: Clifton Brandon. Continuity: Pamela Carlton. Costumes: Bridget Sellers. Make-up: Stuart Freeborn. Hairdresser: Barbara Ritchie. Special effects: Wally Veevers. Travelling matte: Vic Margutti. Aviation adviser: John Crewdson. Executive producer: Leon Minoff.

Cast:
Peter Sellers (Group Captain Lionel Mandrake/President Merkin Muffley/Dr Strangelove); George C. Scott (General 'Buck' Turgidson); Sterling Hayden (General Jack D. Ripper); Slim Pickens (Major T. J. 'King' Kong); Peter Bull (Ambassador de Sadesky); James Earl Jones (Lieutenant Lothar Zogg); Keenan Wynn (Colonel Bat Guano); Jack Creley (Mr Staines); Frank Berry (Lieutenant H. R. Dietrich); Tracy Reed (Miss Scott); Shane Rimmer (Captain A. 'Ace' Owens); Paul Tamarin (Lieutenant B. Goldberg); Gordon Tanner (General Faceman); Glenn Beck (Lieutenant W. D. Kival); Robert O'Neil (Admiral Randolph); Roy Stephens (Frank); Laurence Herder, John McCarthy, Hal Galili (Burpelson defence team).

93 minutes. Black and white.

At the American Burpelson air force base, Group Captain Lionel Mandrake (Peter Sellers) of the British air force – sent there on an officer exchange programme – is called to the office of General Jack D. Ripper (Sterling Hayden) and informed that the base is now on a Condition Red alert and that all radios are to be impounded. Telling Mandrake that the Russians have begun an attack on the US, Ripper issues the coded order to the fleet of B-52 bombers – permanently airborne and never more than two hours from their assigned targets within the Soviet Union – to proceed with Plan R.

On board one of the bombers, Major T. J. 'King' Kong (Slim Pickens) doubts the authenticity of the order – Lieutenant Zogg (James Earl Jones) suggests it may be a test of loyalty – but, once confirmation has been received, Kong tells his men that they are 'about to face nooclear combat toe-to-toe with the Rooskies', with the likelihood of 'promotions and citations for every man jack of you when this thing is over.'

At Burpelson, meanwhile, Mandrake has discovered a radio tuned to a civilian broadcast of dance music and tells Ripper that there must have been a mistake – if the Russians had attacked, then all normal broadcasts would be halted. With typical British reserve, he hesitatingly suggests that Ripper issue the recall order, since 'we don't want to start a nuclear war unless we really have to, do we?' but the distracted Ripper insists that the order will stand, since an all-out attack is the only way to stop the 'Commies from sapping and impurifying our precious bodily fluids.'

Chief of Staff General 'Buck' Turgidson (George C. Scott) is at home, 'working' with his secretary Miss Scott (Tracy Reed) when he is informed by telephone of the events at Burpelson. Reluctantly forced to 'mosey on over to the War Room,' he faces strong questioning from US President Merkin Muffley (Peter Sellers), during which he confirms that the base is completely sealed, with orders to fire on anyone approaching within 200 yards of the gate, that all telephone contact has been blocked and that the nature of Plan R – a 'safeguard' retaliatory plan, designed for use in the event that the president has been incapacitated – is such that the planes cannot be recalled without a three letter code known only to General Ripper. 'I don't want to pass judgment before all the facts are in,' Turgidson tells the president, 'but it's beginning to look like General Ripper may have exceeded his authority.' The recall code, it seems, has a possible 17,000 permutations which will take about two and a half days to transmit to the plane – now within 20 minutes of Russian air-space.

As Ripper had intended, Turgidson suggests a means of avoiding the inevitable retaliatory strike which will follow, by launching an immediate, all-out attack to 'catch them with their pants down' – an action which would result in 'only modest civilian casualties – 10 or 20 million, depending on the breaks'. President Muffley angrily rejects the idea and – against Turgidson's advice – summons Soviet Ambassador, de Sadesky (Peter Bull), to the War Room in order to explain the situation and enlist his help in warning the Russian President Kisov.

Tracking the Russian president to the home of a friend – 'He is a man of the people, but he is also… a man, if you follow my meaning' – de Sadesky warns Muffley that Kisov may be drunk. As the two leaders discuss the problem, it is agreed that, once given the precise flight plans of the bombers, the Soviet air force will be able to bring down the US planes if the recall code cannot be discovered in time. The devastating consequence of failure is that a Soviet 'Doomsday Machine' will be automatically triggered, destroying all animal and human life on the planet and, once set in motion, incapable of being deactivated. When Muffley expresses disbelief that such a machine could exist, his adviser, Dr Strangelove (Peter Sellers) – a wheelchair-bound ex-Nazi scientist – confirms that he had previously carried out research on the possibility of producing a US version of the same device. De Sadesky claims that the Russians – afraid of a Doomsday Gap – had developed their own weapon, after the top-secret American research had been revealed by an unimpeachable source – the *New York Times*.

Meanwhile, a US army force advances on Burpelson as Ripper asks 'Mandrake, did you ever see a Commie drink a glass of water?' further explaining to the increasingly bewildered captain that it is by the fluoridation of water that the American essence is being diluted and that he now drinks only distilled water and grain alcohol. Women, Ripper says, sense his power and seek his essence. 'I do not avoid women,' he says. 'But I do deny them my essence.'

Realizing that his troops have been overrun by the Marine attack, Ripper ignores Mandrake's request to share the recall code with him, and commits suicide, rather than be interrogated by the soldiers now within the compound. By chance, Mandrake discovers what may be the code scribbled on the desk blotter, and urges liberating General Bat Guano (Keenan Wynn) to let him call the president. The suspicious Guano reluctantly allows him to make a call from the public telephone after shooting open a Coca-Cola machine to obtain enough change, and within min-

series of huge nuclear warheads, meaning the end of the human race and civilization.

'Feed me that belt, Mandrake!' – Fearless General Jack D. Ripper (Sterling Hayden) holds off the advancing redcoats, with the cowering Mandrake (Peter Sellers) at his side in *Dr Strangelove*. 'Peace is our profession...'

* * *

At 05:29 and 45 seconds on the morning of 16 July 1945 in the Los Alamos desert, New Mexico, a group of scientists led mankind blindly into a new age via a single, two-second flash of light, 'brighter than a thousand suns' which was to cast a dark, poisonous shadow over the Earth for the next three decades.

As his team prepared to detonate the world's first atomic bomb, Robert Oppenheimer – director of the so-called Manhattan Project – paradoxically claimed to subscribe to the Sanskrit concept of '*ahimsa*' which demanded the 'doing of no harm or hurt,' even naming the test Trinity after the Hindu Vishnu, Brahma and Shiva – the power of life, creator and destroyer. From the *Bhagavad Gita* he quoted the line 'I am become Death, the destroyer of worlds' as the hour of the test approached, although he was later said to have privately considered the most appropriate comment to come from Kenneth Bainbridge, physicist on the project, who observed 'We are all sons of bitches now.'

Across the continent, the main concern in Washington was how soon the new weapon could be put to use in bringing an end to the war with Japan, which some military generals believed could not last much longer anyway. Three weeks later, on 6 August, the first casualties of a new era of atomic warfare fell victim to the American bomb, nicknamed 'Little Boy' and dropped over Hiroshima. More than 70,000 were killed at a single stroke, with an even greater number obliterated three days later at Nagasaki. The ultimate weapon had arrived.

Whether the bomb actually significantly hastened the end of the war has since been the subject of much debate. Carson Mark, in charge of the theoretical department that worked on the post-war hydrogen bomb, reflected 40 years later, to *The Sunday Times*, that 'at the time we thought it would put an end to organized war, because no one can put up with destruction on that scale. But we didn't know how imminent it was that the Japanese would have to call it quits. That might have changed one's feelings: why rub it in and kill all those people if you don't need to? Washington knew how desperate the situation was in Japan and they would have to surrender.'

Some of those connected to the Manhattan Project had initially favoured sharing the technical and scientific developments which had produced the weapon with Russia and Britain, but by the time the first warhead had been constructed, there was no longer any suggestion

utes the great map in the War Room shows the planes retreating from their objectives.

One plane, however, continues on its mission. The radio on board Major Kong's plane has been damaged by an interceptor missile, and the crew are unaware of the recall message. Muffley informs Kisov of Kong's destination but, as the plane loses fuel from a ruptured tank, the ever-resourceful pilot changes course and heads instead for another target.

Back at the War Room, Dr Strangelove – now increasingly addressing the president as 'Mein Führer' – suggests that, with disaster imminent, there is a means of 'preserving perfect specimens' by retreating to deep mine-shafts where they will have to remain for 100 years until the radiation disperses. By taking ten women – chosen for their physical attractiveness – to every one man, the population could soon be replaced. An open-mouthed Turgidson insists that they get to work straight away before the Commies take the initiative and create a Mineshaft Gap.

Approaching his new target, Kong discovers that the plane's bomb doors are jammed and personally goes to investigate. Finally managing to release the door, he is however still sitting on top of the bomb as it is released and falls to Earth – the massive explosion automatically triggering the Doomsday Machine which, in turn, will set off a

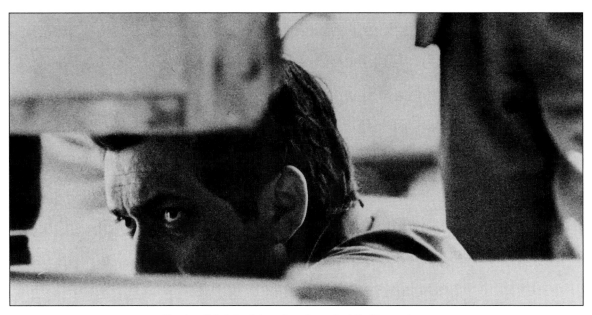

**Stanley Kubrick pictured on the set of *Dr Strangelove*
and, some would say, already going into hiding.**

that such knowledge would be made available, even to the allies. The seeds of the Cold War had already been sown and, shortly, the mutual distrust between the US and USSR was thought to pose an even greater threat to world security.

By the early 1960s, paranoia was at its highest, with nuclear weapons now a reality on both sides and a well-publicized 'secret fleet' of nuclear weapons prepared and ready for virtually instantaneous despatch to 'strategic targets' at the apparent discretion of the American and Russian presidents. People lived in genuine fear of mass destruction at the hands of what were seen as power-crazy political leaders in whom there was failing confidence.

The subject of nuclear warfare and its consequences had been dealt with uneasily by film-makers, who remained unsure of its entertainment value. MGM presented a typically glossy semi-documentary account of the development of the bomb – *The Beginning or The End?* directed by Norman Taurog in 1947 – which concentrated on the scientific breakthrough in a standard Hollywood-style 'Eureka!' fashion, and ultimately suggested that the result was about as much of a threat to mankind as was Don Ameche's invention of the telephone, in *The Alexander Graham Bell Story*.

During the 1950s – apart from the potential for gigantic, rampaging mutant insects, shrinking or, alternately, expanding humans and insane scientists exposed to radiation – an increasing number of films began to feature what was now known as the 'nuclear capabili-

ty' as a backdrop to otherwise conventional stories. Dick Powell's *Split Second* (1953), for example, was a fairly standard crime thriller set within a nuclear testing zone, but few pictures were willing to deal with the horrors of mass destruction, or to consider the circumstances which might lead to the button being pressed.

Seemingly chilling – but at the same time supposedly 'uplifting' – accounts such as *Five* (1951) and *The World, the Flesh and the Devil* (1959) concentrated on the reconstruction of society in an 'Adam and Eve' manner following a pre-credit, often unseen holocaust. Heavy on biblical symbolism, these pictures suggested that, even if the worst came to the worst, the good would still survive, while Ray Milland's *Panic in the Year Zero* (1962) assumed a grimmer tone as survivors ran amok in a lawless, handsomely devastated America until the US Army – with no sense of irony – came to the rescue by restoring law and order.

Stanley Kramer's *On The Beach* (1960) – based on the novel by Nevil Shute and hailed as 'The Biggest Story of Our Time!' – at least avoided an obvious happy ending, as an American submarine crew was spared the devastation by apparently being the sole submerged vessel on Earth at the time of impact – which also spared the viewer from much of the more unpleasant aspects of the attack. Heading for Australia – the last safe place, as the deadly radioactive cloud inexorably follows them – Gregory Peck has the good fortune to meet up with Ava Gardner, although their chances of repopulating the doomed planet seem remote as the film closes.

All of these pictures, however, dealt with the aftermath of a nuclear explosion, without any explanation of the circumstances which led to the triggering of the bomb in the first place. In *On The Beach*, Fred Astaire casually remarks that 'somebody pushed a button,' but cannot recall exactly why – perhaps understandably, from the sane viewpoint of a screenwriter. After all, what possible explanation could there be?

Stanley Kubrick had been interested in nuclear warfare as the basis of a possible movie for a number of years, reportedly reading more than 70 books on the subject and keeping an ever-expanding file of newspaper and magazine articles. Alistair Buchan, director of the Institute for Strategic Studies in London introduced him to a book called *Red Alert* by Peter George (previously published as *Two Hours to Doom* under George's *nom-de-plume* Peter Bryant). Kubrick noted Buchan's recommendation that the book was 'the only feasible, factually accurate fictionalization of the way in which an H-bomb war could start without any sane cause or prompting.'

Among Kubrick's cuttings file was the report of an American serviceman who had tried to set off a thermonuclear bomb, by shooting at it with his revolver. The soldier was apparently already receiving psychiatric treatment, but 'his job was so secret that the psychiatrist never knew his patient had access to the bomb.' An American aircraft crew had also recently dropped its bomb after their plane got into difficulties, 'reasoning that it *probably* contained safety devices' (my italics). True enough, except that all but one of the safety devices failed. To Kubrick, the message was clear – with such figures in charge of the nuclear arsenal, the chances of accidental mass destruction were significantly greater than by deliberate action. 'If the safety devices are 99.9 per cent perfect,' he told one reporter, 'a bomb is bound to go off by accident over a period of thirty years.'

Kubrick and Harris quickly bought the screen rights to *Red Alert* for $3,000 and began adapting it with Peter George at Kubrick's Central Park West apartment. 'We were working on the script as a serious piece,' says Harris today. 'I had set up the deal and I said to Stanley that I felt comfortable about going back to California to pursue a directing career' – something which Kubrick had often asked his friend to consider, despite the producer never having directed a movie, apart from those few experimental efforts with Alexander Singer several years before. 'He just felt that I could do it,' Harris recalls. 'Stanley promised me that the fulfilment of being a director is so much more than being a producer,' although he also warned his partner that 'it can be a lonely business.'

Harris left for California 'with Stanley's encouragement, his advice and his blessings', as the grimness of the subject matter of *Red Alert* – total world destruction

caused by the actions of a deranged individual – began to look ever more senseless to the director. 'After all,' said Kubrick later, 'what could be more absurd than the very idea of two megapowers willing to wipe out all human life because of an accident [and] political differences that will seem meaningless to people a hundred years from now.'

There had been occasions during initial script meetings, 'usually late at night when we were giggly,' says Harris, 'when we used to talk about the humour in the situation: you know, what if everybody in the war room got hungry and had to call down to the deli and we had a guy with an apron come in and take orders, and all these other what-ifs.' In the cold light of day, however, it was considered best to leave well enough alone, as the drama and suspense of the story seemed too strong to meddle with.

Once settled back in California, however, Harris 'got a call from Stanley, who said he had reconsidered, and he now thought the best way to tell the story and get the message over was as a satire. I thought, Jesus Christ, I left him alone for ten minutes and he's going to go right down the drain without me.' As things turned out, Harris now says that the resulting 'nightmare comedy' (Kubrick's description), turned out to be 'my favourite Kubrick picture.'

Renamed *Dr Strangelove* – later acquiring the subtitle *or: How I Learned to Stop Worrying and Love the Bomb*, thus making it one of the longest film titles in movie history – the film was set to go into full-scale production at Shepperton Studios in England in January 1963, following a month of second-unit aerial photography, shot aboard a specially fitted USAF B-17 bomber in the Arctic. Peter Sellers, whose collection of home movies include several glimpses of Kubrick and his wife, as testament to their increasingly friendly off-screen relationship, was signed to play four characters in the film, and it was Kubrick's insistence on Sellers' involvement which dictated that the movie be produced in England – the actor reportedly unable to leave the country for 'domestic reasons' (he was in the midst of a divorce). 'Except for natural locations unique to a particular part of the world,' Kubrick later added, 'pictures can be made anywhere good craftsmen can work. Atmosphere is created by the film-makers, not by the location or the studio.'

Since his appearance in *Lolita*, Peter Sellers had returned to more conventional roles in British comedies like *The Wrong Arm of the Law* (1962) and *The Pink Panther* (1963), when he made his first appearance as the bungling Inspector Clouseau – the role for which he would ultimately be best remembered, but which he eventually played, just once too often, in a series of five increasingly weak sequels.

Kubrick explained his decision to feature the actor so heavily in this film: 'Believe me, it is not a gimmick

The enormously impressive war room set for *Dr Strangelove*, designed by Ken Adam.

by any means,' he said. 'Each of the parts requires the same kind of talent, the same kind of performance. If there is only one man who has that kind of talent, then he must play all four parts.' 'These characters,' the director said, 'must all be played straight, and still be funny,' further predicting that Sellers - 'with no suggestion of aiming for further recognition of virtuosity, he has that already' - would 'score four triumphs' for his work on the picture.

With his second-unit running off some 40,000 feet of film over the Arctic – a task which he had by now decided he would never undertake personally, having flown for the last time when he attended the London

opening of *Lolita* – Kubrick approached novelist Terry Southern, who was writing an article on the making of the film for *Esquire* magazine, to work with him on what was said to be an already-completed screenplay – 'to see if some more decoration might be added to the icing on the cake', according to the *New York Times* – although another source claims that it was the result of two stipulations which Peter Sellers had written into his own contract for the film: that he receive a white Bentley and that Southern be hired as screenwriter.

Southern's own late-1950s novels *Candy* and *The Magic Christian* would later be filmed, the latter starring Sellers himself in 1969, but his work on *Dr*

Strangelove was to become the source of some conflict, when critics assigned much of the film's effectiveness to his contribution alone. When *The Loved One* (1965) was advertised as being the work of 'the writer of *Dr Strangelove*', Kubrick released a statement to the press which read 'Mr Southern was employed from 16th November to December 28th 1962, during which time I wrote in close collaboration with him,' but went on to state that 'during shooting, which began on January 28th 1963, many changes were made in the script by myself and/or Peter George.' Southern, the director, insisted, had no further part to play in the production, either as writer or consultant. 'I guess I was being generous when I gave him the third writer's credit on the picture,' Kubrick later told the *New York Times*. 'But I thought it might help him get more work, if he wanted it.' *Dr Strangelove* certainly boosted Southern's career as he won further, increasingly hip screenplay assignments for over-trendy late-sixties productions like *Barbarella*, *Easy Rider* and *The Cincinnati Kid*. His own comment on his input to *Dr Strangelove* was that Kubrick's 'completed script... quite simply wasn't funny.'

During filming, which continued throughout the summer, news filtered through from Hollywood that Sidney Lumet's *Fail Safe* was also now in production, dealing with an almost identical situation as *Dr Strangelove* – the unintentional launching of a nuclear attack on the Soviet Union by a rogue US plane. This time, it was the result of a computer malfunction, although efforts to recall the bomber were frustrated by the pilot ignoring radio messages because he had been trained to complete his mission, at whatever cost.

Fail Safe was a straight drama, with Henry Fonda cast as the American president forced to negotiate with his Russian counterpart via the so-called 'hot-line' (its real-life existence not yet officially confirmed) and offering to voluntarily bomb New York as recompense for the imminent destruction of Moscow – potentially a situation even more unlikely than that being offered by *Dr Strangelove*, but one which could be easily believed in the paranoia-rife time in which the film was made.

Kubrick's attempt to gain an injunction preventing *Fail Safe* from going ahead included the claim that the novel on which Lumet's film was based – by Eugene Burdick and Harvey Wheeler – had plagiarized *Red Alert*, but the court action eventually proved unsuccessful, and in the end Columbia stepped in and – either over-compensating or just to ensure that they didn't lose out either way – financed and distributed both pictures. *Dr Strangelove* appeared first by several months and almost completely eclipsed *Fail Safe*, which – though praised by critics as a 'gripping narrative realistically and almost frighteningly told' – was elsewhere derided by Julian Smith in *Looking Away: Hollywood and Vietnam* for 'turning disaster into national pride [with] the disaster itself blamed on a machine instead of

on the men who put so much trust and pride in their toys.'

Dr Strangelove instantly announces its satiric intentions with the opening sequence of a bomber refuelling in mid-air – a much-discussed, supposedly symbolic image – against a lush orchestral reading of 'Try a Little Tenderness', and retains that edge until the closing shot of numerous giant spreading mushroom clouds, following the devastating detonation of the Doomsday Device, set against Vera Lynn's war-time rendition of 'We'll Meet Again' – an unlikely sentiment, as it happens... (The original shooting script had included a framing prologue/epilogue narrated by an alien civilization observing Earth's nuclear development – another possible nod to *The Twilight Zone*).

Apart from Kubrick's statement that he and Peter George had rewritten much of the film's dialogue once shooting began, he also revealed that the cast had improvised scenes during rehearsals, in much the same way as had happened during *Lolita*. 'Some of the best dialogue was created by Mr Sellers himself,' Kubrick told reporters, and Sellers later confirmed that the director 'was a great person in that way... You can chuck ideas at each other, and... the end product is all that matters... you can be good friends, but you can argue your bloody heads off on the set.'

Fifteen years later, Sellers maintained that *Dr Strangelove* was 'a wonderful film... I saw it again the other day and it has even more impact now than it had then.' Eventually, he would feature as just three characters instead of four, but Sellers did indeed provide further evidence of his extraordinary versatility, as he was once more allowed free rein by Kubrick as the blustering Captain Mandrake (attempting to placate Ripper over his fear of polluted bodily fluids with 'Do I look all rancid and clotted, Jack?') and President Muffley ('Gentlemen! You can't fight in here – this is the War Room!'). For the role of Dr Strangelove, according to Sellers, 'Stanley suggested I wear a black glove, which would look rather sinister on a man in a wheelchair... I looked at the arm and suddenly thought, 'Hey, that's a storm-trooper's arm,' so instead of leaving it there looking malignant, I gave the arm a life of its own. That arm hated the rest of the body for having made a compromise; that arm was a Nazi.'

Unfortunately, this is the least satisfying part of the film, and quickly becomes a regrettable example of the actor's self-indulgence, which Kubrick really ought to have kept in check. Although some other cast members are seen grinning and smirking behind Sellers as Strangelove ad-libs his dialogue and actions, the sequence has the effect of stopping the film dead in its tracks, coming as it does after almost an hour and a half of non-stop action. This unbalancing of the film was an unwanted side-effect of Sellers' improvisational skills – 'George C. Scott could do his scenes equally well take

Stanley Kubrick on the set of *Dr Strangelove* with Peter Sellers as US president Merkin Muffley.

after take,' Kubrick recalled, 'but Peter Sellers was always incredibly good on one take, which was never equalled,' so that it would invariably be Sellers' best take which would be used.

George C. Scott, in fact, came close to stealing the picture away from Sellers as the gum-chewing, Commie-hating gung-ho General 'Buck' Turgidson, constantly clutching a military tome entitled *World Targets in Megadeaths,* and clearly viewing the whole exercise as little more than an unwelcome intrusion on a weekend spent with his young secretary (played, incidentally, by Tracy Reed, daughter of Sir Carol Reed, director of *The Third Man* (1950) and *Odd Man Out* (1947) – reportedly one of Kubrick's favourite movies).

Speaking in 1970, Scott paid handsome tribute to his director of seven years previously. 'Kubrick has a brilliant eye,' he enthused. 'He sees more than the camera does.' Of the often on-the-hoof style of rehearsing and script rewrites, the actor recalled that 'I used to kid him by saying that I should've gotten the screen credit for *Dr Strangelove* because I wrote half the goddam picture.' A *New York Times* review at the time suggested – somewhat unkindly – that Scott had been 'drawn out to give one of his best performances without the least awareness of what was happening', quoting Scott as recognizing that 'Kubrick is most certainly in command, and he's so self-effacing that it's impossible to be offended by him.' Lyn Tornabene – a writer friend of Kubrick's who once memorably remarked that 'Stanley doesn't believe in biting any hand which might strangle him' – believed that Kubrick had quickly assumed control over Scott by 'simply beating him at chess and showing him who was boss.' 'There's no b.s. with him,' confirmed the actor. 'No pomposity, no vanity. The refreshing thing is that he hates *everything*.'

Turgidson's manic behaviour takes the character perilously close to buffoonery – even, at one point, literally falling over himself in his eagerness to denounce the Commie threat, as he fears the Russian ambassador will see 'the big board.' But Scott skillfully plays him 'with a snarling and rasping volubility that makes your blood run cold', as described by Bosley Crowther. Elsewhere – in a film which has often unfairly been regarded as Peter Sellers' one-man show – there were equally expert performances from Sterling Hayden, Slim Pickens and Keenan Wynn.

The 6'5" Hayden – once alternately dubbed 'The Most Beautiful Man/Blond Viking God in the Movies' by a Paramount publicity campaign – had made headlines by his complete withdrawal from movies in 1958. Described as 'a man who had everything' (a Hollywood career, earning on average $160,000 a year, with 35 pictures behind him), he more than likely considered his two most recent movies – *Terror in a Texas Town* and *Ten Days to Tulara* – to be rather less than 'everything' and, in the midst of a crippling divorce case, defied a court order and set sail with his four children on a voyage to Tahiti. His long-held contempt for stardom surfaced in one of his rare published comments: 'There's nothing wrong with being an actor, if that's what a man wants, but there's everything wrong with achieving an exalted status because one photographs well and is able to handle dialogue.' His agent referred to him simply as 'someone who had been born in the wrong century. He should have been a sea captain in the 1800s.'

Away from the screen for almost six years, Hayden made his overdue return as the almost logically deranged General Jack D. Ripper. With military fear-

The explosive General 'Buck' Turgidson (George C. Scott), catches up on some further light reading matter.

lessness, he is unstoppable from the moment he issues the command for Condition Red. Trapped in his office as the Marines advance, he plucks a machine-gun from his golfing bag ordering the captive, cowering British general to feed an ammunition belt to him – 'Come over here, Mandrake. The red coats are coming.' With bullets shattering the windows and flying about his ears he defiantly calls back 'Nice shooting, soldier – two can play at that game,' before reflecting with Mandrake on the likelihood of how he will stand up under torture, eventually taking the honourable way out.

Keenan Wynn's brief appearance as Colonel Bat Guano – 'if that really is your name,' as Mandrake demands – is one of the best, most controlled sequences in the picture. Delivered entirely deadpan, his 'I think you're some kind of deviated prevert, organizing a mutiny of preverts' is a perfect example of a dumb-Joe US 'gob' soldier. Warned by Mandrake that 'the court of enquiry will give you such a pranging' if he blocks attempts to contact the president, Guano responds with: 'You try any preversions and I'll blow your head off.'

Peter Sellers had privately confided to friends that he was unhappy with his upcoming fourth characterization – that of Major T. J. 'King' Kong – and, soon afterwards, reported to the set with his leg in plaster, saying that he had broken his ankle getting out of the car. A sceptical Stanley Kubrick was faced with the task of finding a replacement. He finally settled on Slim Pickens, who had been signed for *One-Eyed Jacks* during Kubrick's six-month period working on that picture.

Pickens' Major Kong – seemingly more at home on a bucking bronco than at the controls of a B-52 bomber – gave him the best role of his career, first seen reading *Playboy* and relieving the boredom of non-stop airborne patrol by playing games such as flying with his eyes closed. Receiving the initial order to commit to Plan R, he comments, 'Well, I've been to one World's Fair, a picnic and a rodeo, and that's the stupidest thing I ever heard coming over a set of earphones.' Once confirmed, however, he dons his Stetson and follows his sealed orders to the letter, relaying to the men the contents of the standard issue survival kit which contains, as well as a .45 automatic and four days' emergency rations, 'three lipsticks, three pairs of nylon stockings' – still, apparently, universal currency – and, most vitally, 'nine packs of chewing gum'. (Pickens would repeat the exercise when emptying his pockets in Steven Spielberg's *1941*). It is not overstating the situation to say that it is almost impossible to imagine Sellers as Kong, given Pickens' expert, winning performance.

Visually, *Dr Strangelove* is a remarkably impressive picture, from the hand-held camera work of the US Army advance on Burpelson Air Base – entirely convincing, with the complete look of authentic wartime newsreel footage – to the *noir* style of Ripper's semi-lit office and the in-flight shots over the Arctic. With no

military assistance or co-operation on the film, the interior of the bomber was apparently based on a single photograph published in a British aviation magazine. Kubrick had never seen the inside of a B-52 but, he argued, none of the production crew had seen an H-bomb either, although they had built 'two whoppers' at Shepperton. The director oversaw every aspect of the production, with technicians 'frequently standing off to watch him rechecking their work not with hostility, but incredulity.'

Much of the look for the film was due to the inspired work of set designer Ken Adam, here working for the first time with Stanley Kubrick and already established as designer of the James Bond series (beginning in 1962 with *Dr No*, he worked regularly on the Bond movies until *Moonraker*, 1979). In particular, the astonishing and impressively awesome War Room set was conceived by Adam as 'an underground atomic shelter... made in reinforced concrete'. The resulting set, with its gleaming black 13,000 square feet of laconite flooring and circular table 22 feet in diameter was dominated by 'the big board' – three screens showing world maps and statistical data as the US planes approach their targets.

According to the designer, 'Kubrick insisted I build a ceiling in concrete to force the director of photography to use natural light instead of the artificial lighting which we use in studios.' The exchanges between Muffley, Turgidson and the rest of the chiefs of staff were then lit entirely by the circular lighting above the characters gathered 'like a gigantic poker table,' said Kubrick, 'and the president and the generals are playing with the world like a game of cards.' (So convincing was this fictional representation that, it was said, Ronald Reagan was surprised and somewhat disappointed on seeing the real 'War Room' at the Pentagon for the first time, soon after assuming the presidency.)

Completed in November 1963, the premiere of *Dr Strangelove* was postponed until the New Year, since the film was said to be 'not considered suitable for the present moment' – this referring to the events of 23 November when President John F. Kennedy was assassinated in Dallas, Texas. Coincidentally, the late president had recently been seen to support the view of 'most nuclear strategists... that the chance of annihilation through accident, miscalculation or madness is far greater than the possibility of nuclear war being started deliberately by either side.'

With suggestions that the public taste for topical comedy about serious themes was on the wane, Kubrick defended his film, in which there was 'absolutely no relationship between our President, played by Peter Sellers, and any real person... [and] it is clear that no one can see *Dr Strangelove* and take it as just a joke.' The assassination did, however, occasion one change to the film before its release, with Slim Pickens' line following the listing of the survival kit – 'A fella could have a pretty good weekend in

George C. Scott and a spotlessly clean Peter Sellers following the huge custard pie fight in the deleted climax to *Dr Strangelove*.

Dallas with that stuff' – redubbed as 'a weekend in Vegas'.

More substantial was the removal of a closing ten-minute scene in which, as related by Peter Bull, 'all the personnel went berserk and started hurling custard pies from one end of the studio to the other.' With upwards of 2,000 fresh custard pies (mostly made of shaving foam) on order for each day – 'the pastry after a day or two was as lethal as a cast iron brick', said Bull – the shooting of the scene lasted a full week, ending with President Muffley and Ambassador de Sadesky sitting on the floor building pie castles and singing 'For He's a Jolly Good Fellow'. 'It was a very brilliant sequence with a *Hellzapoppin'* kind of craziness,' says Ken Adam, but once the completed film was cut together, Kubrick decided that 'it was too farcical and not consistent with the satiric tone of the rest of the film.' Thrown out, it survives today in a number of production stills which confirm Kubrick's decision to jettison the scene.

Eventually reaching screens at the end of January 1964, *Dr Strangelove* split the critics – Hedda Hopper 'loathed it' (always a good sign) – between those who considered the subject no laughing matter and those who recognized it as a satire on official arrogance and the madness of further involvement with the nuclear arms race. Some reviews, indeed, managed to voice both points of view, as Bosley Crowther did. Accepting that the film was 'one of the cleverest and most incisive satiric thrusts at the awkwardness and folly of the military that has ever been on the screen,' Crowther found his reaction 'quite divided' and was further 'troubled by the feeling of discredit and even contempt for our whole defense establishment, up to and even including the hypothetical Commander-in-Chief.'

The review questioned the characterization whereby 'virtually everybody turns up stupid or insane – or worse, psychopathic,' further demanding 'I want to know what this picture proves' before concluding that the closing image of the film 'isn't funny. It is malefic and sick.' Despite this, Crowther some months later included *Dr Strangelove* on his list of the ten 'best' movies of 1964, prompting Arthur C. Clarke to dub him 'The Critic Who Came In From The Cold'.

If Columbia had been apprehensive about the reception that the film might be given, they were soon celebrating the news that *Dr Strangelove* had broken opening day records in New York, with the Baronet Theatre reporting gross takings of triple the previous high. In London, the Columbia Cinema announced extra late (11pm) screenings of the movie each night to meet the unprecedented demand, with attendances 'up by 25 per cent on any previous film the cinema has shown, and all house records broken'.

Variety noted Kubrick's 'light touch' as director of the 'imaginative and offbeat' screenplay and, although the subject matter 'would seem no setting for comedy or satire... the writers have accomplished this with bit-ing, piercing dialogue and thorough characterizations.' As Kubrick had predicted, Peter Sellers was widely praised, with George C. Scott also scoring well with 'a top performance, one of the best in the film. Odd as it may seem in this backdrop, he displays a fine comedy touch. Sterling Hayden is grimly realistic as the general who blames the Communists for fluoridation of water, and just about everything else.'

In the British press, Penelope Gilliatt of *The Observer* found the film 'very, very sophisticated... as specific as the wound of a stiletto and so close to the facts that it makes you feel ill', although Peregrine Worsthorne rather high-handedly condemned the picture as 'a mammoth sick joke... anti-American propaganda'. Gilliatt agreed that it was 'the most anti-American comedy ever made, and only an American would have had the experience and guts to do it,' finding the 'wit of the screenplay... exhilarating... and every sharp-eared line of it is a pleasure.' To the reviewer who complained that he laughed only once – at Keenan Wynn's shooting of a Coca-Cola machine – Peter Sellers goonishly responded, 'I was tremendously pleased about this because I played the part of the Coca-Cola machine, and shall always regard it as one of my neatest imitations.'

Such glibness was justified as *Dr Strangelove* became a runaway box-office hit, with Kubrick receiving his first Academy Award nomination as Director, and the film also considered for Best Picture, Best Screenplay and Best Actor (Peter Sellers). On the night, however, all prizes went to George Cukor's *My Fair Lady*, apart from the screenplay Oscar awarded to Edward Anhalt for *Becket*. Kubrick was more handsomely rewarded by the New York Film Critics – who named him Best Director – and by the Writers Guild, who voted *Dr Strangelove* Best Written American Comedy.

In a well-reasoned article for *Life* magazine, Loudon Wainwright (a predecessor of singer/songwriter Loudon Wainwright III) answered critics of the movie who, he said, 'attacked [it] with extraordinary bitterness as if it were downright disloyal'. One unnamed reviewer had now written a 'third disturbed review of the picture' in which he argued that 'it passes belief that everyone in command could be as foolish and ineffectual as they're shown here.' To demonstrate with what solemnity the picture was being discussed, Wainwright further quoted a 'professional policy expert' who complained of Kubrick's apparent failure to ascertain what he called 'the publicly available facts... to the detriment of the trust which the American public rightly reposes in the integrity and competence of our political leadership, and of the professional leaders of the armed services'.

Wainwright countered these allegations by stating that 'in their anger, these men have failed to realize that Kubrick... isn't asking people to believe that everybody in command is as foolish in life as in the movie. As a satirist, he is involved in revealing the human folly through burlesque.' He concluded by hoping that 'some... are illuminated by the style and exaggerations of the film. And I don't see why an artist has to do any more than produce an artistic experience that reflects his thinking.'

Before the film's opening, Kubrick had told Eugene Archer that he found it 'interesting to think about ways of influencing people in a medium such as mine. People react, as a rule, when they are directly confronted by events. Here, any direct contact with the bomb would leave very few people to do any reacting. Laughter can only make people a little more thoughtful.'

James B. Harris, meanwhile, was at work on his own first picture as director away from Kubrick – although not too far, as it turned out. *The Bedford Incident* co-produced by Harris with its star Richard Widmark coincidentally became the straight, serious nuclear war drama which *Dr Strangelove* might have been.

This time, the action was based on board the US destroyer *Bedford*, tracking a Russian nuclear submarine – a tactic designed to disrupt the Soviets' routine by forcing them into territorial waters, thereby breaking international marine agreements. Instead, the manoeuvre ends with an over-anxious junior officer launching a torpedo attack on the sub which, before sinking, retaliates by firing off its nuclear warheads. The consequences – as the *Bedford* erupts in a mushroom cloud of destruction – are only too grimly apparent.

Again distributed by Columbia, *The Bedford Incident* was also made at England's Shepperton Studios and proved a highly creditable effort from a fledgling director – albeit one who had already been in the business for more than a decade. Of any similarities between his picture and *Dr Strangelove*, Harris says 'I just thought it couldn't hurt to get the message across once more – that if you put atomic weapons in the hands of right-wing field commanders, they just might by accident or some other way get to use them.' Although their individual approach may have differed, both men were saying much the same thing, and Harris now muses, 'I don't know – if Stanley had made *Dr Strangelove* straight, then maybe I would have done *Bedford* as a comedy.'

On Kubrick's suggestion that he would find himself more fulfilled by the experience of directing, Harris discovered that 'it wasn't as easy as it looked. I watched Stanley direct three films, and it looks easy when he does it. Mine turned out OK, but it was a lot of pain and compromise and trying to second guess. I had a terrific cast [Richard Widmark, Sidney Poitier, Martin Balsam, Eric Portman] and I just got lucky with all those people for a first-time director – I could use all the help I could get.'

Nevertheless he says, Kubrick was right about the up side of the job. 'When you look at the dailies and it works you really feel good about it,' he says. 'Of course when it doesn't play, it makes you sweat, but overall I was wise to listen to him. Watching Stanley is an inspiration – he makes you want to do it too.' Though clearly less acclaimed than Kubrick, Harris continues to direct. 'Stanley thinks I'm pretty good now,' he said proudly. 'He called me when I made *Boiling Point* and said 'You know, you can be a really good director,' but I don't really have the confidence.' Harris does not regret making the move, however, even if it means that he 'didn't get to produce *A Clockwork Orange, Dr Strangelove, Barry Lyndon* – what a body of work'.

Inevitably, during their partnership, there had been times when the director received all of the praise and attention, while, as producer, Harris says, 'You get pushed aside in the photo shoots and, with this swing towards the importance of the director, you couldn't help wanting to be part of that.'

Reflecting on the seven or eight years that they spent working together, Harris still recalls the experience with a warmth rare among former partners: 'One thing I must say about Stanley,' he says, 'is that he always had an open ear for my opinions and suggestions. I was always involved in the writing, but I wouldn't pull up a chair to a typewriter. We discussed things, and I always got my two cents in.' As for the supposed reputation Kubrick has in some quarters as a ruthless megalomaniac, Harris insists that 'he never shut me out or resented other people's ideas, because he was not insecure. He felt that it never hurt to listen and discuss things – something good can come out of it.'

The producer's precise role had been to initially set up any deal – purchasing screen rights of suitable material, where 'we usually had the same ideas. Stanley wasn't going to do something unless he really loved the idea, but I don't ever remember having any arguments about anything artistic.' Once agreed on a subject, Harris compared his job to that of an American footballer, where 'Stanley had the ball and I was getting all of the obstacles out of the way.' Once the project was under way, however, there was no question of the producer retreating to a comfortable office to monitor the company's profits. 'Stanley and I were best friends,' he says today. 'We were together all the time. I'd be sitting right next to him on the set and we would go and play ping-pong while they were lighting – he liked having the company.'

Finally taking up the megaphone for the first time himself on *The Bedford Incident*, Harris was more than ever aware of his and Kubrick's former reliance on each other – 'it's a lonely business when you're making pictures by yourself.'

1968
2001: A SPACE ODYSSEY

Sometimes I think we are alone in the universe and sometimes I think we are not; either way, the thought is staggering.
ARTHUR C. CLARKE

Metro-Goldwyn Mayer.
Produced and directed by Stanley Kubrick.

Screenplay: Stanley Kubrick and Arthur C. Clarke. Special photographic effects designed and directed by Stanley Kubrick. Special photographic effects supervisors: Wally Veevers, Douglas Trumbull, Con Pederson, Tom Howard. Production designed by Tony Masters, Harry Lange, Ernest Archer. Film editor: Ray Lovejoy. Wardrobe: Hardy Amies. Director of photography: Geoffrey Unsworth. Additional photography: John Alcott. Music: Aram Khatchaturian (Gayaneh Ballet Suite), Gyorgy Ligeti (Atmospheres, Lux Aeterna, Requiem), Johann Strauss (The Blue Danube),Richard Strauss (Thus Spoke Zarathustra). First assistant director: Derek Cracknell. Special photographic effects unit: Colin J. Cantwell, Bruce Logan, Bryan Loftus, David Osborne, Frederick Martin, John Jack Malick. Camera operator: Kelvin Pike. Art director: John Hoesli. Sound editor: Winston Ryder. Make-up: Stuart Freeborn. Editorial assistant: David De Wilde. Sound supervisor: A. W. Watkins. Sound mixer: H. L. Bird. Chief dubbing mixer: J. B. Smith. Scientific consultant: Frederick I. Ordway III.

Cast:
Keir Dullea (Major David Bowman); Gary Lockwood (Major Frank Poole); William Sylvester (Dr Heywood Floyd); Daniel Richter (Moonwatcher); Douglas Rain (voice of HAL 9000); Leonard Rossiter (Smyslov); Margaret Tyzack (Elena); Robert Beatty (Halvorsen); Sean Sullivan (Michaels); Frank Miller (mission controller); Penny Brahms (stewardess); Edward Bishop (pilot); Alan Gifford (Mr Poole); Kenneth Kendall (newsreader); Vivian Kubrick (Floyd's daughter); Burnell Tucker (photographer); John Swindell, John Clifford (technicians); Frank Miller; Glenn Beck; Edwina Carroll; Bill Weston; Mike Lovell; Ann Gillis; Heather Downham; John Ashley; Jimmy Bell; David Charkham; Simon Davis; Jonathan Daw; Peter Delmar; Terry Duggan; David Fleetwood; Danny Grover; Brian Hawley; David Hines; Tony Jackson; John Jordan; Scott Mackee; Laurence Marchant; Darryl Paes; Joe Refalo; Andy Wallace; Bob Wilyman; Richard Wood.

160 minutes (cut to 141 minutes). Super-Panavision. Presented in Cinerama. Technicolor/Metrocolor.

The Dawn of Man
In the barren, rocky landscape of prehistoric Earth, a colony of apes live out their lives constantly searching for food and fighting amongst themselves in a society in which the most aggressive tribe eats and the rest go hungry.

Regular confrontations force one group, led by 'Moonwatcher' (Daniel Richter), to retreat to the cold shelter of their cave where they are in danger of starvation, listening to the sound of other creatures outside. The next morning, however, they wake to find a huge black monolith has mysteriously appeared, standing upright in a nearby clearing. Approaching it with a mixture of caution and curiosity, Moonwatcher eventually touches the block's smooth, featureless surface.

Later picking over the remains of a tapir skeleton, the ape now sees how one of the more substantial bones could be put to use as a weapon to kill other animals for food. Soon, he has killed his first wild boar, and the group of apes – now transformed to carnivores – eagerly feed on the meat.

At the next confrontation at the water-hole, Moonwatcher takes his rival by surprise and beats him

with his newly formed club, forcing the other tribe of apes to scatter in fear. The means of securing food has quickly become a weapon with which to kill, and to achieve superiority over fellow creatures.

Three million years later, Dr Heywood Floyd (William Sylvester) is travelling to the semi-colonized moon on an apparently routine trip, although his true mission is to investigate reports of an unusual discovery on the lunar surface. Aboard the orbiting space station, he is questioned by a group of Russian scientists en route back to Earth. Led by Professor Smyslov (Leonard Rossiter), the Russians are curious as to the real purpose of Floyd's visit, and there are rumours of an epidemic at the American base, which the Russians fear could affect their own colony. Floyd remains non-committal and quickly excuses himself to address a meeting of American scientists before leaving with Halvorsen (Robert Beatty) and Michaels (Sean Sullivan) to investigate the find for himself.

Inside the shuttle, Floyd examines aerial photographs showing the crater Tycho and the disturbance to the moon's natural magnetic field caused by the so-called TMA-1 (Tycho-Magnetic Anomaly). Halvorsen reveals that the object they discovered is at least three million years old, given its position and surrounding geological data. Arriving at the excavated site, the group of scientists approach a huge, featureless black monolith standing upright. Circling and photographing the object, Floyd finally comes close enough to touch its surface with his gloved hand and, within seconds, the men are all deafened by a piercing electronic signal apparently emanating from the block itself.

Jupiter Mission, 18 months later
The vast space ship Discovery heads silently though deep space on its nine month voyage to the planet Jupiter. Of the five-man crew on board, three are held in a frozen state of suspended animation while the remaining two, David Bowman (Keir Dullea) and Frank Poole (Gary Lockwood) attend to routine tasks. The ship is maintained and controlled by an onboard talking computer – the latest of the sophisticated HAL 9000 series, said to be completely infallible.

Much of the day-to-day routine aboard Discovery is monotonous, relieved only by occasional broadcasts from Earth – a birthday message from Frank's parents and the transmission of a television interview recorded with the crew at the start of the mission – and chess games between the astronauts and HAL, who is programmed to assess the crew's actions and psychological condition, continuously, while monitoring the efficiency of the ship. When HAL reports that an external

The first shot of *2001: A Space Odyssey* to go before the cameras in December 1965, as scientists explore the discovery of the second monolith on the moon, led by Heywood Floyd (William Sylvester, second right) and Halvorsen (Robert Beatty, right).

communications unit is due to fail within 24 hours, Bowman undertakes the laborious task of replacing the unit, bringing the original in for examination.

When the onboard tests indicate that the unit is in perfect working order, HAL insists that it will fail absolutely at the specified time. Bowman and Poole consult with Mission Control and are advised to replace the unit and observe whether it crashes or not. They are, however, told that their data has been fed into an identical HAL 9000 computer on Earth which finds that Discovery's HAL is 'in error'.

HAL maintains that he is incapable of making an error, and Bowman and Poole secrete themselves in one of the ship's pod shuttles, disconnecting the communications link so that they can discuss the situation in private. Reluctantly they agree that, if HAL really is at fault, they will need to disconnect him, unaware that the all-seeing eye of the computer has been watching them and lip-reading their conversation.

During Poole's space-walk to replace the suspect unit, Bowman sees him suddenly flash past the observation window and away into space with his lifeline apparently severed. Taking one of the pods, he gives chase, eventually reaching Frank and managing to carry him back to Discovery in the pods' mechanical arms, only to find that HAL refuses to allow him to re-enter the ship.

HAL tells Bowman that he cannot allow them to disconnect him and so jeopardize the mission, so is continuing alone. As Bowman searches for another means of entry, HAL terminates the life functions of the three sleeping crew members and Bowman is finally forced, reluctantly, to release Frank's body into space before managing to break into the ship through an emergency air-lock.

Locating the central memory banks of the ship's computer, Bowman begins the process of disconnecting HAL's higher functions, so that he will be able

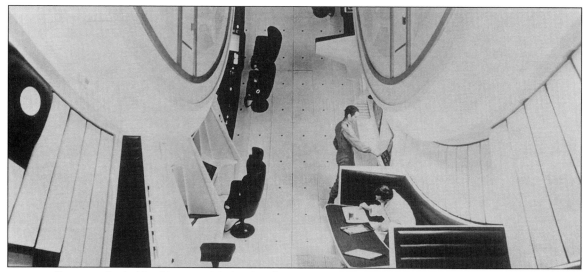

The curved set of the Discovery interior, dwarfing the astronauts (Keir Dullea and Gary Lockwood).

to take control of the ship for himself. As HAL protests and asks for another chance, a pre-recorded message flashes onto a television screen from Heywood Floyd, informing the crew of the true purpose of their mission – to trace the origin of the signal heard on the moon.

Jupiter and Beyond the Infinite

As Bowman approaches the planetary system surrounding the planet Jupiter, he leaves Discovery and, seeing a vast black featureless monolith orbiting among the planet's moons, he enters a 'star gate' – a dazzling succession of cosmic creations, exploding galaxies and new-born worlds which eventually leads him to glide across an alien landscape before finding himself within an elegantly furnished Earth-like room. Silently he observes his own self in various stages of ageing until, at the very point of his own death, he is again confronted by the black monolith and transformed into an unborn child, returning across the universe to the revolving Earth.

In 1865, Jules Verne published *From the Earth to the Moon* – to all intents and purposes the first novel to deal seriously with the idea of space travel – and with H. G. Wells' *The Time Machine* (1895), *The War of the Worlds* (1898) and *Tales of Space and Time* (1900), the newly spawned science-fiction genre opened the 20th century as one of the most intriguing forms of the printed word.

Inevitably, not everyone would prove to be as far-sighted or as skilful as Verne or Wells, and much of the later (1930s onwards) examples of science fiction consisted of lurid scare stories, with pulp magazine stories dealing with monsters from space intent only on conquering the Earth, or else abducting improbably huge breasted, nubile women – apparently at their most vulnerable when semi-clothed, as demonstrated by the remarkable frequency with which this occurred in cover illustrations. The genre became ever more closely linked with horror/shock stories at the expense of believability, with monstrous, eight-armed, swollen-headed beings slithering across the surface of the planet bent on destruction.

At its best, however, science fiction could stimulate and inspire discussion on a far greater scale than most other forms of literature, especially when – as was the case with H. G. Wells – some of those seemingly far-fetched ideas appeared to become realities within the author's own lifetime. Though intrigued by advances in technology, Wells feared man's inability to control his new inventions (how he would have loved *Dr Strangelove*!) and successfully predicted the two world wars which he would live through, before his death in 1946. Some of the more serious writers began to deal increasingly with the scientific aspects of the subject – risking the alienation of some of their less technically minded readers, but acquiring a respectability which the 'bug-eyed monster' tales seldom achieved.

Cinema's first notable encounter with science fiction and space travel had been George Melies' *Le Voyage dans la Lune*, released in 1902 and probably inspired by Wells' *First Men in the Moon*, published the previous year. Melies' film combined primitive special effects with trick photography to create a wholly unbelievable, but delightful film, in which space travel is achieved by means of firing the manned (and womanned) rocket from a huge gun, similar to that used in human cannonball circus acts (although Verne had described just such a method to launch his own people into space in *From the Earth to the Moon*).

While space exploration remained an intriguing, but seemingly far-off, possibility, cinema occasionally mused on its potential – Fritz Lang's *Woman in the Moon* (1928) accurately foresaw the countdown sequence employed by later, real-life space missions, and included a spacecraft convincingly designed by top German rocket experts. Less intellectual, but more fun, were the late 1930s serials like *Flash Gordon Saves the Universe*, starring Buster Crabbe pitted against the all-but indestructible Ming the Merciless of the planet Mongo, with Flash and his assistants – dependable but dull scientist Dr Zarkov, and the less academic but decidedly more glamorous Dale – jetting from planet to planet in extraordinarily bulbous, wobbly spaceships.

Fantasy stories such as these all but disappeared from the screen during the war years, but in the 1950s – as sightings of flying saucers were being reported with ever increasing frequency – film-makers began again to 'Look to the skies', as one advertising campaign loudly announced itself. Most often this dealt with invasion from other planets – *War of the Worlds* finally reached the screen in 1953 – or escape from a doomed Earth on collision course with a rogue meteorite or out-of-control planet (*When Worlds Collide*, 1951). The future promised to be somewhat gloomy should mankind ever be confronted by – invariably hostile – alien life forms.

In reality, the quest for space exploration had begun in October 1957, when Russia launched *Sputnik I*, the first artificial Earth satellite, followed, a month later, by *Sputnik II* containing the first mammal in space – the unfortunate dog, Laika, less gloriously doomed also to be the first Earth creature to die in space.

Even with the United States entering what would soon be known as the 'space race' (a term which could almost have been lifted straight from *Dr Strangelove* – 'We must avoid a Space Gap, Mr President!'), Russia continued to lead the way, with the first probes to reach the moon and the first photographs of its 'dark side' (the 1959 *Lunik* series), first animals recovered from space (another two pioneering dogs, Belka and Strelka on board *Sputnik V*), first man in space (Yuri Gagarin, 12 April 1959), first – unsuccessful – Mars probe, first woman in space (Valentina Tereshkova, 16 June 1963), first space walk (March 1965) and first soft landing on the moon (January 1966, unmanned).

Not that America was far behind – John Glenn became their first astronaut in February 1962, with *Ranger IV* becoming the first American craft to reach the moon two months later. The first US space walk followed the Russians' by just three months and, in December 1965, the first space rendezvous was carried out, with a successful space docking – a vital feature of future space shots – four months later and an unmanned soft moon landing on 30 May 1966.

In such a climate, science fiction on the screen had taken a decided back seat. Few films now dealt with space travel – hardly surprising, since how could they compete with the breathtaking real-life images being sent back to Earth by orbiting satellites and moon probes? Wells' *First Men in the Moon* was finally filmed in 1964 as one of those unfunny 'comic' Victorian adventure films and, along with the improbable *Robinson Crusoe on Mars*, was practically cinema's only contribution to the growing interest in space exploration during the period.

'Somewhere along my wandering reading,' Stanley Kubrick told reporters – he had already acquired a reputation as an avid reader between (and in search of) new film projects – 'I came across some Rand Corporation statistics on the probability of life in outer space.' The likelihood of finding life on the moon was as yet still undetermined in 1964–5, when Kubrick considered his follow-up to *Dr Strangelove*, although pictures being sent back by ever more adventurous probes revealed what seemed a dusty, lifeless surface.

'Our galaxy is made up of about a hundred billion stars,' Kubrick continued. 'Each is made of the same chemical stuff as our own [with] an estimated 640,000 Earth-type planets in our own galaxy... Most astronomers and other scientists interested in the question are strongly convinced that the universe is crawling with life: much of it... equal to us in intelligence, or superior simply because human intelligence has existed for so relatively short a period.'

Most science-fiction films had presented the potential existence of extra-terrestrial life as a threat to Earth's security – *The Day the Earth Stood Still*, directed by Robert Wise in 1951, was a rare exception, with the alien representative (played with such convincingly other-worldliness by Michael Rennie that he was later called upon to appear as aliens of varying beneficence in television series' *Lost in Space* and *The Invaders*) sent to Earth accompanied by a huge, protective robot on a mission to warn mankind of its folly in meddling with atomic energy and set it back on the right road. This was later reinterpreted as a veiled warning against the advancing march of communism, as was Don Siegel's *Invasion of the Body Snatchers* (1957). With the limitless universe to play with, it seemed, some could still see no further than their own paranoia.

What intrigued Kubrick was not alien invaders or shoot-outs with dodgy looking ray-guns. 'We decided that the most interesting story we could tell would be the first contact between our own and an extra-terrestrial civilization,' he said. To come up with a convincing and feasible storyline, Kubrick decided that he must work on the screenplay with an established writer in that field, although he possibly took the decision with some misgivings. 'I can see their difficulty,' he said of those authors working in science fiction – most of which he found to be of little interest – 'It's a hell of a job to imagine the unimaginable.' Among the most respected of sf writers, Kubrick finally approached Arthur C. Clarke as a potential collaborator.

Clarke – considered to be 'the most scientifically grounded' writer of the genre – was born the son of a farmer in Somerset in 1917, and had graduated from Kings College, London. A radar specialist during the Second World War, in 1945 he had not only forecast but actually designed a communications satellite which was published in a magazine for amateur radio enthusiasts. US satellites built 20 years later, it was said, used much of his original idea, although Clarke 'at the time believed his ideas to be a little far-fetched [so] took out no patent, and consequently draws no royalties.' For several years he was president of the British Interplanetary Society, and also a Fellow of the Royal Astronomical Society. According to one publisher's blurb, he 'has written several *serious* works on Space' (my italics), 'but is best known for his science fiction' – this including such successful novels as *Childhood's End*, *Prelude to Space*, *The Sands of Mars* and *Imperial Earth*.

Clarke later recalled his first contact with Kubrick by letter in the spring of 1964, when the director asked that he make a contribution to the 'proverbial good science-fiction movie.' When they met for the first time, on 22 April in New York, the director 'had already absorbed an immense amount of science fiction, and was in some danger of believing in flying saucers: I felt I had arrived just in time to save him from this gruesome fate.'

According to the author, Kubrick 'had a very clear idea of his ultimate goal... He wanted to make a movie about Man's relation to the universe... a work of art which would arouse the emotions of wonder, awe – even, if appropriate, terror.' Within a month, an agreement had been signed for Arthur C. Clarke to work with Stanley Kubrick on a screenplay – provisionally entitled *Journey Beyond the Stars* but privately referred to as *How the Solar System Was Won* – to be based on a number of Clarke's previously published short stories and climaxing with the discovery of irrefutable evidence of extra-terrestrial life as Clarke had speculated in one of those short stories, *The Sentinel*.

Written in 1948 and entered for a BBC competition – 'It wasn't placed,' Clarke recalled many years later, musing 'I'd like to know what did win,' – *The Sentinel* told of an alien artefact discovered on the moon during a routine expedition in far-off 1996. This crystal pyramid had been left behind, centuries earlier 'before life had emerged from the seas of the Earth,' acting as a beacon which, once disturbed, would signal to its makers that the inhabitants of the nearby third planet had 'proved our fitness to survive – by crossing space and escaping from the Earth, our cradle.' The story ended by speculating on the likely response of those ancient travellers, now that contact had been established – 'I do not think we will have to wait for long.'

It was Kubrick's idea that he and Clarke should begin by writing the story as a novel, well before any shooting schedule was even considered. 'It seemed to me a better kind of attack,' said Kubrick later. 'If you do a screenplay from an original story idea you tend to leave out those ideas you can't find a ready way of dramatizing. But by doing it as a novel first, you have a chance to really think everything out, after which you can figure out ways of dramatizing what you now know are valuable points of the story.' These points would be discovered during endless brainstorming sessions which included Kubrick setting Clarke 'a 100 item questionnaire about our astronauts, e.g. do they sleep in their pajamas, etc.' and occasional outrageous (non-serious) suggestions such as 'seventeen aliens – featureless black pyramids – riding in open cars down Fifth Avenue surrounded by Irish cops.'

With the benefit of 20/20 hindsight, Clarke later found the 'initial schedule... hilariously optimistic, as it allowed some 12 weeks for writing, two for discussion and a further four weeks for story revisions, a mere 20 weeks each for art design, shooting and editing – 'a total of 82 weeks... I was very depressed by this staggering period of time, since I was (as always) in a hurry to get back to Ceylon; it was just as well that neither of us could have guessed the project's ultimate duration.'

Seven months went by as the two bounced ideas off each other, with Clarke continually working on the novel, now retitled *Universe*, then *Tunnel to the Stars* and *Planetfall*. During this time, *Ranger VII* crash-landed on the moon and sent back the first close-up pictures of the lunar surface, prompting Kubrick to approach Lloyds of London to see if he could insure against the 'forthcoming Mars probes [showing] something that shoots down our story line.' The proposed policy was a non-starter.

Clarke, meanwhile, underwent more sleepless nights, his journal recording a number of nightmares in late September: 'Dreamed that shooting had started. Lots of actors standing around, but I still didn't know the story line.' By Christmas Eve 1964, however, he considered the novel complete, with Kubrick convinced that it would be a best-seller (a fairly safe bet, given Clarke's previous track record) and that 'we've extended the range of science fiction.'

Despite this optimism, much of 1965 was spent on further rewrites – 'strange and encouraging how much

The scene at Elstree Studios with the huge, rotating set for the Discovery spacecraft fully lit and ready to roll.

of the material I thought I'd abandoned fits in perfectly after all' (2 May) – and discarding other ideas – 'long session with Stanley discussing script. Several good ideas, but I rather wish we didn't have any more' (16 November). Unforeseen delays included Clarke's response to a first sight of the newly constructed Earth-orbit ship, when he 'happened to remark that the cockpit looked like a Chinese restaurant. Stan said that killed it for him and called for revisions' – the author ruefully deciding that it would be prudent for him to 'keep away from the Art Department for a few days.' By Christmas Day 1965, he was still 'hack[ing] my way to Jupiter – slow but steady going.'

The deal to finance *2001: A Space Odyssey* – as the film was now called (the title arrived at in April 1965 and, according to Clarke, entirely Kubrick's idea) – had meanwhile been agreed with Robert O'Brien, president of MGM, who promised that 'it won't be a Buck Rogers type of space-epic,' and the production was booked into the MGM-British Studios at Elstree, Borehamwood (not to be confused with the old Associated British-Elstree Studio, just a few hundred yards away on the opposite side of Elstree Way, where *Lolita* had been made – with MGM cash – three years previously).

Shooting actually began, however, at Shepperton on 29 December 1965, where a huge excavated moon-set had been constructed, containing the second black monolith TMA-1. Shepperton Stage H had been chosen for its immense size – the second largest in Europe – and that it should be required for the first shot of *2001* instantly gave some idea of the scope of the production – now finally under way, after almost 18 months of preparation. By contrast, this first scene would need to be completed within a week, as the set was due to be dismantled to make way for another production booked in for the New Year, when Kubrick and his team would return to Borehamwood. Robert Beatty later recalled that the filming of this scene – with all of the actors securely locked into authentic-looking, air-tight space-suits, supplied by compressed air bottles on the actors' backs – was not without its problems. 'While you were acting,' he said, 'you had to keep an ear cocked for the hissing sound. If it stopped you waved frantically for help – even if you were in the middle of a scene.' Quite understandably, Beatty said he 'did not relish being the first dead man on the moon.'

Although casting of the film would be completed with Kubrick's usual thoroughness, it is safe to say that the actors in *2001: A Space Odyssey* were destined to become the least significant aspect of the picture – reflecting man's own relative insignificance in relation to the vastness of the universe. Above all, this is what impresses about the film – the sheer scope, immensity and wonder of space. Those who complained that the human characters were bland or unsympathetic may

well have a point, but the story's subject matter makes this almost necessary, yet at the same time acceptable – should we be concerned with romance, personal problems, small-scale dramas and relationships when faced with the enormity of space and the possibility of contact with an alien civilization?

That there were no major stars involved with the film – many of the cast, including William Sylvester, Robert Beatty and Ed Bishop were American and Canadian actors resident in the UK – may have raised some eyebrows after the high-profile casting of both *Lolita* and *Dr Strangelove*. As the nominal star, Ohio-born Keir Dullea had made his Broadway debut in 1956 and his first screen appearance five years later (*The Hoodlum Priest*). Immediately prior to his casting by Stanley Kubrick, he had completed D. H. Lawrence's *The Fox* in Canada for Mark Rydell and worked opposite Laurence Olivier and Noel Coward in Otto Preminger's *Bunny Lake is Missing*, finding the director 'truly a bully... working with him was terrible.' On *2001: A Space Odyssey*, however, he found Kubrick 'extremely supportive,' even at those times when the actor 'didn't know what was going on.' Thirty years later, however, he still recalled his time on the film as 'a unique and wonderful experience.'

Co-star Gary Lockwood was rumoured to have been an extra in *Spartacus* but had since starred in a successful US television series *The Lieutenant* and appeared in two films with Elvis Presley, while the most familiar face to British audiences would have been Liverpool-born comic actor Leonard Rossiter, previously seen in many television plays and feature films including *A Kind of Loving, This Sporting Life* and *Billy Liar*. Here he was improbably cast as Russian scientist Smyslov, quizzing William Sylvester's tight-lipped Professor Heywood Floyd on a possible epidemic at Moon base.

Totally unrecognizable – even to those who knew him well – would have been the leading player in the opening sequence to *2001*, Daniel Richter, a celebrated teacher and performer of mime theatre, who had been living in England since the mid-1960s, and made his film debut in this movie as the ape 'Moonwatcher'. Richter had apparently not been first choice for the role, for which the initial casting requirements were, reportedly, that the ape-actors should be 'no more than five foot tall with long upper lips'. Scottish television comic entertainer Ronnie Corbett was an early candidate, undergoing a number of experimental make-up tests which, it was reported, transformed him into a 'grotesque apparition that sent studio secretaries shrieking along the corridors' before he decided to withdraw from the production.

Most crucial, however, was the crew behind the camera which would create *2001*, which Kubrick alternately suggested would be 'a hopeful look at the skies' or 'a majestic visual experience'. With scrupulous attention to even the tiniest detail, Kubrick had enlisted the help of a number of companies including IBM, Eastman Kodak, du Pont, Minneapolis-Honeywell, Bausch & Lomb and General Mills, who all contributed – apparently free of charge – their predictions on how their individual products – furniture, machinery, computers, clothing (even the fabric they were made from) – were likely to look 30 years into the future. The NASA Space Agency made their own computers available to calculate a flight path for the journey to Jupiter (initially Saturn), with former NASA scientists Frederick I. Ordway III and Harry K. Lange recruited as consultants on engineering and design. From the Massachusetts Institute of Technology (MIT), Professor Marvin Minsky – a leading authority on artificial intelligence and the construction of automatons – confirmed for Kubrick the likelihood that computers of the year 2001 would be capable of those actions which the story suggested.

On a more filmic level, Kubrick claimed to have seen almost every science-fiction movie produced thus far, including – at Arthur C. Clarke's suggestion – William Cameron Menzies' 1936 film of *Things To Come*, written by H. G. Wells himself. After the screening, however, he told a deflated Clarke that he would '*never* see another movie I recommend.' Visiting American physicist Jeremy Bernstein found himself accompanying Kubrick and his wife to a North London cinema, one Saturday afternoon, to catch a Russian movie bearing the unpromising title *Astronauts on Venus* – 'a terrible hodgepodge of pseudo-science and Soviet propaganda', which Kubrick reportedly 'insisted we stick out to the end, just in case.'

More impressive had been a National Film Board of Canada documentary called *Universe* – coincidentally, an early title for *2001: A Space Odyssey* – which had combined animation and special effects to create a convincing impression of outer space. Kubrick was said to have attempted to hire the entire team from that film, but ultimately designed and directed the effects himself, heading a team of special effects supervisors including the veteran Wally Veevers, Douglas Trumbull, Con Pederson and Tom Howard, all of whose reputations were enhanced considerably by their association with this one movie – none more so than Douglas Trumbull, who had previously been involved with a Graphic Films documentary on NASA and whose first feature film assignment this was.

As with Terry Southern's contribution to *Dr Strangelove*, Trumbull was later often named as having created the effects for *2001*, which eventually led Kubrick and MGM to issue an open letter to Hewlett-Packard following a 1984 advertising campaign announcing 'The year was 1968. But for the audience it was 2001. And they were not in a movie theatre, they

were in deep space – propelled by the stunning Special Effects of Douglas Trumbull.'

Hewlett-Packard immediately withdrew the ad, on being notified that this created a false impression, and the open letter continued by stating that the film's end credits listed the effects team in 'non-alphabetical order to reflect the comparative contributions of the people principally responsible for the Special Effects work'. Kubrick appeared first on the list, having 'Designed and Directed' the effects, followed by 'Special Photographic Effects Supervisors' Veevers, Trumbull, Pederson and Howard in that order – each allowed their own individual full screen credit. Even with later, Oscar-nominated effects work on such spectacular, effects-laden films as *Star Trek, Blade Runner* and *Close Encounters of the Third Kind* – as well as his own directorial debut *Silent Running* - it seems likely that Douglas Trumbull will remain best known as the 'special effects man' for *2001: A Space Odyssey* – not least with those who wish to minimize Kubrick's own contribution. There are still those, after all, who insist that Herman Mankiewicz – and not Orson Welles – wrote *Citizen Kane*...

2001's effects would famously become the dominant factor in making the film the ultimate science-fiction movie, taking 18 months to perfect (the live action sequences were completed as early as May 1966) at a cost of six and a half million dollars, from a total budget of ten and a half million. 'I felt it was necessary,' said Kubrick, 'to make this film in such a way that every special effects shot in it would be completely convincing' – a definite rarity in cinema, with even the best of those previously produced movies relying on all-too obvious models and often unconvincing effects.

It would be all too easy to become bogged down with relating stories of *2001*'s ever more innovative special effects and how they were achieved, and in the process lose most of my readers as well as myself. Those keen on exploring such matters are best referred to articles which appeared in journals such as *American Cinematographer* or *Positif*, but suffice to say that the look of *2001: A Space Odyssey* was entirely unlike anything seen on screen before – and in many respects has never been surpassed since. Filmed in Super Panavision and presented in Cinerama, the film always promised to be a major spectacle, with unusually sharp, clear images even during the most complex of effects shots – the dazzling star gate sequence involved photographing tiny objects in huge close up, with powerful lenses to achieve some effects, while the actual light corridor recalled the brief nightmare scene in *Killers Kiss*, some 13 years previously, though enormously more impressive. Not least because of the era in which *2001* was released, this wondrous ten minutes, it was claimed, could only have been envisaged and created by the use of mind-expanding substances – and fully appreciated under the same conditions. Arthur C. Clarke found himself the recipient of a packet which contained 'some powder and an anonymous note of thanks, assuring me that this was the best stuff,' which he promptly flushed down the toilet. Kubrick's view was that 'drugs are basically of more use to the audience than to the artist,' since he believed that any state of artificially induced euphoria and contentment worked against a creative temperament, 'which thrives on conflict and on the clash and ferment of ideas.' Clarke had insisted that 'consciousness-expanding' drugs served only to expand 'uncriticalness,' while Kubrick agreed that 'perhaps when everything is beautiful, nothing is beautiful.'

In designing the effects for the film, Kubrick had rejected much of the conventional method of achieving backgrounds with 'travelling mattes' and some scenes were filmed in ultra-slow motion in order to catch enough light to focus on miniatures and other far-off objects – 'It was like watching the hour hand of a clock,' said Kubrick, who revealed that a scene showing a door opening by four inches had taken five hours to film. 'This type of thing required endless trial and error,' he said, 'but the final results are a tribute to MGM's great precision machine shop in England.'

Not everything was as high-tech and sophisticated as that, however, and Trumbull later told *Sight and Sound* that some effects were achieved by almost primitive means – close-ups of Keir Dullea, with flashing control panel lights reflecting in his spacesuit visor, were the result of projecting film of the panel either directly onto the actor's face, or onto a small screen off-camera, which would then reflect back onto the glass. 'It was crazy,' said Trumbull, 'but it looked great.'

One contributor to *Universe* who did make it to the production of *2001* was the actor Douglas Rain – narrator of the Canadian documentary and chosen as the voice of the talking computer HAL over Nigel Davenport (who, according to Jeremy Bernstein, had 'been hired to read the computer's lines... to give Dullea and Lockwood something more professional to play against') and Martin Balsam (supposedly considered 'too emotional').

Undergoing several changes during the writing of the source novel, HAL had originally been – somewhat grandly – named Socrates, later becoming female and renamed Athena. At that stage, he/she/it was more conventionally described as a walking, talking robot open to comparison with Robby the Robot of *Forbidden Planet* (1956). The decision to make HAL the on-board talking computer created an entirely new concept in science-fiction machines, although Clarke was particularly embarrassed at 'one annoying and persistent myth' that he had deliberately named his creation 'one letter ahead of IBM, and... that Stanley and I were taking a crack at that estimable institution.' The writer claimed that, since IBM had been one of those companies who lent their own

expertise to the making of the picture, he would certainly have changed the name had he spotted this coincidence which, he says, defied odds of '17,576 to 1'. HAL, meanwhile, officially 'stands for Heuristically programmed ALgorithmic computer' – though, like the denials that *Lucy in the Sky with Diamonds* refers to LSD, this is far less fun to those who like to investigate such coincidences.

Early stages of filming, meanwhile, had prompted the construction of ever more elaborate sets and props as the orbiting space station and interior of the ship *Discovery* were created in the hangar-like spaces of the Elstree studio. Dominant among these was the giant centrifuge, first proposed by Arthur C. Clarke as a solution to weightlessness in his short essay *Vacation in Vacuum* in 1953. The Sky Grill, as it was then called, was the main room in a huge rotating drum which 'if you could see right across – and maybe it's just as well that you can't – you'd see that the people on the other side were upside down, with their heads pointing at you.'

A calculation which took account of the size of the rotating drum and the speed at which it turned would recreate a form of gravity through centrifugal force and, although it was clearly unnecessary for Kubrick to recreate genuine weightlessness in a studio, the realistic design of the futuristic spaceship would need to convincingly reflect this. The renowned Armstrong-Vickers Engineering Group were commissioned to build an actual centrifuge, at a reported cost of $750,000 and taking six months to complete. Standing 38 feet in diameter and eight to ten feet deep, the Ferris/hamster wheel (depending on your point of view) was large enough to contain several necessary props including the computer console, an artificial sunbed and five beds, three of which contained the hibernating members of the crew placed in suspended animation for the nine-months duration of the voyage – all of this securely bolted to the 'floor' around the inner surface of the wheel and capable of functioning throughout a 360-degree rotation.

Most impressively, the rotating centrifuge allowed Kubrick to track his actors either with a moving or stationary camera as they took their exercise jogging around the rim of the 'ship', effectively running up a curved wall, upside down and back down the other side. Shifting the camera at right angles gave even more confusing, disorienting effects as the two actors moved in seemingly impossible opposite directions. Asked how he had achieved this, Kubrick replied to Jeremy Bernstein that he was 'definitely, absolutely not going to tell me.'

Although it eventually became the opening sequence of the film – after a documentary prologue featuring several eminent scientists discussing the possibility of extraterrestrial life was scrapped – the pre-

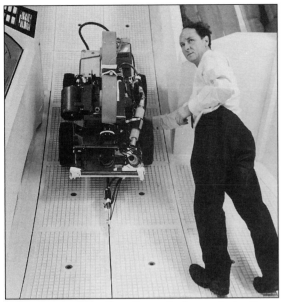

Cameraman Geoffrey Unsworth demonstrates the tracking camera inside the drum which allowed actors to complete a 360-degree exercise run upside down and back again.

historic Dawn of Man was actually added later, when Clarke and Kubrick had finally decided on the form that the story would take. Astonishingly, this entire sequence was shot in the studio apart from the skull-smashing scene which, Clarke revealed, 'was shot in a field, a couple of hundred yards away... [with] cars and buses going by.' (Incidentally, the closing shot of this prologue, with the bone being transformed into a spacecraft, has been much praised for its originality in effecting a flashforward of three million years in a split-second. Though not as vast a leap, however, the same trick had been used in Michael Powell and Emeric Pressburger's 1944 *A Canterbury Tale* which substituted a medieval hunter's swooping falcon for a World War Two spitfire.)

The remainder, and the ravishingly beautiful landscape – consisting of ten projected colour transparencies photographed in South West Africa – were the result of front projection; an ingenious process which, when explained to Clarke, produced the response, 'What crazy nut invented this? I might have known it would be an sf writer' (Will Jenkins). *2001* popularized the process as opposed to the more common but less impressive back projection, with front projection using a 45-degree semi-transparent mirror, to reflect a projected background onto both a highly reflective screen and the actors themselves. Any shadows cast were then hidden by the actors, on whom the projected image disappeared with the use of additional lighting. One mis-

take which this caused in the film was the brightly shining eye of a leopard reflecting the light of the projector, although this was paradoxically a pleasing effect.

At this stage there were few reports leaking out to the press concerning the plot of the new movie (Gary Lockwood later said that there had never been a complete screenplay throughout the entire shooting schedule). In response to the suggestion that his films tended toward the 'brilliant but baleful', Kubrick told *The Sunday Times*, 'Emotionally, I am optimistic. Intellectually, I'm not. I do things in spite of all the things I'm intellectually aware of, such as the burden of my own mortality.' At the age of 37, he teasingly revealed that *2001: A Space Odyssey* would not be 'gloomy... but it is full of apprehensions.' Whatever the feelings on set – and the natural sense of achievement, as bold experiments such as the giant centrifuge came together – Keir Dullea told Bernstein during filming that 'This is a happy set, and that's something.'

Kubrick, it was said, was involved in every aspect of the production – approving or rejecting designs, discussing possible logistical problems with production staff, consulting with Arthur C. Clarke (still!) over questions of a scientific nature, as well as considering the comparative merits of anteaters, pigs and tapirs for use in the opening prehistoric Dawn of Man sequence. Revealingly, when Bernstein observed Kubrick's hands-on involvement with the actual lighting and photographing of the film and asked if this were common practice among directors, he was told that Kubrick 'had never watched any other movie director at work.'

Behind the camera as director of cinematography was Geoffrey Unsworth, a master craftsman, whose early experience included work as camera operator, under Jack Cardiff, on the Powell/Pressburger films *The Life and Death of Colonel Blimp* and *A Matter of Life and Death*. Coincidentally, Unsworth's departure from *A Matter of Life and Death* to accept a lighting cameraman job on another production, led to Christopher Challis taking over from him, and eventually becoming Powell's regular cinematographer from then on. Now, on *2001: A Space Odyssey*, Unsworth was, again, called away after six months of shooting to begin another film, with Kubrick making the bold decision to promote first assistant John Alcott into his place. According to Alcott's wife Sue, speaking to *American Cinematographer* in 1987, '*2001* was the most incredible experience for John. I'm sure he became the great cinematographer he became because of that film.' With no previous experience of such a major role, Alcott was rightly 'proud to be shooting the movie,' says his wife, 'and he worked incredibly hard. The hours were horrendous.' Keir Dullea confirms that the director was already an 'absolute' perfectionist although, he says, 'it never affected me in any negative way. I think he'd drive a few technicians up the spout, though.' Sue

CAUTION WEIGHTLESS CONDITION

Stanley Kubrick and
Arthur C. Clarke on the
set of *2001: A Space Odyssey.*

Alcott adds that 'Stanley was such a hard taskmaster [but] the experience of working with that man and his constant repeating to get it right stood John in good stead.' Alcott would be Kubrick's first choice cinematographer for the next 15 years.

By February/March of 1966, Kubrick had put together a few rough-cut scenes to show the anxious MGM executives, nervous over the scale of their investment in what was still something of an unknown quantity. Arthur C. Clarke saw one test reel, which featured an accompanying soundtrack from Mendelssohn's *A Midsummer Night's Dream* and Vaughan Williams' *Antarctica Symphony* 'with stunning results. I reeled out convinced that we have a masterpiece on our hands – if Stan can keep it up.' Jeremy Bernstein later watched Gary Lockwood exercising in the revolving *Discovery* to a Chopin waltz – 'picked by Kubrick because he felt that an intelligent man in 2001 might choose Chopin for doing exercise to music.'

The choice of suitable music for the film was by

now becoming a significant factor in Kubrick's method of film-making. Although earlier movies had relied on relatively basic – and fairly unremarkable – music scores, Alex North's music for *Spartacus* had been rightly acclaimed, though still within the mainstream Hollywood tradition. By contrast, *Dr Strangelove* had used a recording of Vera Lynn, or a lush orchestral version of a standard, to point up the irony of the storyline – music as an active feature of the film itself. For the upcoming space epic, Kubrick – whose opinion was that 'in most cases, film music tends to lack originality' – initially thought that 'a film about the future might be the ideal place for a really striking score by a major composer.' The director spent endless hours listening to a wide range of contemporary recordings – including electronic – searching for 'something that sounded unusual and distinctive but not so unusual as to be distracting.' One source later claimed that Pink Floyd had been considered at one point – highly unlikely, since they had yet to even release their first single while Kubrick was filming *2001* and, by 1968, had just sacked their main songwriter, Syd Barrett, and were yet to achieve anything like the fame and respect which 'Dark Side of the Moon' would give them five years later. It was in December 1967 – probably at MGM's suggestion – that Alex North was brought on board to score *2001: A Space Odyssey*.

According to North, he was 'ecstatic at the idea of working with Kubrick again,' not least because of reports that the likely two-hours-plus *2001* would contain only 'about twenty-five minutes of dialogue and no sound effects.' By this time, Kubrick had already been using existing recordings during editing, which he later said was not an uncommon practice, since it was 'very helpful to be able to try out different pieces to see how they work with the scene.' North later agreed that Kubrick 'was direct and honest with me concerning his desire to retain some of the temporary music tracks, but the composer felt 'I could compose music that had the ingredients and essence of what Kubrick wanted and give it a consistency and homogeneity and contemporary feel.'

North's supporters and admirers have, in recent years, painted a picture of the following events as 'a charade of monumental proportions', with Kubrick encouraging the composer to continue with his score when, in fact, he never intended to use any of it. Kubrick later told Michel Ciment that, although he and North had examined the edited film – still with its music by Johann and Richard Strauss, Khatchaturian and Gyorgy Ligeti – and the composer 'agreed that they worked fine and would serve as a guide for the musical objectives for each sequence he, nevertheless, wrote and recorded a score which could not have been more alien to the music we had listened to, and much more serious than that, a score which, in my opinion, was completely inadequate for the film.'

North had, in fact, recorded a total of about 40 minutes of music to accompany the opening hour of the film when Kubrick told him that no more would be needed, since 'he was going to use breathing effects for the rest of the film.' The composer claimed he was never informed that his completed recording would not feature in the film, and was unaware of this until he actually attended the New York premiere, in April 1968, although Kubrick insisted that MGM had been contacted by North's agent on hearing that his client's score would not be used. The director was supported by MGM president, Robert O'Brien, who Kubrick later recalled as 'a wonderful man, and one of the very few film bosses able to inspire genuine loyalty and affection from his film-makers.'

Perhaps spurred more by what they saw as an injustice to their friend, North's colleagues loudly hailed his lost score to *2001: A Space Odyssey* as a masterpiece, eventually sponsoring a new recording in 1993 of what they boldly claimed to be 'one of the most important pieces of film music ever written'. Typical of the tone of the album sleeve-notes was the fulsome description of North's score to *Spartacus* as 'perhaps the greatest in film history' – an impossible statement, dismissing as it does such magnificent works as Hugo Friedhofer's *Best Years of Our Lives*, Bernard Herrmann's *Vertigo* or *The Ghost and Mrs Muir* or any one of a dozen others. Kevin Mulhall's notes on the music conceded that 'No one can deny that *2001: A Space Odyssey*, as it exists now, is a masterpiece of visual, non-narrative film-making,' but went on to claim that 'after listening to [the lost score], there is no doubt that *2001* would have been even better if Kubrick had used North's music.'

In fact, this unused score – the main opening theme aside – is, as Kubrick said, quite unsuited to the film for which it was written. There are echoes of the composer's own score to *Spartacus* and even themes reminiscent of Americana in selections written for the opening Dawn of Man sequence – which Kubrick intended would not feature any music at all – and an attempt at a Ligeti-style piece in *Moon Rocket Bus*. The space docking sequence, which ultimately took place to the strains of the 'Blue Danube', was heavily criticized by Mulhall, who claimed that North's 'sublime waltz... would have solved the perceived defects of the Danube' although the extract, as featured in the movie, confirms that Kubrick wanted something more substantial than the two-and-a-half minute composition which North provided, and which has none of the flow and tranquillity of the Strauss. Only the main title theme bears any resemblance to the feel of the music finally featured in *2001* – and, here, what emerges is little more than a pastiche of Strauss' 'Also Sprach Zarathustra' - a piece destined to become renowned the world over as representative of the power and grandeur of man's quest for space flight and exploration.

Played alongside the film today, North's music cannot honestly be said to improve the images, and Kubrick's inspired choice of musical pieces remains one of the many startlingly innovative features of this landmark movie, perfectly complementing the frequently beautiful images of spacecraft and astronauts floating through space. This aspect of the film prompted Baird Searles of US radio station WRVR-FM to warn 'Dancers beware! Stanley Kubrick may come to be regarded as the major choreographer of the twentieth century.'

On such a large-scale movie on such an extraordinarily massive subject, there was still room for humour in the film: the much-loved 'Zero-Gravity Toilet' which Floyd encounters *en route* to the Moon, the video phone-call to his daughter (actually played by Kubrick's own daughter Vivian) who requests a bush-baby for her birthday, the broadcast to the *Discovery* from BBC12 (the British Broadcasting Corporation in England had – and still has – only two television channels) introduced by Kenneth Kendall, then a contract BBC newsreader, and the serio-comic disconnection of HAL by Bowman as the computer pleads – with alarmingly emotional responses – for another chance, eventually disintegrating into a shambling, mindblown wreck singing 'Daisy, Daisy, give me your answer do.'

Overall, however, it is the sheer visual brilliance of the film which retains the greatest power – as Kubrick had said, there was very little dialogue: none at all in the first 20 minutes, nor in the final 20. Released in the US on 3 April 1968, the film quickly divided critics, with the *New York Times* simultaneously praising the effects as 'the best I have ever seen [with] all kinds of minor touches expertly done' while suggesting that 'its real energy seems to derive from that bespectacled prodigy reading comic books around the block.' The effect of the movie, they said, 'is somewhere between hypnotic and immensely boring,' and its 'uncompromising slowness makes it hard to sit through without talking.' Kubrick, they said, 'seems as occupied with the best use of the outer edge of the screen as any painter, and he is particularly fond of simultaneous rotations, revolving, and straight forward motions – the visual equivalent of rubbing the stomach and patting the head.'

Many of the film's most scrupulously realized effects gave a previously unseen impression of the likely true condition of space travel – the first image we see in modern times is of Dr Floyd, asleep in his seat, as his pen floats weightlessly around him (achieved by invisibly attaching the pen to a huge, slowly rotating perspex disc invisible to the camera). Kubrick later commented on what he saw as an unavoidable error in this section when Floyd enjoys a taste of pre-packaged space food, which has to be taken through a tube: when the actor stopped sucking, Kubrick said, the food in the tube ought to have either remained where it was or continued coming out of the tube, instead of falling back to the container, as it would in Earth's gravity. Anybody else notice it?

The *Washington Post* meanwhile, called the film 'unique and awesome... as a philosophical musing on man in infinity it is on the side of the optimistic angels – its fascination lies in stating questions which Kubrick and Arthur C. Clarke are too wise to answer.' Some dissent was voiced by the *International Herald Tribune*, who considered 'the human beings [in the film] a dreary lot... it is impossible to care about any of them. Hal is what we care about... because [he] possesses the human attributes that Kubrick has denied his people.'

British critics were equally split when the film opened in June. *Films in Review* pulled no punches when it bluntly announced, 'whether or not *2001* cost MGM $5,000,000, as they say, is not so important as the deplorable fact that, whatever the amount, all of it was wasted.' Even accepting that the film's effects and photography were worthy of Academy Awards, they considered Kubrick's movie a 'meaningless, adolescent

muddle... [resulting in] a 159 minute bore [which] makes no sense.'

Such a stinging, vicious attack was thankfully rare, although *Sight and Sound* remained on the fence, admitting that 'Kubrick has won the ultimate technical triumph in that his film is beautiful to watch from start to finish,' but hinting that 'one realizes afterwards that one has been almost hypnotized by the visual magnificence of the film [with] the suspicion that all the artifice has simply been used to disguise what was an artificial premise to begin with... Kubrick's greatest achievement has been to persuade us to believe him.'

Most troubling to reviewers – apart from the film's deliberate pacing and lack of explosive set-pieces – was the seemingly inconclusive ending. Clarke's novel based on the screenplay would not reach the bookshelves for at least another month, and the appearance of the drifting star-child approaching Earth at the film's close confused many – even after they had read the book. *Monthly Film Bulletin* noted that 'the film's enigmatic ending may seem something of an anti-climax, a bewildering speculation which provides no answers to the question it raises,' but finally decided that 'this is purely how it should be.' Kubrick himself had already told an American interviewer that essentially, the film is a mythological statement, 'Its meaning has to be found on a sort of visceral, psychological level rather than in a specific literal explanation.'

This, however, seemed something of a cop-out to some critics – the *Films in Review* article dismissed it as '...the stock eye-wash with which poseurs in all the arts are now defrauding the general public', while the *Evening News* – with apparently all the collective brilliance it could muster – declared 'Oh, Mr K – what an odd Odyssey!' adding that 'it's a change from Lady Penelope' – their main point of reference seemingly no more advanced and sophisticated than Gerry Anderson's children's puppet series *Thunderbirds*.

Among those more open to discussion, however, *2001: A Space Odyssey* was quickly hailed as a major work – the *Washington Post* had placed it 'in the evolving tradition of *The Lost World* and *The Cabinet of Dr Caligari*.... immensely imaginative' – and, as the year's awards ceremonies approached, it was clear that Kubrick's film would be a contender in several categories. By that time, however, there had already been a number of changes made to the film: after only three days on release in New York, Los Angeles, Washington and Boston, *2001* was cut by a total of 19 minutes. No scenes were cut entirely, but sections of the Dawn of Man prologue, scenes on board the Orion spaceship, of Frank Poole exercising, and Bowman later returning from his space-walk with the faulty unit were all edited – or 'tightened', as Kubrick called it – with the addition of a couple of title cards dividing the film into three sections: 'The Dawn of Man' (which, significantly, included not only the prehistoric ape-man sequence, but

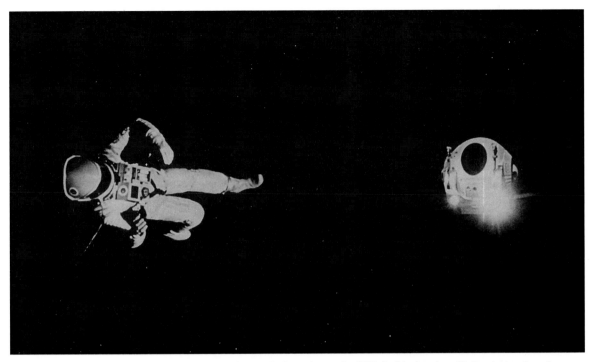

Kubrick and Clarke avoided the 'bug-eyed monster' syndrome in *2001*, but instead – with the help of costume design – produced a race of 'bug-headed astronauts': the end of Frank Poole (at least until 3001) set adrift in space by HAL as Bowman vainly attempts to retrieve him.

also the discovery of the monolith on the moon, three million years later), 'Jupiter Mission 18 Months Later' and 'Jupiter and Beyond the Infinite'.

Variety explained that, even after a full two years in production, Kubrick had finally been up against a studio deadline which meant that he had seen the final cut only eight days before release. (An old Hollywood tradition had been the previewing of major films before an unsuspecting audience, whose comments – via completed questionnaire cards handed in as they left the theatre – were keenly examined by the heads of the studio before a film was set to go on general release. Now, studios were afraid of unfavourable word-of-mouth reaction to big-budget movies, which might damage their investment, so that – as *Variety* pointed out – 'the most expensive and important Hollywood pix get less post-production care than many programmers.')

Kubrick himself defended the cuts by explaining that he had done the same with both *Paths of Glory* and *Dr Strangelove*, and the new, 141–minute version received significantly more positive reviews. The *Chicago Daily News* raved 'I have seen Stanley Kubrick's mind-bending, maddening, awesome, debilitating, demoniacal, dehumanizing and miraculous extraterrestrial fantasy-drama. At first I thought Kubrick had flipped his lid. Now I believe he is a genius who *sees* with incredible clarity a vision of earth-man turning himself into a total nonentity as he pushes on and on... into the limitless void.'

Chicago American rightly predicted that the film 'is going to start a lot of arguments at cocktail parties. Some people will hate it. Some will call it the best movie of the year. And everybody who sees it will argue about what it means.' Kubrick's only concession to those seeking an easy solution to the film's meaning was 'How could we possibly appreciate the *Mona Lisa* if Leonardo had written at the bottom of the canvas: 'The lady is smiling because she is hiding a secret from her lover.' This would shackle the viewer to reality, and I don't want this to happen to *2001*.'

Soon after the film had opened in the United States, the National Catholic Office for Motion Pictures (NCOMP) announced that they had rated *2001* 'morally unobjectionable for adults and adolescents' – as opposed to a general audience – causing MGM to amend their advertising campaign, which until then had promoted the picture as family entertainment. The NCOMP considered that 'small children... would likely be more frightened and confused than entertained. This film is for youth and imaginative adults; the curious and the adventurous.' MGM accordingly aimed their marketing at what was called a 'specific youth hip' audience, hailing the film as 'The Ultimate Trip'.

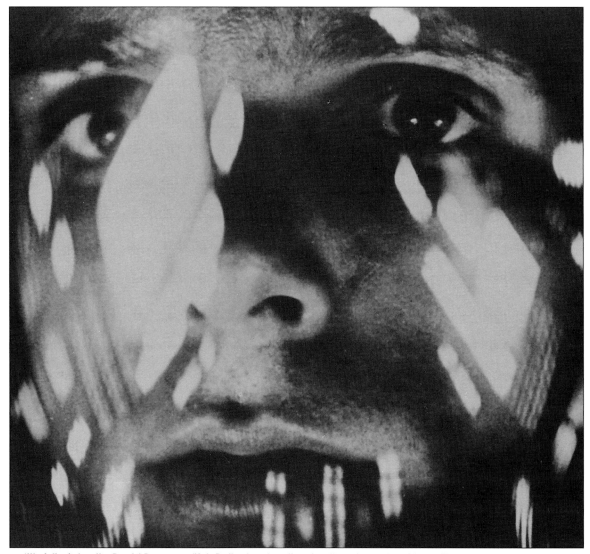

'It's full of stars!' – David Bowman (Keir Dullea) enters the dazzling star gate which will lead him to the ultimate revelation of the future of mankind.

2001: A Space Odyssey became Kubrick's most successful picture to date – one which wins instant recognition even among those with no interest in such technicalities as the names of film directors – and was well recognized at awards time: the New York Film Critics named it in the Best Film, Best Direction and Best Screenwriting categories while, at the Academy Awards, Kubrick won his first personal Oscar for the film's special effects and was nominated as Best Director, losing out to Carol Reed for *Oliver!* (named Best Picture – a category in which *2001* was mystifyingly overlooked). Kubrick and Clarke's screenplay was also nominated (losing to James Goldman's *The Lion in Winter*), as was

the art direction/set decoration of Harry Lange, Tony Masters and Ernest Archer (the prize went – again – to *Oliver!*). Clarke later noted 'to my fury... [that] a special Oscar was presented for make-up – to *Planet of the Apes*!' and suggested that the 'judges had passed over *2001* because they thought we used real apes.'

It may have been some comfort to the film-makers that, at the British Academy Awards soon afterwards, although the film again lost out, it was honoured for its art direction, sound recording (Winston Ryder) and photography (Geoffrey Unsworth) and, a little later, received its ultimate accolade when it featured as a *Mad* magazine movie satire under the title *201 Minutes of Space Idiocy*.

2001 influenced many, both on release and in later years – mostly positively – and this was not confined to movie-makers either: the pop singer formerly known as David Jones left behind his group the Lower Third, changed his name to David Bowie (*almost* Bowman) and wrote and recorded 'Space Oddity' – a chart-topping single which had no actual connection with the film other than a storyline which left its hero (Major Tom) floating helplessly in space ('Planet Earth is blue, and there's nothing I can do.')

In the cinema, Douglas Trumbull 'thought at the time that *2001* would start a big new trend,' but found the reverse to be true. 'The main effect,' he says, 'was that people said no one's ever going to have the patience, the money or the talent to do this again,' and the hoped-for science-fiction 'boom' failed to materialize – at least not until some years afterwards. Only Andrei Tarkovsky's *Solaris* – in production for four years and finally released in 1972 – could be said to rival *2001* in terms of scope and intellectual content although, inevitably, a mammoth (three-hour) and intensely complex Russian film with English subtitles would struggle to find a sizeable audience, although those who did make the effort to see it were well rewarded.

Trumbull's own *Silent Running* (1972) became a minor cult success, but it was not until George Lucas' *Star Wars* (1977) that sf/space movies achieved mass popularity – not least as a result of the merchandising opportunities they offered – although Lucas admitted that 'I just wanted to forget about science [and] make a space fantasy that was more in the genre of Edgar Rice Burroughs' – a return to the intellectual level of the *Flash Gordon* Saturday-morning serials. 'Stanley Kubrick made the ultimate science-fiction movie,' said Lucas, 'and it's going to be very hard for someone to come along and make a better movie, as far as I'm concerned.'

Star Wars was closely followed by Steven Spielberg's monumental *Close Encounters of the Third Kind* and, two years later, *Star Trek: The Motion Picture* (1979) – both with effects supervised by Douglas Trumbull. Furthermore, the first of the *Star Trek* pictures – directed by Robert Wise – clearly owed more to *2001: A Space Odyssey* than to its own origins as a television series – leisurely, balletic shots of circling spacecraft, unlike the fast action of the TV episodes or the later entries in the ongoing film series. Some effects in *Star Trek* – the alien landscape as the Enterprise approaches the signalling V-Ger entity – clearly echoed the star gate sequence of *2001*, as did *Time after Time* (1979) an unlikely sf-drama directed by Nicholas Meyer, in which fact and fiction became increasingly confused as H. G. Wells (Malcolm McDowell) hunts down Jack the Ripper (David Warner) after the latter has fled into the future using Wells' own time machine. The film contained a definite bargain basement version of the star gate effects as Wells was thrown through time.

In 1974, the most blatant *2001*-inspired film of all, *Dark Star* appeared. Originally an amateur student film, made by John Carpenter and Dan O'Bannon, it was expanded and theatrically released to only limited interest, despite being one of the funniest examples of the genre. Carpenter, it was said, was not a fan of *2001*, which may explain why *Dark Star* appears to be almost the opposite of everything which *2001* is: with filthy, cramped conditions on board a malfunctioning ship peopled by bored, irritable crewmen who clearly do not like each other much. Those areas where the two films could be said to coincide – like, talking machinery – differ in that the *Dark Star* computer has the seductive tone of a movie starlet, while it is the irrational talking bomb which actually has more in common with HAL, which eventually brings about the ship's destruction.

Carpenter was not alone among film-makers to be less than overwhelmed by Kubrick's masterpiece: François Truffaut later confessed that he simply 'didn't understand' the film at all, adding that 'there was too much machinery.' Despite this, he said, 'people whom I respect, like Roman Polanski, have said very complimentary things about it,' although, so far as Truffaut was concerned, 'I must admit that I have an anti-scientific mind. It bores me to look at rockets.' Whether or not Truffaut's opinion altered in later years is not clear, but it may be noted that he reached perhaps his largest ever cinema audience by appearing as a French scientist in *Close Encounters of the Third Kind* a decade later – rockets everywhere!

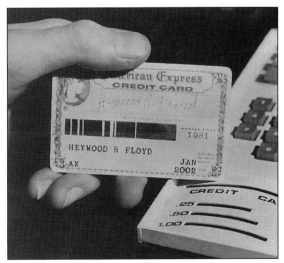

The level of attention to detail in the making of *2001: A Space Odyssey* extended even to the issuing of an American Express card to Heywood Floyd – still with a couple of years left on it.

As for *2001: A Space Odyssey* the book, it became an instant best-seller, credited as 'a novel by Arthur C. Clarke, based on the screenplay by Stanley Kubrick and Arthur C. Clarke'. Four years later, Clarke produced *The Lost Worlds of 2001*, subtitled *The Ultimate Book of the Ultimate Trip*, in which he recalled the ideas discussed and discarded during the screenplay's protracted gestation and, with the subject still obviously very much alive, produced a sequel *2010: Odyssey Two*. Later filmed by Peter Hyams (1984), this saw Keir Dullea briefly reprise his role as a ghostly David Bowman, although the actor later admitted 'I wasn't happy with it. It was just another film,' which is probably the kindest thing one could say about the picture which starred Roy Scheider glumly musing at its conclusion on his inability to explain anything that has happened! Apart from supplying the source novel, Clarke had no further involvement with the film other than as an image on a mock-up *Time* magazine cover in which he and Kubrick were depicted as the Soviet premier and US president.

Clarke went on to pen *2030, 2060* and, in 1997 and reportedly lured by a phenomenal advance from his publishers, *3001: The Final Odyssey*, with the author telling reporters that only Stanley Kubrick could transfer it to the screen, should the need ever arise. Interestingly, *3001* resurrected the character of Frank Poole – last seen somersaulting lifelessly off into deep space as Bowman attempts to re-enter *Discovery*. During early development of *2001*, Clarke noted that he was 'fighting hard to stop Stan from bringing Dr Poole back from the dead. I'm afraid his obsession with immortality has overcome his artistic instincts.'

Thirty years later, it is becoming increasingly difficult to view *2001: A Space Odyssey* in the form in which it was first envisaged. Apart from Kubrick's early trimming of the film's length, there remain few theatres capable of screening any film in Cinerama, although the film has been reissued periodically in impressively restored prints. In October 1994, the National Museum of Photography Film and Television in Bradford presented a rare 70mm screening of the film on their new Cinerama screen, but noted that it was available for one week only before it was needed in Australia! 'We receive regular requests to show the film – more than any other,' wrote Bill Lawrence of the NMPFT, 'and the screenings in October by no means satisfied demand.'

Inevitably, the film is most often seen today on television or on video, but even in these limited formats there have been appalling results: when first screened on BBC Television – in widescreen format – someone had the bright idea of filling in the black spaces above and below the picture with stars – which remained static throughout the entire film, even for scenes not set in space! A flood of complaints led the BBC to admit that it had made 'an error' on this occasion, and subsequent screenings on British TV have usually been in the best available widescreen, though at absurdly late hours. On video, a 1997 re-release in the *MGM Modern Classics* series promised a definitive version but, following the original theatrical trailer and the opening titles, the image inexplicably switches to full screen, with the remainder of the film subject to either the irritating panning left to right during a scene which should remain fixed or – even worse – sections of the picture missing altogether: none more alarmingly so than the Star Child's final return to Earth. In this version the embryo is not even on screen until the closing seconds! And this for a film which, the packaging assures us, is 'the most influential science-fiction film ever... Epic in length and visually stunning... in Cinerama and Super Panavision.'

How influential the film remains is beyond doubt, and in the regular critics' poll held by *Sight and Sound* each decade to vote for the Best Film of All Time, *2001: A Space Odyssey* appeared in the Top Ten in 1991 – the first science-fiction movie to do so, and only the second (nominally) British film in the poll's 40-year history (the first had been David Lean's *Brief Encounter* in the very first list of 1951).

With such a lasting influence and reputation, it is amusing to consider Arthur C. Clarke's opinion in 1969 when, despite his obvious and understandable pride in the film, he felt 'its success has been so overwhelming that it poses the embarrassing problem 'Where do we go from here?'... yet in a very few years it will probably seem old-fashioned, and people will wonder what all the fuss was about.'

1971
A CLOCKWORK ORANGE

Stanley told me I had the Debbie Reynolds part.
ADRIENNE CORRI

Polaris Productions/Hawk Films. (Warner Brothers)
Produced and directed by Stanley Kubrick.

Screenplay: Stanley Kubrick, based on the novel by Anthony Burgess. Associate producer: Bernard Williams. Assistant directors: Derek Cracknell, Dusty Symonds. Director of photography: John Alcott. Film editor: Bill Butler. Production designer: John Barry. Art direction: Russell Hagg, Peter Shields. Costumes: Milena Canonero. Sound editor: Brian Blamey. Sound recording: John Jordan. Sound re-recording: Bill Rowe, Eddie Haben. Technical adviser: Jon Marshall. Stunt arranger: Roy Scammell. Special paintings and sculpture: Herman Makkink, Cornelius Makkink, Liz Moore, Christiane Kubrick. Electronic music score created and performed by Walter Carlos, including excerpts from: Music for the Funeral of Queen Mary (Henry Purcell), William Tell Overture and The Thieving Magpie (Rossini), Pomp and Circumstance Marches Nos. 1 and 4 (Edward Elgar), Ninth Symphony (Ludwig van Beethoven). Other music: Overture to the Sun (Terry Tucker), 'I Want to Marry a Lighthouse Keeper' (written and performed by Erika Elgen), 'Molly Malone' (James Yorkston), 'Singin' in the Rain' (Arthur Freed, Nacio Herb Brown, performed by Gene Kelly).

Cast:
Malcolm McDowell (Alex de Large); Patrick Magee (F. Alexander); Miriam Karlin (Cat Lady); Adrienne Corri (Mrs Alexander); Michael Bates (chief guard); Warren Clarke (Dim); James Marcus (Georgie); Michael Tarn (Pete); Anthony Sharp (minister of the interior); Carl Duering (Dr Brodsky); Madge Ryan (Dr Branom); Aubrey Morris (P. R. Deltoid); Philip Stone (Mr de Large); Sheila Raynor (Mrs de Large); Paul Farrell (tramp); Clive Francis (Joe, the lodger); John Clive (stage actor); Virginia Wetherill (stage actress); Steven Berkoff (constable); Michael Gover (prison governor); Godfrey Quigley (prison chaplain); Pauline Taylor (psychiatrist); John Savident, Margaret Tyzack (Alexander's conspirators); Lindsay Campbell (inspector); David Prowse (Julian); John J. Carney (CID man); Richard Connaught (Billy-Boy); Gillian Hills (Sonietta); Barbara Scott (Marty); Katya Wyeth (girl at Ascot); Cheryl Grunwald (rape girl); Jan Adair, Vivienne Chandler, Prudence Drage (handmaidens); Carol Drinkwater (Nurse Feeley); Barrie Cookson; Gaye Brown; Peter Burton; Lee Fox; Craig Hunter; Shirley Jaffe; Neil Wilson.

136 minutes. Colour.

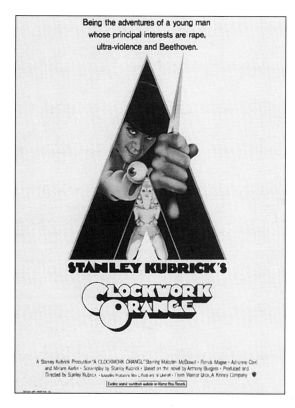

Being the adventures of a young man whose principal interests are rape, ultra-violence and Beethoven.

STANLEY KUBRICK'S

CLOCKWORK ORANGE

A Stanley Kubrick Production "A CLOCKWORK ORANGE" Starring Malcolm McDowell · Patrick Magee · Adrienne Corri and Miriam Karlin · Screenplay by Stanley Kubrick · Based on the novel by Anthony Burgess · Produced and Directed by Stanley Kubrick · Executive Producers Max L Raab and Si Litvinoff · From Warner Bros., A Kinney Company

Exciting original soundtrack available on Warner Bros. Records.

Somewhere in the not too distant future, Alex de Large (Malcolm Mcdowell) and his gang of 'droogs' spend their time in any one of a number of 'milk-plus' bars, where the milk is served spiked with hallu-cinogenic drugs. At odds with a society which cares little anyway, the droogs even invent their own lan-guage - Nadsat - understood only by themselves.

Leaving the Korova Milk Bar one night, they come across a tramp lying in a subway gutter and merci-lessly beat him before moving on to a local deserted casino where Alex's rival Billy-Boy and his mob are about to gang-rape a young girl. The droogs' arrival allows the girl to escape, and a vicious gang fight follows - complete with baseball bats - from which Alex, Dim, Georgie and Pete emerge the victors.

Stealing a car, they drive out into the country at breakneck speed, stopping at a remote, futuristic country house. Pretending that there has been an accident and they are in need of help, the gang trick their way into the house and savagely beat the owner, Mr Alexander (Patrick Magee) before forcing him to helplessly watch the rape of his young wife (Adrienne Corri).

Back home later, Alex relaxes by listening to Beethoven's Ninth Symphony at ear-shattering vol-

ume, oblivious to the pleas of his parents. Next day, he plays truant from school and is visited by his 'post-corrective adviser' P R Deltoid (Aubrey Morris), who warns Alex that he is heading for serious trouble unless he changes his ways.

Unconcerned, Alex spends the rest of the day having sex with two girls he meets in a local record shop, before meeting up again with his droogs in the evening. Georgie (James Marcus) – supported by Dim (Warren Clarke) – suggests that the gang ought to be run along more democratic lines in future, to which Alex apparently agrees. As they are walking alongside the river, however, he attacks the two rebels, pushing them into the water and slicing Dim's hand with a concealed knife, to reassert his position as leader.

After another milk-plus session, the gang decide to repeat the previous evening's revelry at a local health farm, but find that the owner (Miriam Karlin) – alone in the house apart from a huge number of cats – is wary following reports of the attack on the Alexanders' home, and refuses to open the door to them. Alex enters the house, through an open upstairs window, and confronts the woman who, unknown to him, has already telephoned the police. As she defiantly orders him out of the house and attacks him with the nearest heavy object to hand – a bust of Beethoven – Alex dodges her swipes and picks up a huge sculpture of a phallus, with which he beats her unconscious, as the sound of the police sirens approaches. Making his escape through the front door, Alex is confronted by the still resentful Georgie and Dim, who break a bottle of milk in his face before leaving him to be caught by the law.

At the station, a belligerent Alex is beaten by the police before Deltoid is summoned to speak with his 'client'. The adviser angrily spits in his face and tells him that the woman he attacked tonight has died in hospital and that Alex is, indeed, in serious trouble as he had predicted. Sentenced to 14 years in jail for the murder, Alex is inducted into prison by the bureaucratic chief guard (Michael Bates), but quickly uses his wits to feign good behaviour and gain remission of his sentence. After two years working with the chaplain (Godfrey Quigley) in the prison library, Alex asks him if he has ever heard of the new 'Ludovico Technique' which, it is claimed, can 'cure' violent criminals who will then be fit to be released safely back into society.

Soon afterwards, the Minister of the Interior (Anthony Sharp) visits the prison, planning to use the Ludovico treatment as a vote-catching experiment which will

Stanley Kubrick discussing a shot on the extraordinary Korova Milk Bar set of *A Clockwork Orange*.

demonstrate that the government is taking action to resolve the problem of street violence. Alex ensures that he is voluntarily 'chosen' for the experiment, intending that it will merely help him to secure an early release. Transferred to a local hospital, he is injected with the new serum by Dr Branom (Madge Ryan) – who tells him that they are 'merely vitamins' – before being taken to a screening room. Here, he is fitted with clamps preventing him from closing his eyes, and forced to watch a series of films of increasing brutality and sexual violence, watched over by Dr Brodsky (Carl Duering). As the films become more vicious and sadistic, so Alex becomes more and more nauseous as the drug treatment takes effect.

The two weeks of relentless treatment continues, with Alex responding as the doctors had hoped, although his loudest complaint is reserved for the use of a recording of Beethoven's Ninth Symphony to accompany a film of Nazi war atrocities. At the end of the sessions, Alex is paraded before a group of interested parties including the Minister, the Prison Chaplain and the sceptical Head Guard. When an actor attempts

to goad him into retaliating in an aggressive manner, Alex - overcome by nausea - is unable to respond, and is finally forced to lick his boots in submission. To follow this, a young, semi-nude girl is brought before him only for Alex to find himself again sickened by the thought of sex as he cowers at her feet.

The Minister declares the experiment a great success, predicting that it will soon be possible to release all violent criminals from prison with the guarantee that they will be unable to reoffend. Only the Prison Chaplain speaks against what has happened, arguing that Alex is not good through choice, but only incapable of being bad - the treatment has left him no longer a human being but a programmed machine. The Minister shrugs this off, replying that he is not concerned with motives and ethics - only with cutting down crime and reducing the overcrowding in prisons.

The next day, Alex is released, with the newspapers hailing the government-backed tests a turning point in the war against crime. Arriving home, however, Alex finds that his parents – unaware of his impending

The demonic Alex (Malcolm McDowell) takes his droogs for a spin in the country.

arrival – have let his room to a lodger (Clive Francis) and sold all of his possessions to raise the compensation demanded for the upkeep of his victim's pet cats. Bullied by the lodger, Alex becomes physically sickened again and leaves.

Disconsolately walking along the embankment, he is confronted by the same tramp that he and his droogs had beaten previously. Now incapable of defending himself, Alex is set upon by an angry mob of tramps and only rescued by the arrival of two policemen. The police officers, however, turn out to be Dim and Georgie who, still seeking revenge for his past behaviour as their former leader, and aware of his new condition, take him into the countryside and brutally beat him before leaving him in the woods semi-conscious.

Stumbling through the rain-sodden night, he comes across a house and begs to be let in – not realizing that this is the home of F. Alexander, the political reactionary writer they had attacked earlier. Alexander – crippled as a result of the assault and now looked after by a bodyguard (David Prowse) – later identifies Alex as the 'victim' of the dehumanizing Ludovico Technique and suggests that, with his help and that of a few friends and associates, they can bring down the government. While waiting for the arrival of his friends, however, Alexander hears Alex absent-mindedly singing – 'Singin' in the Rain', which he had sung during the droog attack, and realizes just who his house guest is.

During the dinner which follows, Alexander reveals that his wife had died shortly following the attack – officially due to pneumonia but, Alexander says, 'a victim of the modern age' – and becomes increasingly manic, as Alex relates his own tale of abuse and ill-treatment before falling, drugged, into his food. On waking, he finds himself locked in an attic room, with Beethoven's Ninth being played at him through the floorboards at full volume.

Nauseated by the music, as a result of the treatment, he sees that his only option for escape is to leap from the window to his death. The fall, however, does not kill him and he wakes in hospital, to learn that the press are now branding the government as no more than murderers over the case. A psychiatrist interviews him and it is clear from the dreams he relates, and from his responses to a series of slides, that much of his old aggression has returned.

The government minister now reappears, announcing that Alexander has been 'safely put away' and the doctors who ran the experiments have been struck off. The government, he assures Alex, are his 'new friends' and will take good care of him, in return for his support during the forthcoming election. Alex – quickly sizing up the situation – plays along with the minister, who reveals that he has brought him a present – a huge stereo system, with speakers eight feet high on which Alex requests to hear 'the lovely Ninth', without suffering any ill-effects.

As the media circus is brought in to snap photos of the recovered youth, shaking hands with the minister, for the morning editions, Alex daydreams of sex in the snow with a blonde girl, as respectable society ladies and gentlemen look on and applaud him.
Triumphantly, he tells us, 'I was cured all right.'

* * *

Within a month of the UK opening of *2001: A Space Odyssey*, the *London Evening News* carried a report that Stanley Kubrick had begun preparing his next picture – a screen biography of Napoleon, for which Felix Markham of Hertford College, Oxford had been engaged as historical adviser. Kubrick later told *Time* that the film would 'be the first to deal gracefully with historical information and at the same time convey a sense of day to day reality.' Jack Nicholson – yet to land a serious starring role in any picture of note – was said to be in line to play the Little General.

Such a subject would inevitably afford great opportunities for the spectacle and epic sweep that Kubrick had already shown he could deliver in *Spartacus*, although the director intended also to present an altogether more human side of the story. 'Most people,' he said, 'are unaware that Napoleon spent most of his time on the eve of a battle doing paperwork.'

As discussions continued – and with the release in 1970 of Sergei Bondarchuk's massively budgeted Italian/Russian co-production of *Waterloo* with its top-heavy cast including Rod Steiger as Napoleon – Kubrick's version was ultimately shelved as too costly, at least for the time being. He turned, instead, to a book which he said had been 'given to me by Terry Southern during one of the very busy periods of the making of *2001*.'

This would become Kubrick's third consecutive picture to fall under the loose heading of 'science fiction,' although clearly that was about the only thing that either *Dr Strangelove* or *2001* would have in common with the new project, to be based on Anthony Burgess' novel *A Clockwork Orange*.

Born and educated in Manchester, Anthony Burgess

(the pen-name of John Burgess Wilson) had been a teacher of English literature before and after army service during the Second World War, but also spent considerable time abroad working as an education officer in Malaya throughout most of the 1950s. By the time he became a full-time writer and returned to England in 1960, he had already written three novels and a history of English literature, as well as composing a number of full-scale orchestral works, regularly performed in concert halls across the US. What apparently spurred him on to writing – not only as Burgess but also under his real name and as Joseph Kell – was a medical diagnosis that he would be dead within 12 months from an inoperable cancer (he survived another 30 years).

A Clockwork Orange had been published in 1962, soon after Burgess returned to an England in which Teddy Boys had all but had their day and Mods, Rockers and Skinheads were still some two or three years in the future. Much of the book – narrated by its central character, Alex – was written in an almost incomprehensible teen dialect invented by the author – further evidence of his keen interest in linguistics, which later saw him engaged to create an entire 'language' of subtly distinguishable (at least to their creator) grunts and snorts for the 1981 movie *Quest for Fire*. Nadsat, as the chosen speech of *A Clockwork Orange*'s gang of droogs was called, combined cockney rhyming slang, cod-Russian and other unfathomable elements, only attributable to Burgess' own idiosyncrasies, but with occasional similarities to the nonsense verses of Edward Lear and Lewis Carroll, which would later have such an influence on John Lennon's published writings. (A later US paperback edition of Burgess' novel included a Nadsat glossary – neither compiled nor apparently authorized by the author, and quickly removed from subsequent editions.)

The screen rights to the book had, at one point, been co-owned by Andy Warhol and photographer David Bailey, who intended to film the story with The Rolling Stones – a project which folded when the group reportedly 'demanded exorbitant fees' and the rights were subsequently allowed to lapse.

Earlier, Terry Southern had, written a screenplay with Michael Cooper which – as was the tradition in British cinema – had been submitted to the British Board of Film Censors (BBFC) in May 1967, as a forerunner to the London International/Paramount co-production. Although the subsequent BBFC report admitted that the story 'does contain a moral message, which I take to be an indictment of a world in which violence is the only law and human beings are programmed like computers,' Paramount were advised that the proposed script 'could not possibly get into even the X-category unless we are willing to turn our existing standards upside down for the sake of this one film.'

With John Trevelyan, secretary of the BBFC, insisting that any film of this script would not be shown in Britain, Paramount quickly abandoned any thought of proceeding, although Southern – despite any differences which may have lingered with the director over credit for *Dr Strangelove* – later brought it to the attention of Stanley Kubrick, who 'just put [the book] to one side and forgot about it for a year and a half.' Eventually – and almost accidentally – Kubrick 'picked it up and read it. The book had an immediate impact: 'I was excited by everything about it.' The rights were acquired and a screenplay written by Kubrick alone – the first time he had worked on a complete script without a collaborator – which closely followed the structure of the book and, as Kubrick later told *Sight and Sound*, 'was principally a matter of selection and editing, though I did invent a few useful narrative ideas and reshape some of the scenes.'

Most noticeably, Kubrick's script ended with Alex's return to his former self in his hospital bed, omitting Burgess' final chapter which suggests that the once-uncontrollable Alex will, after all, outgrow his violent behaviour naturally and settle down, as his former droog, Pete, had done – now married and soon to be a father. Despite all that had gone before, this reflective – somewhat maudlin – closing section ultimately transforms the story into a mere variation of a 'younger generation/bloomin kids'-style drama, in which 'when I had my son I would explain all that to him when he was starry enough to like understand. But then I knew he would not understand or would not want to understand at all and would do all the vesches I had done... and I would not be able to really stop him. And nor would he be able to stop his own son, brothers. And so it would itty on to like the end of the world, round and round and round.'

Kubrick justifiably found this ending 'unconvincing and inconsistent with the style and intent of the book,' although fortuitously, his own copy of the book had not contained that final chapter anyway (cut by its American publishers and not restored until 1986). 'I wouldn't be surprised,' Kubrick told Michel Ciment, 'to learn that the publisher had somehow prevailed upon Burgess to tack on the extra chapter against his better judgement, so the book would end on a more positive note.' In fact, the reverse seems to be true, with the British version published 'complete' and the US edition cut, against Burgess' wishes. In any case, Kubrick 'certainly never gave any serious consideration to using it,' and on the one occasion when the two men spoke by telephone, there was no suggestion that the author would be involved with the screenplay. 'It was mostly an exchange of pleasantries,' said Kubrick, who didn't feel the need to consult Burgess further. 'In a book as brilliantly written as *A Clockwork Orange*,' he said, 'you would have to be lazy not to be able to find all the answers

Filming the beating of the tramp in the subway: Kubrick (left with back to camera)
watches as Alex applies pressure...

to any question which might arise within the text of the novel itself.'

Kubrick's main additions to the telling of the story – retaining, but simplifying, much of the difficult (and ultimately annoying) Nadsat dialogue – included the invention of a lengthy sequence involving Alex's arrival at the prison, with some humorous over-the-top playing by Michael Bates, as the slightly ridiculous prison officer. Although the film is remembered as being notorious for its level of violence, Kubrick also injected considerable humour into the story, such as the apparently painful groans which answer Alex, as he gradually regains consciousness in the hospital, but which turn out to be a nurse sharing the curtained-off bed opposite with a junior doctor. As explained to *Sight and Sound*, most of Kubrick's 'contributions merely clarify what was already in the novel – such as the Cat Lady telephoning the police, which explains why they appear at the end of the scene.'

The remarkable look of the film, of course, was where Kubrick and his crew came into their own, creating a near-future environment which was not too bizarre to be believable – Kubrick's future, unlike that of many other film-makers, did not rely on silver suits and impractically awful furniture and architecture. Most extraordinary of all was the Korova Milk Bar, designed by John Barry, after Kubrick had seen an exhibition of sculpture which displayed female figures as furniture. 'John photographed a nude model in as many positions as he could imagine would make a table,' he said, adding 'There are fewer positions than you might think.'

The famous 'droog look' too, was created entirely for the film – utterly unlike the novel's descriptions of black tights over a strategically placed jelly mould (most uncomfortable, surely?), waistcoats with padded shoulders and cravats. Kubrick's droogs dressed in virtually all-white, with braces and huge bovver boots as were the style of skinheads of the late sixties, and most notably, a prominent false eyelash applied to one eye only. This costume/uniform – though worn only in the opening third of the film – is probably the image most people have of *A Clockwork Orange* – even those who have not seen the film are dimly familiar with the striking and menacing look of this gang of young thugs.

There were few star names to be found in the entirely British cast, which consisted of mainly television and stage performers including Adrienne Corri, Patrick Magee, Anthony Sharp, Miriam Karlin, Michael Bates and David Prowse (the future Green Cross Code Man of children's TV safety commercials, and physical presence of Darth Vader in the *Star Wars* movies, where his voice was provided by James Earl Jones). The pivotal lead role of Alex went to Malcolm McDowell, best known up until then for his debut performance in Lindsay Anderson's *If...* (1968).

McDowell had never met Kubrick when he received a phone call asking him to go visit the director at his home, where he was given a copy of Burgess' novel and asked to read it. A little later, McDowell called back to say he considered the book 'a modern classic,' and asked the director to 'come to my house and talk, not realizing that Stanley *never* leaves home unless absolutely forced to.' Nevertheless, Kubrick arrived on time and 'finally, I said "Uh, Stanley, you're going to make a film of this? And you want me to play it?" He looked quite startled. "Oh, yeah, Malc – that's what this is all about".' Kubrick later told Michel Ciment that McDowell was 'without the slightest doubt the best actor for the part' of Alex who is, however, just 15 years old at the novel's outset. '[His] age is not that easy to judge in the film,' said Kubrick. 'It might have been nicer if Malcolm had been seventeen, but another seventeen-year-old actor without Malcolm's extraordinary talent would not have been better.'

Warren Clarke recalls that 'it was one of the biggest movies to be made at the time... And Stanley made it the way he wanted to make it – he just took a year for what should have been a ten-week shoot. No one seemed to worry about the fact that we were going on and on.' Filmed on location around London, the production of *A Clockwork Orange* did not use any studio facilities at all, with just four sets having to be built in a deserted factory at Borehamwood, 'a few hundred yards from the old MGM studio.' In sharp contrast to Kubrick's earlier works (notably *Fear and Desire* and *Killer's Kiss*), in which all sound had been added to the film afterwards, *A Clockwork Orange* required no post-synchronization whatever. The use of radio transmitters and advanced microphones now made it possible for all dialogue to be recorded on location – so sophisticated was the equipment, in fact, that for the scene on the embankment between Alex and the tramp 'there was so much traffic noise that you had to shout in order to be heard, but we were able to get such a quiet soundtrack that it was necessary to add street noise in the final mix to make it realistic.'

Visually, *A Clockwork Orange* is often filmed in a straight, dispassionate manner with a minimum of tricks – 'If a scene plays well in one camera set-up and there is no reason to cut, then I don't cut' – although Kubrick's use of different lenses at certain points served to heighten a sense of unreality – most especially during the prison sequence and the distorted wide-angle views of Patrick Magee, as he realizes his visitor's true identity. Much of the film was, in fact, shot by Kubrick personally: 'All of the hand-held camerawork is mine,' he said, explaining that, 'In addition to the fun of doing the shooting myself, I find it is virtually impossible to explain what you want in a hand-held shot to even the most talented and sensitive camera operator.'

Although he does not consider Kubrick an actor's director – 'he is very difficult to communicate with,' Malcolm McDowell spoke later of his first discussions with the director when, 'just feeling him out, I asked Stanley how he worked, and all he said was "Well I never shoot anything I don't want," and walked away. That seemed terribly glib at the time, but I learned that was the key to his film-making. "Never a wasted screen moment" would be his motto.'

Kubrick independently confirmed this when speaking to *Sight and Sound* in 1972, when he revealed that he enjoyed the editing process the most. 'It's the nearest thing to some reasonable environment in which to do creative work,' he said, comparing it to 'the actual shooting of a film [which] is probably the worst circumstances you could try to imagine for creating a work of art.' Editing, too, remained 'the only aspect of the cinematic art that is unique.'

Editing *A Clockwork Orange* had taken almost six months – working seven days a week – during which time Kubrick's 'only concern is with the questions is it good or bad? Is it necessary? Can I get rid of it? Does it work? My identity changes to that of editor... I look at the material with completely different eyes [and] cut everything to the bone.' Even with a running time of around two hours and 20 minutes, it is hard to see any unnecessary material remaining in the picture.

As Kubrick's first work since *2001: A Space Odyssey*, *A Clockwork Orange* contained several visual references to the earlier film – or at least such was the considered opinion of the inwardly/downwardly school of criticism, as each clue – deliberate or otherwise – was seized upon and minutely scrutinized. The *2001* soundtrack album, placed centre screen during Alex's visit to his local record store, was undeniable, but – although taken direct from Burgess' novel – the early encounter with Billy-Boy's gang had striking similarities with the confrontation scene between the rival bands of apes, during the Dawn of Man sequence,

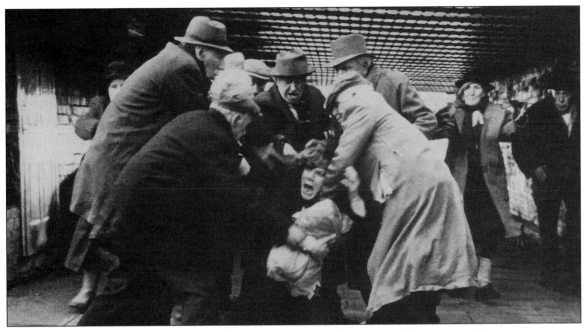

What goes around comes around, as the 'cured' Alex is set upon by a group of tramps who recognize his former self.

in which a crude social hierarchy is created.

This identification of the droogs with the savagery of the ape was seemingly reinforced during Alex's reassertion of his status as gang leader. Having pushed the disloyal Georgie and Dim off the embankment and 'swished with the britva... drew a malenky drop of krovvy [to show them] who was master and leader – sheep, thought I,' Alex is seen brandishing his stick in a low-angle shot recalling Moonwatcher's bone-crunching moment of revelation.

Other – less self-evident – allusions to *2001*, included the droogs' silhouetted stroll down a subway slope, compared by some to the astronauts approaching the excavated monolith on Moon Base (although it might well be wondered just how many ways there are of a group of people walking down a slope together?), and the final scene, in which Alex's present from 'the Minister of the Inferior' – the enormous stereo system – is photographed from Alex's point of view, as the two vast speakers at the foot of his bed unmistakably echo the final appearance of the monolith at David Bowman's feet.

The placing of such visual clues continues to excite comment – as with all of Kubrick's films – but even if we accept that at least some of them are deliberate, this does not necessarily imbue the remainder with any remarkable significance above the possibility that they merely form part of an in-joke which, as ever, has been over-analysed.

One aspect of the film which did draw considerable attention, was the electronic music score by Walter Carlos, much of it based on classical works by Mozart, Purcell and, of course, Alex's 'lovely Ludwig van' Beethoven. Carlos had been a pioneer of electronic music, collaborating with the engineer Robert Moog to create the first Moog Synthesizer and, in 1967, recording the album *Switched On Bach*, which became the best selling classical record of the decade.

For *A Clockwork Orange*, Kubrick – as with *2001* – 'had some [music] in mind from the start,' but, although the film eventually did include standard orchestral versions of some pieces, he invited the composer/musician to London to discuss the score, after having been sent a copy of *Switched On Bach* by Carlos' agent. Kubrick later said that he considered Carlos 'the only electronic composer and realizer who has managed to create a sound which is not an attempt at copying the instruments of the orchestra and yet which, at the same time, achieves a beauty of its own employing orchestral tonalities.' The director even went so far as to suggest that the electronic rendition of Beethoven's Ninth 'rivals hearing a full orchestra playing it, and that is saying an awful lot.'

Carlos' slightly discordant 'Title Music from A Clockwork Orange', based on Henry Purcell's 'Music for the Funeral of Queen Mary', was a perfect opener for the film, creating just the right, unsettling effect as Alex and his droogs are visually introduced in the

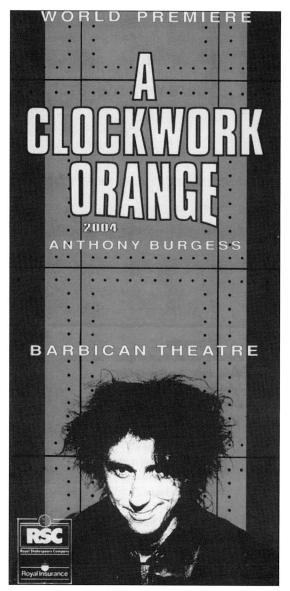

WORLD PREMIERE

A CLOCKWORK ORANGE

2004

ANTHONY BURGESS

BARBICAN THEATRE

RSC
Royal Shakespeare Company

Royal Insurance

Anthony Burgess's scripted stage version of the story, in a production which 'contains scenes which some people may find disturbing, and is not recommended for those under 16.'

Korova Milk Bar. This theme had been suggested to the composer by Kubrick himself: 'The piece just occurred to me,' he said, 'and after I listened to it several times in conjunction with the film, there was simply no question about using it.'

Once again, Kubrick went to considerable lengths to compile a strikingly original, yet highly suitable, score from his own vast researches and knowledge of music. Some pieces were almost obligatory from Burgess' novel,

but for the remainder Kubrick explained his use of classical music – 'in its correct form, or synthesized' – instead of employing a contemporary composer 'who, however good he may be, is not a Mozart or a Beethoven.' This hand-picked method, he said, 'gives you the opportunity to experiment... early in the editing phase, and in some instances to cut the scene to the music' – the exact opposite of the traditional method of scoring a picture, but one which had been used previously, to often startling effect, by Orson Welles (in collaboration with Bernard Herrmann) on *Citizen Kane* and Michael Powell on *The Red Shoes, Tales of Hoffmann* (1951) and, most notably, *Black Narcissus* (1947).

Effective and acclaimed as Carlos' contribution was, it was the inclusion of 'Singin' in the Rain' which became the most discussed aspect of the soundtrack. First heard during the brutal attack on the Alexanders, Kubrick's recollection was that 'this scene... appeared to be going nowhere. We spent three days trying to work out just what was going to happen and somehow it all seemed a bit inadequate.' The director says that 'the idea popped into my head – I don't know where it came from or what triggered it off,' although Malcolm McDowell claims that 'Stanley suddenly called, "Hey, Malcolm, can you sing and dance?"' to which the actor, who admits he can do neither, replied 'Oh yes, Stanley, sure, and just sort of started 'Singin' in the Rain' as it's the only song I know.' The use of such a globally popular item – with its innocent, Golden Age of MGM Hollywood aura – to accompany the ferocious rape and beating of the couple led to charges that Kubrick was a cold, calculating cynic, perverting what was once a thing of innate decency.

McDowell explained the purpose of the song at this point: 'This was the sort of thing I knew I must look for,' he said. 'Alex larking about happily while doing this terrible violence. It's the kind of contradiction, the extra dimension that I had to find for him.' Burgess' novel contained no such identifying moment, which Kubrick later uses as the plot device which brings about Alex's downfall – Alexander, recognizing Alex through association with the song, and quickly plotting his revenge. Finally, the more famous Gene Kelly version of the song is heard over the closing credits – recalling the use of Vera Lynn's recording of 'We'll Meet Again' at the close of *Dr Strangelove*. As a counterpoint to Alex's final 'I was cured all right,' everything is as it was at the beginning.

The subject matter, however, was always going to present difficulties when brought before film censors. Though Burgess' novel could describe the attack on the writer (Alexander) and his wife from Alex's point of view, and without too much detail, it was quite another thing to see the appalling, brutal assault and events leading up to the rape in such graphic detail, even though the entire scene – from the gang's entry into the house to the cut back to the Korova – lasts little more than three minutes.

That opening quarter hour of *A Clockwork Orange* in fact contains virtually all of the film's most discussed scenes of violence – the unprovoked beating of the tramp, the imminent gang-rape of the young girl (halted by the droogs, but only so that they can beat the rival gang) and the crippling and humiliation of the Alexanders. 'It's all in the plot,' Kubrick told the *New York Times*. 'Part of the artistic challenge is to present the violence as he sees it, not with the disapproving eye of the moralist but subjectively as Alex experiences it.' On another occasion, he said 'this may have some effect in distancing the violence. Some people have asserted that this made the violence attractive. I think this view is totally incorrect.'

In a 1995 *Films in Review* article on 'The New Violence', Michael Eric Stein noted that, 'for some moviegoers, Kubrick's reputation never recovered from those 15 minutes of carnality and crime, which sparked one of the angriest controversies over screen violence of the seventies.' Kubrick himself went to considerable lengths to discuss the film with journalists, and explain the reasoning behind it. 'The central idea of the film has to do with the question of free will,' he later said. 'If we are deprived of the choice between good and evil, do we become, as the title suggests, a Clockwork Orange? Recent experiments in conditioning and mind-control on volunteer prisoners in America have taken this question out of the realm of science fiction.'

In response to charges that the movie was little more than an orgy of gratuitous screen violence and misogyny which served to glamorize brutality, Kubrick told the *New York Times* that 'Alex is a character who by every logical and rational consideration should be completely unsympathetic, and possibly even abhorrent to the audience. And yet in the same way that Richard III gradually undermines your disapproval of his evil ways, Alex does the same thing and draws the audience into his own vision of life... you respond to the basic shape of the story on a subconscious level, as you would respond to a dream.'

In a major *Sight and Sound* interview to mark the film's release, Kubrick insisted that 'there is no positive evidence that violence in films or television causes social violence,' equating this with 'the scientifically accepted view that, even after deep hypnosis, in a post-hypnotic state, people cannot be made to do things which are at odds with their nature.' He suggested that much of the hostility towards the film was based on a 'basic psychological, unconscious identification with Alex. He is within all of us. In most cases this recognition seems to bring a kind of empathy from the audience, but it makes some people very angry and uncomfortable. They are unable to accept this view of themselves and, therefore, they become angry at the film.

It's a bit like the King killing the messenger who brings him bad news.'

Viewed by a BBFC team which included the same censor who had rejected Southern's 1967 script, it was now decided that the violence of the early scenes was justified in the overall context of the story, and an X certificate was granted to the full-length 136-minute version of the film which had already premiered in New York on 20 December 1971 – also as an X. It was this occasion which prompted Kubrick to have the interior walls of the New York cinema repainted from a shiny white to something which would not reflect light. With only days to the premiere, the theatre manager complained that there was not enough time for this work to be done, but Warner Brothers publicist Julian Senior recalls that 'after checking through the Manhattan directory, Stanley sent them a list of firms' he considered suitable to carry out the job, discovering later that they had used black gloss paint, which reflected just as much as the original white had done. 'They had to repaint it in matte black, as he wanted,' confirms Senior. 'That gives you some idea of his precision in technical matters.'

In the UK, coming soon after the release of a number of violent and controversial movies – *Straw Dogs* (1971), *Soldier Blue* (1970) and (uniquely for a British movie) *Get Carter* (1971) – *A Clockwork Orange* was seized upon by campaigners such as the newly formed Nationwide Festival of Light, who claimed that, 'while no individual film by itself would make any significant public impact, collectively [they] contributed to an atmosphere in which social violence could flourish and expand.'

Among the Festival of Light's leading figures was Peter Thompson, a public relations expert converted to Christianity, following a sermon by the US evangelist, Billy Graham, in 1954. Eleven years later, he had suffered a nervous breakdown, attacking three young women with a knife and being sentenced under the Mental Health Act to be detained at Broadmoor mental institution. By 1969, however, he was released and claimed that his problems had stemmed from the watching of a number of films portraying sex and violence.

Associating himself with the Festival of Light, Thompson soon became both a committee member and the group's public relations spokesman, which he self-servingly intended would 'extend my film censorship campaign.' Testing their influence with an (unsuccessful) campaign aimed at forcing the withdrawal of Ken Russell's film *The Devils* (1970), they turned their attention to the UK release of *A Clockwork Orange* in January 1972, by which time the movie had already been voted the Best Film of 1971 by the New York Film Critics, with Kubrick named as Best Director.

Within days, conflicting reviews and editorials claimed the film as either a 'masterpiece' or 'Muck in the name of Art' – this last, the verdict of the aptly-named Peregrine Worsthorne, who had been invited to a special screening of the picture, arranged by Lord Longford's self-appointed Pornography Commission of Enquiry. Thompson had also attended the same screening and, embarrassingly for the Festival of Light, was quoted afterwards as declaring the film to be 'the best I have ever seen,' and one in which he could 'relive his own experiences.' Elsewhere, both he and Lord Longford were said to have some reservations over the level of violence in the movie, while Worsthorne – in the grand manner of sloganeering journalism – pompously and somewhat obviously labelled it 'a sick film for a sick society.'

Kubrick had actually toned down the amount of violence described in Burgess' original – he omitted both the first beating of a 'doddery starry schoolmaster type veck,' and the unrelieved cruelty and depravity of prison life which eventually leads to the murder of a fellow prisoner by Alex and his cell-mates (also cut from the film version). The book's drink-induced seduction of two ten-year-old girls by Alex now involved highly willing, late-teenagers (this scene played almost for comic relief and accompanied by a speeded-up version of the William Tell Overture) and – if Kubrick had really been intent on merely showing sickeningly violent images, then those films which Alex is forced to watch as part of the Ludovico treatment would have given him more than ample opportunity. Although we witness a couple of brief sequences, most of the remaining sessions are depicted only by Alex's facial and verbal reactions. One technician who worked with the director – though not on *A Clockwork Orange* – told me of a particularly gruesome scene which he had completed with Kubrick, apparently to his satisfaction, only to be told later that three-quarters of the scene would have to be deleted. 'Stanley obviously thought that it was much too gratuitously violent,' says the technician, who wishes to remain anonymous. 'I don't think he has any taste at all for ghoulish violence just for its own sake.'

Michael Wood in *New Society* clearly recognized this, and reasoned that 'Readers of Anthony Burgess' [book] will expect to see violence in the film... There is less than you'd expect – the minimum, I think, that the movie requires to make sense.' Wood also suggested that there was significantly more violence to be seen in other 'acceptable' movies, citing John Boorman's *Point Blank* (1967) and – ironically – Brando's *One-Eyed Jacks* as examples.

Andrew Sarris of *Village Voice* merely found *A Clockwork Orange* 'an ultimately pointless futuristic fantasy' in a review which – surprisingly – made no mention of the growing controversy surrounding the picture. 'Don't take my word for it,' he continued. 'See [it] for yourself and suffer the damnation of boredom,' finally dismissing the picture as a 'pretentious failure.'

In general, however, the more conservative press complained loudest of the dangers of such a film being unleashed on the public. The *Daily Mail* demanded to know 'What on earth induced our censors to pass those startling scenes of rape and violence?' although they still considered 'Kubrick and his film far too good to need bolstering up with such repellent shock tactics.' Praising Malcolm McDowell's 'superb performance,' the review still feared that 'all the shoddy directors will jump on the sex and brutality bandwagon in the scramble to turn out lesser and more leering imitations of *A Clockwork Orange*.'

In *The Sunday Times*, the venerable Dilys Powell could not fault Kubrick's technique and skill in making the picture, which had 'no hanging on to the tail of movement; every scene snaps to an end at the exact moment when its usefulness is exhausted,' but warned that 'one must not be conned by one's admiration into soft-soaping Mr Kubrick's film [which] has passages savage to the point of nausea' – an interesting and appropriate observation, given the precise effect that scenes of violence have on Alex during the Ludovico experiment and later.

If Kubrick was at all inviting his audience to identify with Alex, he considered it 'absolutely necessary to give weight to Alex's brutality, otherwise I think there would be moral confusion with respect to what the government does to him.' The instant, knee-jerk reaction would be that the government action, in applying the Ludovico treatment to obliterate aggression, is an attractive alternative if this will produce a less violent society but, in reality, this is not the case. '[By] the immense evil of turning him into something less than human in order to make him good, then the essential moral idea of the book is clear,' said Kubrick. Only the prison chaplain voices this fear, with other authority figures shown as either ruthless, two-faced opportunists (the minister), weak-willed (the prison governor), hopelessly out of touch (the prison officer), callous (the dispassionate doctors conducting the experiment), morally corrupt (Deltoid – a flesh-crawlingly effective performance by Aubrey Morris) or even more brutal than the villains (most notably, the police force on Alex's release from prison – his former droogs are now officers of the law, and legally more vicious than ever).

With the film less than a month into its initial run in London, the Festival of Light urged local councils to exercise their own powers to prevent it being seen throughout the country, prompting the BBFC to defend their own position: Stephen Murphy – successor to John Trevelyan, who retired in 1971 – wrote to one authority that 'censorship of this film would undoubtedly be seen, publicly, as the censorship of ideas.' Admitting that the board had been 'disturbed by the first half of the film,' Murphy declared himself 'satisfied by the end that it could not be accused of exploitation: quite the contrary, it is a valuable contribution to the whole debate about...

the social problem of violence, and it would be quite wrong to prevent the serious film-maker from making his contribution to its examination... I can think of no other film that more clearly illustrates the dilemma we are all in about the treatment of violence by the media.' A press report that Home Secretary Reginald Maudling had personally asked to see the film appears not to have been correct. He apparently did request an explanation from the BBFC over their decision not to cut the film, but took no further action, nor did he comment publicly on the picture.

Nevertheless, *A Clockwork Orange* could be seen at only one cinema in London during the whole of 1972, while winning high praise in other countries, including an award for Best Foreign Film at the Venice Film Festival. At the US Academy Awards, it was nominated for Best Film, Direction, Writing (both personal nominations for Kubrick – and welcome recognition for his first solo screenplay) and Editing (Bill Butler) but lost in all categories to *The French Connection*. Problems remained, however, with the film's American X certificate, which not only limited the number of theatres willing to screen the picture, but also led to the refusal of some newspapers even to accept advertising. Miriam Karlin – the 'Cat Lady' of the movie – was to be seen on US television chat shows 'waving pages of obscene ads for massage parlours and the like, and pages full of crime and violence reportage' from freely available respectable publications to support her argument that *A Clockwork Orange* 'should never have been given an X certificate in the first place.'

In April, Kubrick wrote an open letter to the *Detroit News*, challenging their decision 'to refuse to give space to advertising, publicizing or reviewing X-rated or unrated films,' even though the paper had already reviewed *A Clockwork Orange* – describing it as a 'porno movie' – shortly before imposing its blanket ban. Kubrick complained that 'for any newspaper to deliberately attempt to suppress another equally important communications medium seems especially ugly and short-sighted,' and compared this with 'the words of another arbiter of public morals and national taste [who declared] "works of art which cannot be understood and need a set of instructions to justify their existence... will no longer reach the public... We have set out to rid our nation and our people of all those influences threatening its existence and character." The speaker was Adolf Hitler... in Munich in 1937.'

Explaining the importance of the X-rating as set by the Motion Picture Association of America, Kubrick insisted that such a certificate 'does not stigmatize or condemn a film, but merely places it in the adult film category... there is no power, legal or otherwise, which should be exercised against the rights of adults to select their own entertainment.' He ended by accusing the *Detroit News* of acting under 'anti-democratic princi-

ples [which] many readers may find offensive. They may find that they are censoring their readers rather than their advertisers.' The newspaper responded briefly a few days later by claiming that Kubrick's references to Nazi Germany 'do not fit the issue,' adding that, 'in our opinion the MPAA code is weak and unsatisfactory; if it topples we cannot accept the blame.'

Difficulties remained with the distribution of the picture in some parts of the US, where X-rated films were still considered poor box office and, by August, it was announced that Kubrick would be withdrawing the movie from circulation for 60 days from the end of October, in accordance with rules governing a change in rating. 'I have now replaced thirty seconds with less explicit film from the same scenes,' Kubrick said. 'The film has been resubmitted to the MPAA who viewed it and, who now having no further reason to rate it X have changed it to an R.' Warner Brothers made it clear that this R version (i.e. Restricted - no one under the age of 17 allowed unless accompanied by an adult) was available for those areas where X films were not permitted, while the original edition would also remain in circulation. Paradoxically, *A Clockwork Orange* remains one of the least cut of Kubrick's movies: after the post-premiere editing of *Spartacus*, *Dr Strangelove*, *2001* and, later, *The Shining*, which had removed between five and 20 minutes from each picture, *A Clockwork Orange* – once approved by censors – remained uncut, other than for this compliance with the US rating system. This did not reduce the overall length of the picture, however, and it is seen today – in those places where it can be seen – in the same version as that first screened in 1971.

Kubrick told reporters that he was 'very pleased with *A Clockwork Orange*,' and considered it 'the most skilful movie I have ever made. I can see almost nothing wrong with it,' and, in the UK, the film finally went on general release in early 1973, only to attract further adverse comment which would ultimately prove too much for its director. (Interesting to compare the reception given to Kubrick's film with that afforded Alfred Hitchcock's *Frenzy*, released in the midst of the *Clockwork* debate. A surprisingly shabby, cold and vicious piece of film-making, *Frenzy* – with its own crudely explicit rape and murder scene, and a relentlessly violent stance against women – was nevertheless seen as a creditable entry to the catalogue of works by the Master of Suspense.)

The Festival of Light meanwhile remained vocal in its condemnation of *A Clockwork Orange*, with leading *illuminata* Mary Whitehouse calling for it to be banned after she had watched (presumably the first) 20 minutes of the picture. A couple of local authorities duly obliged, with isolated screenings in those towns blocked.

What finally pushed *A Clockwork Orange* beyond the pale was the sensationalist reporting in national newspapers of supposed 'Clockwork Orange gangs' roaming the streets, acting out the violence of the film and book. A tramp was beaten to death in Bletchley, near Oxford, by a teenager who, it was said in court, 'was play-acting in the most ghastly fashion.' Claiming that 'momentarily, the Devil had been planted in this boy's subconscious,' his counsel continued 'it is the irresistible conclusion that what was planted there was this book, the violence of *A Clockwork Orange*.'

More was to follow, with a Manchester judge sending a 16-year-old boy to Borstal for attacking a younger boy, while apparently wearing white overalls and a bowler hat. The judge condemned the recent trend in violent behaviour, which he said supported the 'unassailable argument for a return of film censorship' – a curious statement since, as BBFC chairman Lord Harlech observed, such censorship was already in place, adding that 'a boy of sixteen should not legally have been able to see the film anyway.'

Even this was not the end, with the Reverend John Lambert – described as former chaplain to Pinewood Studios – making an astonishing attack on both Kubrick and Anthony Burgess whose only motive, he claimed, was 'Money... Dirty, grubby money.' Of this 'celluloid cesspool,' Reverend Lambert argued, 'you have given nothing to the world that is of worth... may the money rot in your pockets. Perhaps it is too much to hope that you will have remorse in your bones.' He ended by forecasting that 'most balanced, mature men today will find you guilty... and so will God.'

Throughout, Kubrick remained silent, even when pressed by Burgess in August 1973 to defend the movie. Calling the film 'a remarkable work, probably already a classic,' the writer announced himself 'increasingly exasperated by the assumption that it was my duty to defend the film against its attackers... It is surely the duty of the maker of the film to speak out for his own work.'

As with later – often unsubstantiated – reports of so-called 'copycat' crimes and violence following the release of Oliver Stone's 1994 film *Natural Born Killers* (actually, more objectionable as a vacuous piece of superficial, technique-filled garbage), in 1973 it seemed anyone committing any particularly vicious form of assault had only to cite a viewing of *A Clockwork Orange* as justification for a serious lapse from their normally law-abiding behaviour: even six months after the film had completed its initial theatrical run, a 21-year-old man on trial at the Old Bailey claimed his exposure to the film as a mitigating factor in the murder of a 79-year-old woman.

No official announcement was made concerning the future of *A Clockwork Orange* – whose run had, despite the adverse publicity, been highly successful at the box office, recouping its production costs and quickly showing a profit. Kubrick, however, had privately informed Warner Brothers of his decision to withdraw the movie from circulation in the UK which – as owner of the British distribution rights – he was fully entitled to do. The picture was, however, still available elsewhere and, apart from its recognition at the Venice Festival, New York Film Critics and American Academy, was picking up numerous other prizes including Best Picture at the London *Evening Standard* awards (with Malcolm McDowell named as Best Actor), Germany's Golden Rose, Frankfurt's Golden Spotlight, Denmark's Ekstra Bladet Five Stars and the Hugo Award at the 30th French Sci-Fi Convention.

Over the next couple of years, *A Clockwork Orange* gradually faded into the distance as do most movies, to be overtaken by more violent and controversial pictures – this week's tabloid fodder – and its disappearance was not fully noted until 1979 when the organizers of a National Film Theatre Kubrick retrospective season were informed by Warners that the film was 'absolutely withdrawn from circulation' in the UK (although a 1993 report in *Sight and Sound* claimed that another party had attempted to hire a 16mm print of the film, but was told it was available for screenings only in 'hospitals, prisons and borstals').

Having earlier demanded that the film be banned, the press would now on occasion question the film's status, often demanding that Kubrick reissue the picture which, after all, could be seen almost anywhere else in the world both on video and in the cinema. There were attempts at defying the ban (although, officially, *A Clockwork Orange* has never been 'banned' other than in those few towns where local authorities refused to grant a certificate) and in 1988 it was announced that Oxfordshire's 'Artweek 88' would present free, late-night showings of the movie at the Picture Palace film club, as part of a science-fiction festival which also included *2001: A Space Odyssey* and *Dr Strangelove*.

Writing in *The Sunday Times*, Joan Bakewell asked 'What are we to make of a film, passed by the censor, but taken out of circulation by its own maker?' She mused that 'The idea of a genius trying to recapture the work he has unleashed upon the world is one that might take Kubrick's own fancy... yet once it is released, a film of the force of *A Clockwork Orange* does, for good or ill, enter the public imagination.' This is certainly true – most people in the UK have not seen the picture in over a quarter of a century, yet those who did catch it at the time retain a strong impression of their reaction – one person I spoke to recently recalled only that she was 'livid' when she came out of the cinema in 1973. Bakewell added that 'Kubrick's action in consistently withholding it merely lends forbidden glamour to its already dangerous reputation.'

At the end of 1989, Anthony Burgess went on record urging Kubrick to make the film available once again, although the same report quoted Adrienne Corri as being wholly in support of the director's unspoken decision not to do so. 'Stanley was appalled by the reaction to the film,' she said, adding that she 'had not seen the film since its first release.' Further media interest was generated by the mounting of a stage musical under the title *Clockwork Orange 2004* – as Philip French noted, a title which 'deliberately evokes and involves *2001: A Space Odyssey*' even though Kubrick had no involvement with the production, which was written entirely by Burgess and featured music by U2's Bono and The Edge (titles including 'Alex descends into Hell for a Bottle of Milk/Korova 1').

As an increasing number of columnists resorted to composing open letters to Stanley Kubrick on the subject – an easy way of announcing credibility to your readers ('I've seen the film and you haven't'/'I'm open-minded enough not to be shocked by it' etc.) – a London cinema went ahead and screened *A Clockwork Orange* in April 1992, with the theatre manager immediately facing charges of breaching the film's copyright. At the court hearing, conflicting evidence claimed that the print had either been 'screened two or three years before and... was stored in the cinema' – unlikely since it had been withdrawn almost 20 years previously – or newly supplied by a mysterious figure who the manager 'never met [and who] never gave any indication of his rights to the film.' 'It is rather analogous,' said the prosecuting counsel, 'to the buying of stolen goods from a mythical man in the pub.'

Although the theatre claimed to be unaware of any ban on the film – again, the legend being that it had been banned rather than withdrawn – the cinema projectionist who had run the film told the court 'everyone knows that Kubrick has spies out every day to keep an eye on the copyright,' (a monumental waste of resources had it been true) thereby adding to the suggestion that the legal action had been brought against the theatre manager 'on the express orders of Stanley Kubrick.' In fact, the Federation Against Copyright Theft (FACT), who actually brought the case, insisted that this was 'absolute rubbish... [the cinema] wasn't prosecuted because it was *A Clockwork Orange* – it was prosecuted because they gave a public viewing of a film without the copyright owner's permission.' The FACT spokesman added, 'I'd have done the same thing if it was *Aladdin*.'

The theatre manager was conditionally discharged and ordered to pay a £1,000 fine, only for the story to apparently resurface within a week, as an independent cinema in Liverpool announced its intention to defy the courts and go ahead with their own screening of the film. An injunction was issued against the cinema the day before the proposed showing, with the local press accusing the organizer of mounting a publicity stunt, with no real intention of showing the film at all. Later in the year, a Channel Four television documentary featuring clips from the movie was blocked by a court injunction brought by Warner Brothers. When the decision was overturned on appeal as 'legitimate review and criticism', the programme was transmitted three weeks later, complete with the 'dangerous clips'.

At the time of writing, *A Clockwork Orange* remains unavailable for public viewing either in cinemas or on video in the UK, and seems likely to remain so for the foreseeable future. Kubrick made no public statement about the film following its withdrawal, although Philip French hinted in 1990 of the 'latest rumour – that Kubrick was re-editing the film' – presumably for reissue? Many of those involved with the making of the picture maintain that it was 'a fabulous experience,' as Warren Clarke recalls: 'You know, you're 22 years old and you're working with one of the biggest geniuses that ever made a movie, and you just think, "Christ, this is amazing, I'm doing a Kubrick movie".' The feeling was apparently shared throughout the company, with John Savident – featured only for a few minutes of screen time as one of Alexander's conspirators – having 'nothing but happy memories of the experience... Stanley was a joy to work with.'

Though still divided in his personal feelings about Kubrick – 'I have my personal angst with him, but he's a brilliant director and an extraordinary man, and I loved pretty much 98 per cent of the time I spent with him' – Malcolm McDowell insists that the film is 'one of the greatest pieces of work that I will ever do – one of the greatest parts written for a film actor... the Hannibal Lecter of its generation.' As recently as 1997, he appeared at the Venice Film Festival to introduce a newly struck print of the movie in an evening entitled 'Malcolm McDowell revisits *A Clockwork Orange*'. Any credit for the lasting strength of the film – still playing to packed theatres in Europe – he gives entirely to Anthony Burgess' novel which, he told BBC radio in 1998 'was a very great book – as far as I was concerned it was the Bible. The brilliance of making the central character this immoral person – it's a tremendous decision that the audience have to make. It's easy to hate him, and yet he has a vulnerability.' As for his own performance, McDowell insists that Kubrick gave him no real direction on how to play the character, and that he eventually turned to Lindsay Anderson for advice on how to create Alex for the screen. 'I went over to see him and said "Well how the hell am I going to play it?" and he said, "Well I'll tell you very simply, Malcolm. There's a shot in *If...* when you come into the gym to be beaten. You open the doors and there's a close-up on you – and you smile. That's the way you play it." And that's what I did.'

With the passage of time, it is difficult – in fact near impossible – to consider *A Clockwork Orange* dispassionately, so fierce were the arguments raised both for and against it. In the UK there are few people under the age of 40 who can have seen the picture at all and, as noted by several writers, receive their impression of it from regularly reprinted sources such as Leslie Halliwell's popular *Film Guide*, which condemned the movie as 'a repulsive film in which intellectuals have found acres of social and political meaning. The average judgement is likely to remain that it is pretentious and nasty rubbish for sick minds who do not mind jazzed-up images and incoherent sound.'

This remarkable outburst does raise a number of significant points: the mention of 'intellectuals' is clearly meant in a derogatory sense, suggesting that these unfortunate and gullible creatures have been taken in by some pretentious nonsense – better to be a non-intellectual who 'knows what I like' and so is presumably more than capable of arriving at whatever passes for average judgement.

A shame that the normally level-headed Halliwell should have taken such pains to discredit the film: his rant has unpleasantly strong echoes of Derek Hill's piece on Michael Powell's *Peeping Tom* (1960), which urged 'the only really satisfactory way to dispose of [it] would be to shovel it up and flush it swiftly down the nearest sewer. Even then the stench would remain.' On that occasion, the film was quickly pulled by its distributor, leaving Powell virtually unemployable in the UK for the remaining 30 years of his life. Fortunately, Kubrick was in a position – fully supported by Warner Brothers – to ride out the storm and resolve it in his own fashion.

Nevertheless, it is instructive to compare the outraged reactions of the national press with those of the showbiz media. While most UK dailies – and even the upmarket Sundays – found their sensibilities offended by the violence of the picture, *Variety* hailed Kubrick's movie as 'a brilliant nightmare [which] employs outrageous vulgarity, stark brutality and some sophisticated comedy' – a point invariably missed by most tabloid reviewers – 'to make an opaque argument for the preservation of respect for man's free will – even to do wrong.'

In Britain, *Monthly Film Bulletin* described Kubrick as 'an intrepid explorer of closed universes,' who revelled in the 'no-exit situations through which he rotates his characters.' This latest exercise, they said, 'emerges as his most cynical and disturbing film to date... by the time Alex regains consciousness in his hospital bed, Kubrick has us rooting for him to resume his thuggery – the only way left to us or him of saying no to this dehumanized society.'

Films and Filming rated *A Clockwork Orange* as 'not to be missed' and concluded that 'much praise is due to Malcolm McDowell as Alex, a performance in perfect balance: a creature who is extrovert enough to be hateful, introvert enough to be pitiful.' The review went on to highlight the achievements of John Barry (production designer), Russell Hagg, Peter Shields (art directors) and John Alcott (cinematographer) as 'worthy of special commendation in what is essentially a director's film – and a ferociously good one.'

Whatever the future of *A Clockwork Orange* may be – whether it remains withdrawn in the UK while legally available in (and importable from), say, France or the US, or if a recut version ever does see the light of day – the inescapable truth remains that, during its absence from the screen, violence on the streets and in society as a whole has increased alarmingly and disturbingly. Now – who is responsible for that?

1975

BARRY LYNDON

If you work with Kubrick, you're one step ahead of the game.
It's like going to finishing school.
RYAN O'NEAL

Hawk Films/Peregrine. (Warner Brothers)
Produced and directed by Stanley Kubrick.

Screenplay: Stanley Kubrick, based on the novel *The Memoirs of Barry Lyndon, Esq.*, by William Makepeace Thackeray. Executive producer: Jan Harlan. Associate producer: Bernard Williams. Director of photography: John Alcott. Production managers: Douglas Twiddy, Terence Clegg, Rudolf Hertzog. Assistant directors: Brian Cook, David Tomblin, Michael Stevenson. Second unit photography: Paddy Carey. Editor: Tony Lawson. Production designer: Ken Adam. Art directors: Roy Walker, Jan Schlubach. Set decoration: Vernon Dixon. Costumes: Ulla Britt Soderlund, Milena Canonero. Hairstyles and wigs: Leonard. Make-up: Ann Brodie, Alan Boyle, Barbara Daly, Jill Carpenter, Yvonne Coppard. Choreography: Geraldine Stephenson. Music adapted and conducted by Leonard Rosenman from works by Handel (Sarabande), Mozart (Idomeneo), Schubert (German Dance No 1 in C-Major, Piano Trio in E-flat), Paisiello (Il Barbiere Di Siviglia), Vivaldi (Cello Concerto in E Minor) J S Bach (Concerto for Two Harpsichords and Orchestra in C-Minor), Hohenfriedberger March from Frederick the Great and Traditional tunes ('British Grenadiers' , 'Lilliburlero'). Music composed by Sean O'Riada ('Mna Na H Éireann'/'Women of Ireland',' Tin Whistles') and Traditional Irish tunes ('Piper's Maggot Jig', 'The Sea Maiden') arranged and performed by Paddy Moloney, Sean Potts, Derek Bell and The Chieftains. Sound editor: Rodney Holland. Historical adviser: John Mollo.

Gambling adviser: David Berglas. Stunt arranger: Roy Scammell. Fencing coach: Bob Anderson. Horsemaster: George Mossman. Wrangler: Peter Munt. Armourer: Bill Aylmore.

Cast:
Ryan O'Neal (Redmond Barry/Barry Lyndon); Marisa Berenson (Lady Lyndon); Patrick Magee (Chevalier de Balibari); Hardy Kruger (Captain Potzdorf); Steven Berkoff (Lord Ludd); Gay Hamilton (Nora Brady); Marie Kean (Mrs Barry); Leonard Rossiter (Captain Quin); Diana Koerner (German girl); Murray Melvin (Reverend Samuel Runt); Frank Middlemass (Sir Charles Lyndon); André Morell (Lord Wendover); Arthur O'Sullivan (highwayman); Godfrey Quigley (Captain Grogan); Philip Stone (Graham); David Morley (Bryan Lyndon); Leon Vitali (Lord Bullingdon); Dominic Savage (young Bullingdon); Anthony Sharp (government minister); Michael Hordern (narrator). With: John Bindon, Roger Booth, Billy Boyle, Jonathan Cecil, Peter Cellier, Geoffrey Chater, Anthony Dawes, Patrick Dawson, Bernard Hepton, Anthony Herrick, Barry Jackson, Wolf Kahler, Patrick Laffan, Hans Meyer, Ferdy Mayne, Liam Redmond, Pat Roach, Frederick Schiller, George Sewell, John Sharp, Roy Spencer, John Sullivan, Harry Towb.

187 minutes. Eastman Colour.

'One of the most astonishingly beautiful movies ever made'; Barry Lyndon (Ryan O'Neal) and the German peasant girl (Diana Koerner).

Ireland in the eighteenth century. Training for a career in the law, Harry Barry is killed in a duel over the purchase of some horses, leaving his wife Mrs Barry (Marie Kean) to bring up their only son Redmond (Ryan O'Neal) alone. It becomes her ambition to turn him into a gentleman.

Redmond, however, falls in love with his cousin, the flirtatious Nora Brady (Gay Hamilton) who encourages his advances until her eye is taken by wealthy English army Captain John Quin (Leonard Rossiter), who offers to pay off her family debts. The jealous Redmond challenges Quin to a duel, apparently emerging the victor, and is advised by Nora's brothers to flee to Dublin before he is arrested by the police. On the road, he encounters the notorious highwayman 'Captain' Freeney (Arthur O'Sullivan), who steals all of the money that Barry's mother has given him, as well as his horse.

Penniless, Redmond has no alternative but to enlist in the army, which is willing to take men to fight in the Seven Years War without inquiring as to their background. He meets up with an old friend, Captain Grogan (Godfrey Quigley) who tells him that Quin is, in fact, still alive and married to Nora. The duel had been a charade, designed to get rid of the lovestruck Barry and force the hesitant Quin into proposing. Redmond's gun had been loaded with harmless tow by Nora's brothers who, Grogan says, were anxious to hold on to a catch worth £1500 a year.

When Grogan is mortally wounded fighting overseas, he leaves all of his money to Barry, who soon sees his chance of escaping the army by taking the identity of a Lieutenant Fakenham and setting off under the guise of delivering urgent despatches. After spending a few days with Lischen, a German peasant girl (Diana Koerner), he continues on his way and meets a Prussian officer Captain Potzdorf (Hardy Kruger), but is soon unmasked as a deserter and forced to enlist in the Prussian army. Saving the injured Potzdorf from a blazing building, Barry is rewarded for his gallantry and sent to spy on the Irish Chevalier de Balibari

Lit entirely by candlelight – the gaming room sequence in *Barry Lyndon*.

(Patrick Magee), himself suspected of espionage. On meeting a fellow-countryman, however, Redmond reveals his true mission to the Chevalier and, together, they escape Prussia and embark on a career as gamblers.

The ambitious Barry wheedles his way into the affections of the wealthy English countess, Lady Lyndon (Marisa Berenson), who quickly falls under his spell. When her husband, Sir Charles (Frank Middlemass) dies, Redmond marries Lady Lyndon and in the process reinvents himself as English nobleman Barry Lyndon, although his roving nature soon leads him to neglect his wife in favour of other women. The marriage does, however, produce a son - Bryan - a year later, although Lady Lyndon's elder son by Sir Charles, Lord Bullingdon (Leon Vitali) deeply resents his new 'father,' and is rewarded for his insolence by several beatings. When Mrs Barry warns her son that, should anything happen to Lady Lyndon he would be left destitute, Barry sets about cultivating Lord Wendover (Andre Morell) in the hope that it may lead to a peerage.

The increasingly jealous Bullingdon, meanwhile, publicly accuses Barry of mistreating Lady Lyndon and swindling her estate. Before a gathering of many influential guests, Bullingdon vows to leave his home for as long as Barry remains there, and is set upon by the sorely provoked Barry. The fierce brawl which follows only serves to expose the fact that the older man is

not of true nobility and, as Wendover drops away from him, so his chances of the peerage are ruined, with mounting bills from creditors threatening to bring him to poverty.

Ill-fortune continues to dog Barry now, as his beloved Bryan dies following a horse-riding accident and Lady Lyndon turns increasingly to Reverend Runt (Murray Melvin) for spiritual consolation. Mrs Barry assumes management of the house and estate, attempting to break the clergyman's influence by forcing Runt to resign now that the estate no longer requires a tutor.

With Barry lost in drink and both her children gone, the heartbroken Lady Lyndon makes an unsuccessful attempt at suicide, which leads her adviser Graham (Philip Stone) to send for Lord Bullingdon. Together with Runt, they plan her rescue, with Bullingdon confronting a drunken Barry and challenging him to a duel.

As they face one another, Bullingdon's pistol misfires, and Barry honourably despatches his own bullet into the ground, only for his rival to insist that he has not 'received satisfaction' and fire off a shot at the second attempt, which hits its target. The wound is serious enough for Barry to lose a leg and, now led by Bullingdon, the family send Graham to visit the tavern where he is being cared for by his mother. Informed that he will receive an annual income of five hundred guineas from the Lyndon estate only on the understanding that he leave England forever, the crippled and defeated Barry sets off first for Ireland and then Europe, where his fortunes continue to decline. At Hackton Castle, Lady Lyndon again assumes control of her estate, surrounded by Lord Bullingdon, Graham and Reverend Runt.

* * *

With *A Clockwork Orange* still showing only in the London area as debates on that film's merits raged in the national press, a *Variety* report of October 1972 announced that Warner Bros were 'still in the dark over new Kubrick pic,' as information on a follow-up amounted to little more than confirmation that *Napoleon* had been shelved (again) and that the director's next - as yet untitled - picture would star Ryan O'Neal.

O'Neal was by that time one of the major box-office stars in Hollywood, having made his big screen debut just three years earlier in the unpromisingly titled *The Big Bounce* (1969) after 514 episodes of the television series *Peyton Place*. The nauseating but massively successful *Love Story* followed in 1970, with two comedies for the consciously knowing cinephile Peter Bogdanovich - *What's Up, Doc* (1972) and *Paper Moon* (1973) - fixing his screen persona as likeable if somewhat lightweight (in *Paper Moon* he had even been mercilessly upstaged by his ten-year old daughter Tatum - at the time the youngest ever recipient of the Oscar for best supporting actress).

Kubrick had originally presented Warner Brothers with a plot outline in which all 'names, places and dates were changes so no-one could filch from him a story in the public domain.' The story was eventually revealed to be William Makepeace Thackeray's long out-of-print first novel *The Memoirs of Barry Lyndon, of the Kingdom of Ireland, by Himself*, originally published as a serial in Fraser's magazine in 1844, as *The Luck of Barry Lyndon: a Romance of the Last Century*, with Thackeray using the pen-name of George Savage Fitzboodle. The scheming character of Redmond Barry was said to have been based in part on that of Andrew Robinson Stoney, an Irish adventurer whose tale had been told to Thackeray one evening by his friend John Bowes-Bowes, a descendant of the colourful Stoney himself.

Stoney had married a wealthy Newcastle heiress who he then mistreated, inheriting her fortune on her death. Turning his attention to the widow of the Earl of Strathmore, he assumed her aristocratic ancestral surname of Bowes when they married, but ended his days in prison after abducting his wife when she attempted to leave him. Redmond Barry's adventures loosely fol-

lowed this pattern, but the resulting book did not prove a great success when it first appeared, with the author apparently dismissive of it in later years, despite - or perhaps as a result of - the struggle of preparing each installment to order.

Stanley Kubrick's decision to film the tale was, if anything, the most surprising of his career, coming as it did on the heels of a couple of futuristic tales requiring the total creation of a society as it might be imagined to exist in years to come. As ever, his reasoning for choosing the subject was simply that he liked the story - he later revealed that of the full set of Thackeray's works on his bookshelf, he had first considered adapting *Vanity Fair* - previously filmed as *Becky Sharp* by Rouben Mamoulian in 1935 (the first feature to be filmed in three-strip Technicolor) - before settling instead on *Barry Lyndon*.

A full year was spent in preparing the picture - in which he again wrote the script alone - before Kubrick began filming the picture in late 1973. For the first time since his move to England a decade earlier, the director was unable to find a suitable location close to his home or in the surrounding area and, says designer Ken Adam, was 'against the idea of shooting in the studio and even of mixing studio sets with real ones,' so made the radical decision to go on location to Ireland - the setting of the early part of the book. This seems to have begun well enough, although a break in filming occurred when the owners of several country houses 'wanted them back over Christmas,' according to a *Sight and Sound* update. Shortly afterwards, the production moved back to England - partly, it was reported, the result of a telephoned threat supposedly from the IRA objecting to a film portraying the British Army being made in Ireland.

Whether this was the sole reason or not, Kubrick set Adam to work in finding locations in the English countryside and, in particular, finding suitable - i.e. architecturally authentic - houses and rooms to double as Lady Lyndon's Hackton Castle. These exteriors were eventually made up from at least four different houses, including Longleat in Wiltshire, Wilton (Salisbury), Petworth (Sussex) and, further north, York's Castle Howard (later famed as the location of television's *Brideshead Revisited*), with interiors hand-picked from an ever wider range of houses, as the film's end credits reflected 'special acknowledgements' to Corsham Court, Glastonbury Rural Life Museum, Stourhead House and the National Trust. John Alcott confirmed that 'every shot is an actual location. We didn't build any sets whatsoever. All of the rooms exist inside actual houses in Ireland and the south-west of England.' This ready-made system, however, could also create its own problems, with several of the houses open to the public. Alcott recalled that the crew often 'used certain rooms with visitors virtually walking past in the corridor' and, on other occasions, 'we had to work when they weren't

The beautiful Marisa Berenson as the gullible Lady Lyndon.

touring. We would shoot when they were changing from one group of visitors to another.' Other brief landscape shots were filmed in Germany by a second unit - as ever, under Kubrick's strict supervision.

In casting the picture, Kubrick retained several players from *A Clockwork Orange* - Philip Stone, Steven Berkoff, Anthony Sharp and Godfrey Quigley - in minor characterizations, with the excellent Patrick Magee again assuming a substantial supporting role as the disreputable Chevalier de Balibari. Also returning was Leonard Rossiter, seven years after his performance in *2001: A Space Odyssey* and turning in an expert semi-comic performance as the flamboyant but cowardly Captain Quin. Seen increasingly on television since his last spell with Kubrick, Rossiter was soon to begin his most successful period on the small screen with a long running and much-loved comedy series *Rising Damp* (1974-8), to be followed by the acclaimed *The Fall and Rise of Reginald Perrin*. Reviewing his screen progress

a few years later, he pinpointed a recurring feature in his career when he noted 'I do tend to work for directors a second time' - apart from his two pictures for Kubrick, he also worked with John Schlesinger (*A Kind of Loving*, *Billy Liar*) and Lindsay Anderson (*This Sporting Life*, *Britannia Hospital*) - 'and invariably in a much bigger role, which is a great compliment to me.' If nothing else, the significant number of players appearing for a second time ought to have silenced the notion that actors did not want to work with Kubrick more than once (a feature, as always, conveniently ignored in some quarters).

The remaining cast was again chiefly British and drawn from theatre and television, apart from leading lady Marisa Berenson, hailed by French fashion magazine *Elle* as 'the most beautiful girl in the world' - a title which usually proves unfounded and more than a little hindrance to any serious acting career (Vivien Leigh had once complained that she was considered 'too beautiful to be taken seriously'). The American-born daughter of a Parisian fashion designer, today Berenson would be labeled a 'supermodel,' but such titles had yet to be coined when she appeared on the covers of *Vogue* and *Playboy* in the late sixties. Making her screen debut at the age of 25, she was seen in quick succession in Luchino Visconti's *Death in Venice* and *Cabaret*, directed by Bob Fosse in 1972.

Unlike *A Clockwork Orange*, where Kubrick's screenplay remained almost slavishly faithful to the book (apart from the 'lost' final chapter), for *Barry Lyndon* he made a number of skilful and significant changes to the original - the first being in the film's opening scene, where Barry's father is killed in a duel (in Thackeray's original he dies of apparent natural causes during a visit to the races). Kubrick also invented the scene which followed, between Redmond and cousin Nora, before either streamlining or dispensing altogether with much of the incidental detail of the original. As with many Victorian novels, Thackeray's work contained numerous sub-plots and minor characters who could be lost without detriment to the overall story.

While Redmond is held up by highwaymen in Kubrick's version, Thackeray had his young hero taking pity on Mrs Fitzsimons - the victim of such a robbery - ultimately wasting most of his money on her. Further on, the German girl Lischen helps Barry to masquerade as Fakenham, the British officer, after both men have been brought wounded into her home. Kubrick had Fakenham robbed while enjoying a dip in the lake with a fellow officer, and Barry encountering the 'innocent' Lischen on the road, where he introduces himself as Jonathan Fakenham before agreeing to stay with her for a few days (although, at their parting, she bids him 'Auf Wiedershein, Redmond').

With one of those coincidences so beloved of Victorian literature, the Chevalier de Balibari had turned out to be no less than Redmond's own 'Uncle Barry' from his home town in Ireland, although Kubrick - wisely, given the extraordinary and not altogether convincing coincidence - did not mention any such relationship, with the screen Chevalier later disappearing without explanation following his attendance at Barry's wedding. Other changes saw Thackeray's Lady Lyndon merely threaten to kill herself ('knowing her character full well, and that there was no woman in Christendom less likely to lay hands on her precious life than herself'), while in the movie she did actually attempt suicide, although the narration suggests that this, too, was not an entirely serious effort, since she succeeded 'only in making herself ill by the small amount she had swallowed.'

Within the film, Kubrick used duels as a recurring feature of the story - apart from the opening shot and the Thackeray-based encounter between Redmond and the trembling Quin, Barry later shows his skill with a sword in maintaining the 'firm' of Balibari and Barry and ensuring that losing gamblers honour their debts as they make their way across Europe. Most devastatingly, the film-maker created the climactic final pistol duel between Barry and Lord Bullingdon - even more of a quivering wreck than Quin had been - which had not been in the novel. Thackeray's story was resolved by having Barry unmasked as a swindler and forced to leave England by Lady Lyndon's friends. After failing to recapture his former success as a gambler, he returns to England and is thrown into prison, where Lady Lyndon nevertheless insists on maintaining the agreed payments to him. Bullingdon has meanwhile been reported killed fighting in the American War of Independence, only to reappear many years later to give Barry a sound beating. Lady Lyndon - still in love with her estranged husband - refuses to see her son and Barry finally dies in prison as a penniless and pitiful drunk with only his old, doting mother for company.

Kubrick's skilled handling of the entirely new ending was both satisfying and dramatic. The recalled Bullingdon finally manipulates his mother into paying off the now-crippled Barry, whose screen incarnation has been notably less ruthless than in the novel (although, immediately following their marriage, we are told that Lady Lyndon 'was soon to occupy a place of not very much more importance than the carpets and fine paintings which formed the pleasant background of Barry's existence.'). The earlier courting of Lady Lyndon, as described by Penelope Houston in *Sight and Sound*, had involved his having 'to work very hard and very unpleasantly to net his heiress [in the book] .. with a combination of bullying, blackmail and cold connivance worthy of *Les Liaisons Dangereuses*... In the film, the business is virtually done with an exchange of meaningful looks across the gaming table.' Also omitted was Barry's wooing of another heiress prior to his setting his sights on Lady Lyndon, and the now unnecessary figure of Lord George Poyntings, an old flame who came to her rescue in banishing Barry from England. The Barry who emerges is admittedly an opportunist and social climber, but one who - at least in the early stages - is seemingly swept along by events taking place around him. Finally realising his ambition to join the rank of gentlemen, he is unable to cope with it, being unfaithful to his wife and ineptly squandering her fortune as well as any small amount of his own. Despite this, he ultimately attains a true moral decency during the duel - sparing the defenceless but unforgiving Bullingdon - only when it is too late for it to do him any good.

Significantly, Kubrick altered the narration of the story from the first-person, with Michael Hordern engaged as the all-knowing storyteller whereas Barry had revealed himself in the book to be 'essentially a braggart and poltroon,' as Richard Schickel wrote in

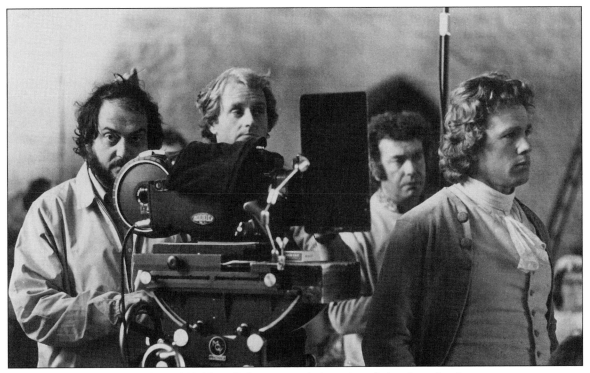

Ryan O'Neal (right) waits for a scene to be set up during *Barry Lyndon*,
as Stanley Kubrick (left) looks the other way.

Time, by 'so obviously exaggerat[ing] his claims to exemplary behaviour.' (Thackeray himself had once good-naturedly described the Irish as 'a nation of liars'). Kubrick, the article continued, 'uses silence to make the same point,' with the director explaining that 'People like Barry are successful because they are not obvious - they don't announce themselves.' More than any other Kubrick picture (every one of his features up to this point apart from *Spartacus* and *2001: A Space Odyssey* had employed a voice-over) - and perhaps more than any other sound feature - *Barry Lyndon* made extensive (but not intrusive) use of its narrator who, at certain points, even informed the viewer of events before they had actually taken place, while at the same time softening the often harshly cynical tone of the source book with its constant dismissals of females as either fat, slatternly, weak or faithless.

As was becoming customary with any new Stanley Kubrick picture, the project was to take a full three years to reach the screen from its first announcement in the press - a year of preparation, five months of shooting and a further lengthy period of editing and laying in the soundtrack. Originally budgeted at around $3 million, this had later reportedly swelled to $11 million, with Warners production chief John Calley insisting that 'It would make no sense to tell Kubrick, "Okay fella,

you've got one more week to finish the thing." What you would get then is a mediocre film that cost $8 million, instead of a masterpiece that cost $11 million. When someone is spending a lot of your money, you are wise to give him the time to get it right.'

This confidence that *Barry Lyndon* would prove to be not only a masterpiece but a profitable one, was not entirely shared by some members of the press, who speculated that Kubrick was out of step with current cinema trends and, at last, about to fall flat on his face (if anything, the director was anticipating by a decade the surge of interest in costume period drama). In the mid seventies, the most popular movies to be seen were *Jaws*, *The Exorcist*, *The Godfather*, *One Flew Over the Cuckoo's Nest* and *The Towering Inferno* - fast action, violent, controversial, star-studded movies more easily digested by audiences than a seemingly slow-paced, densely constructed tale of the eighteenth century.

Further doubts were voiced concerning the suitability of Ryan O'Neal as star. Even with the twelve months prior to shooting spent taking fencing lessons, German lessons, minuet lessons and reporting for a reported 51 costume fittings, O'Neal was still perceived by some as little more than a romantic light comedian. Kubrick maintained that he was the best actor for the part. 'He looked right,' said the director, who 'was confident that he possessed much greater acting ability than he had been allowed to show in many of the films he had previously done.' Following the film's release - to predictably mixed reviews in which O'Neal was often cited as a weakness in the movie's overall effectiveness - the director still felt his 'confidence fully justified by his performance, and I still can't think of anyone who would have been better for the part.'

For his part, Ryan O'Neal later echoed the views of many who had worked with the director before and since, when he noted that 'I loved working with Kubrick. Stanley brought out aspects of my personality and acting instincts that had been dormant. I had to deliver up everything he wanted, and he wanted just about everything I had.' The work was typically demanding and lengthy - eight and a half months - with the star nevertheless convinced 'that I was involved in something great.' His opinion of Marisa Berenson, however, had initially been less generous, apparently describing her as 'overbred, vacuous, giggly and lazy' on his first meeting with the model-turned-actress. Kubrick considered there to be 'a sort of a tragic sense about her,' which made her apt for the role of the somewhat ineffectual Lady Lyndon, with O'Neal later agreeing that her personal qualities actually suited the role perfectly, and predicting that she would be nominated for an Oscar (she wasn't).

In discussing *Barry Lyndon* later, Kubrick revealed a surprisingly flexible and versatile approach to directing the material, confounding those who considered that he worked to a strict, pre-determined blueprint. According to the *Time* article, Kubrick 'is unable to determine how to shoot a scene until he sees it fully dressed and lit,' with Ryan O'Neal adding that 'the toughest part of Stanley's day was finding the right first shot.' Kubrick was later quoted as saying that 'the visual part of film-making has always come easy to me,' but that the 'writing process never really stopped. What you have written and is yet unfilmed is inevitably affected by what has been filmed.' This might suggest that Kubrick was deliberately creating chaos where his actors would never know what was expected of them next, with scenes constantly rewritten on the set, but 'As long as the actors know the objectives of the scene, and understand their characters, this is less difficult and much quicker to do than you might imagine' - a notable difference to the working methods of, say, Alfred Hitchcock, who was said to have so rigidly pre-planned his own movies that he could virtually direct them from the back seat of his car.

With the lengthy shoot and switch of locations pushing the film well over budget, once again there were reports of multiple takes, with Murray Melvin asked to repeat one scene fifty times. Regardless of this, the actor - as the insidiously sly Reverend Runt - enthused over his director as 'a great believer in the man. I knew he had seen something that I had done, but because he was a good director he wouldn't tell me what it was.' To an outsider this might seem churlish on Kubrick's part, but Melvin insists that 'if someone tells you you've done a good bit, then you know it and put it in parentheses and kill it. The better actor you were, the more he drew out of you.' Richard Schickel made clear that Kubrick did not push his actors too hard unless he thought they were up to it - the relatively inexperienced Marisa Berenson and the film's child actors escaped such attention, which was reserved for 'only the established professionals he knew could stand up under his search for the best.' Schickel sensibly noted that 'there is no sadism in Kubrick's insistence on huge numbers of retakes.'

What was undeniable was the sheer ravishing visual beauty of the film - though, as Penelope Houston remarked, some critics even faulted this as being 'too deliberately beautiful.' Designs were heavily influenced by paintings of the period - Gainsborough, Hogarth, Stubbs and the like - especially, says Ken Adam, the work of 'Chadowiecki, an artist who intrigued both of us: a Pole who worked on the Continent, with a marvellously simple style and a remarkable gift for composition.' Star Ryan O'Neal relates that, at one point searching for the correct setting for a scene, Kubrick 'began to search through a book of eighteenth-century art reproductions,' looking for a particular painting and, once found, 'posed Marisa and me exactly as if we were in that painting.'

Costumes were replicas of genuine clothing of the period, even down to copying the way the clothes were originally made, while Ken Adam says that he even researched such minute details as 'the toothbrushes of the period, a mass of things which finally didn't appear on the screen.' What made the film so visually extraordinary was Kubrick's decision to shoot entirely by 'natural' light - comparatively simple enough in outdoor scenes, but requiring far greater care for interiors. John Alcott - again engaged as Director of Photography - produced the most impressive work of his career, later explaining that he and Kubrick maintained a 'close working relationship because we think exactly alike photographically.'

For *Barry Lyndon*, Alcott revealed, Kubrick returned to an idea discussed during pre-production of *Napoleon* - that of filming 'the way we see things.' Kubrick had 'always tried to light my films to simulate natural light' and, for this latest picture, 'we studied the lighting effects achieved in the paintings of the Dutch masters, but they seemed a bit flat - so we decided to light more from the side.' In many of the great houses used for filming, this was a natural way of presenting a scene, since all available light came from windows on one side of the room, which would have been 'virtually their only source of light during the period of the film.' As shooting took place throughout the winter, however, it was necessary to extend the hours of daytime available for filming by 're-creating natural light' outside of the window.

Elsewhere, however, the ultimate goal was to film by candlelight alone, if only a suitable lens could be found to achieve this. According to Alcott, 'Stanley finally discovered three 50mm Zeiss still-camera lenses which were left over from a batch made for use by NASA in their Apollo moon-landing programme.' To adapt this for use on a movie camera, however, was a major problem, and 'the kind of challenge that Stanley enjoys - there are few film-makers willing to pose such questions and take the time necessary to solve them. It took three months to perfect the new lens.'

Visual 'keys' which resurfaced in *Barry Lyndon* included the filming of the British Army near the opening of the picture as they provide an impressive display in the fields around Barrytown. Starting in mid-shot, the camera pulls out (the first of many such extra-long zoom shots switching the focus from the intimate to give a wider perspective) to reveal an extraordinary long-shot of the troops marching with military precision, clearly reminiscent of the wide-angle battle scenes from *Spartacus*. The later onward march of Grogan and his men into battle, felled like cards as they advance towards cannon-fire, recalls the tortuous attempt at taking the Ant Hill in *Paths of Glory*. Bearing in mind the amount of source material which Kubrick omitted, it is worth noting that the futility and barbarity of war was once again a theme in *Barry Lyndon*, albeit a minor one. Although the words were lifted almost straight from Thackeray's novel, Kubrick retained and refined the sentiment for his narrator to impart 'Gentlemen may talk of the age of chivalry - but remember the ploughmen, poachers and pick-pockets whom they lead. It is with these sad instruments that your great warriors and kings have been doing their murderous work in the world.'

The dividing of the story into sections was another familiar Kubrick device - Part I: *By what means Redmond Barry acquired the style and title of Barry Lyndon*, and Part II: *Containing an account of the misfortunes and disasters which befell Barry Lyndon* had the authentic style of Thackeray's novel even if these titles do not appear in his narrative. The closing, sombre and appropriate, epilogue - 'It was in the reign of George III that the aforesaid personages lived and quarreled. Good or bad, handsome or ugly, rich or poor, they are all equal now' - was another inspired invention of the screenwriter.

For a director who has often faced accusations of his pictures as being impersonal, soulless and empty, Kubrick revealed a surprisingly delicate approach to the story, with scenes of tenderness and even sentimentality - notably the romantic interlude between Barry and Lischen, and Redmond's early relationship with Captain Grogan, whose dying words to young Barry are 'Kiss me my boy, for we'll never meet again.' The death of the young Bryan Lyndon, too, was handled with great sensitivity - foreshadowed by an exterior shot of Castle Hackton under dark, brooding skies and a thick mist covering the lake, in stark contrast with the bright sunlit views of the house previously.

Unlike his previous couple of pictures, where Kubrick had been able to select a musical score from a variety of different styles, for *Barry Lyndon* this clearly would be inappropriate - synthesizers and avant-garde atmospheric pieces would simply destroy the period effect. The director had already chosen potentially suitable pieces of music before contacting composer Leonard Rosenman in Hollywood, whose previous credits included two mid-fifties movies starring his friend James Dean - *East of Eden* and *Rebel Without a Cause* - and, more recently, *Fantastic Voyage* (1966) and *Beneath the Planet of the Apes* (1971).

'Stanley called me on a Monday,' Rosenman said later, 'and said to come to England on Wednesday - the picture was finished. He said he had all the music picked out and all I had to do was arrange it. They told me Stanley worked this way.' According to the composer, Kubrick told him that 'the first thing I want to do is buy the theme from *The Godfather*' - an extraordinary choice if true, although Rosenman's objection - that 'the last time I saw *The Godfather*, it was about gangsters' - reveals a surprisingly static attitude for someone who presumably appreciated the value of music to create differing moods in different situations. That said, could Kubrick really have been considering Nino Rota's theme, given the sophistication he had shown with his choice of music previously? Quite apart from its recent familiarity to audiences, and the inevitable association with Coppola's epic, it is difficult to imagine it applied to *Barry Lyndon*.

Rosenman, it seems, was less than happy over his time spent with the director, subsequently claiming to have selected 'about half' of the music featured in the released picture. 'When I saw it,' he said later, 'I saw this incredibly boring film with all the music I had picked going over and over and over again. I thought, 'My God, what a mess!' He further claims that he 'was going to refuse the Oscar,' when *Barry Lyndon* was voted Best Original and/or Adapted Score Music at the Academy Awards (he didn't) but, with a superiority worthy of Andre Previn, stated that, as a 'Bach and Haydn specialist... the classical music used in the film is much closer to me, because I am a pianist.'

Seemingly less fraught - though not without its own peculiarities - was Kubrick's relationship with the renowned traditional Irish folk group The Chieftains, whose beautiful recording of 'Women of Ireland' ('Mna Na H Éireann') he was keen to include. According to John Glatt's biography of the group, Kubrick first telephoned chief Chieftain Paddy Moloney in Dublin as he was in the studio producing a new album. Apparently unfamiliar with the name of his caller, Moloney said he was simply too busy to get involved in anything else at the moment. A later conversation was more productive, with the Irishman invited to Kubrick's home where they discussed and agreed on using further Chieftains music in the film, although a suggestion that the group come to London to record was met with a pronounced lack of enthusiasm by the remaining members of the group who, Moloney said, were just back from an American tour and keen to take a holiday.

The situation was eventually resolved when Kubrick arranged for the entire seven-piece group - together with their families - to spend their holiday in London while recording a new track - eventually cut from the picture during final editing. Despite this - and although it was Rosenman, as the credited adapter/arranger, who accepted the Oscar - it was The Chieftains' haunting contribution which proved more effective - their recordings featured almost continuously throughout the first hour or so of the picture - and provided further evidence of Kubrick's eclectic taste and uncanny choice in music. (One sharp-eared reviewer - Kenneth Robinson in *The Spectator* - suggested that 'if you were wondering how Schubert's music could be played several years before he was even born [the composer lived from 1797 to 1828 - the closing shot of *Barry Lyndon* fixes the year as 1789], then that, no doubt, is what Kubrick hoped you would wonder. He is not the sort of director to make a mistake.' There was no argument concerning the authenticity of the remaining classical pieces, with Handel, Mozart, Bach and Vivaldi all born between 1685 and 1756).

Released in December 1975, *Barry Lyndon* confounded many reviewers who - no doubt thinking themselves the first to do so - queued up to impress their readers with suitably literary/period comparisons: Pauline Kael cleverly noted that 'if you were to cut the jokes and cheerfulness out of the film *Tom Jones* and run it in slow motion, you'd have something very close to *Barry Lyndon*,' while others were even critical of the obvious amount of care which had gone into the film. Marjorie Bilbow in *Screen International* complained that 'Kubrick's meticulous care in composing and collating these impeccable vignettes of the eighteenth century leaves his cast isolated in a clinically sterile vacuum.' Striving to draw a suitable comparison, she continued 'Like porcelain figures behind glass in a museum, they look wondrous lifelike but they do not sweat or weep real tears.'

Leslie Halliwell also pursued this line of criticism when he compared the picture to 'an art gallery in which the backgrounds are sketched in loving detail and the human figures totally neglected.' He found the movie to

be 'a curiously cold-hearted enterprise,' although *Variety* more generously considered it 'a most elegant and handsome adaptation.'

As was becoming the regular pattern, it was left to the serious film periodicals to fully explore the complexities of the picture - the *Daily Telegraph* merely remarking that 'It is a great curiosity of his *Barry Lyndon* that no reason at all emerges for [Kubrick's] personal enthusiasm [for the story] - unless it is a desire to present a series of pretty pictures.' This review conceded that the film was 'elegant,' but equated this with 'static,' further complaining of 'Ryan O'Neal, whose appearance, although romantic is hardly heroic, and who suggests throughout a meek rather than ambitious nature.'

Kenneth Robinson in *The Spectator* was more willing to adjust to the picture's demands as he hailed it as 'one of the most astonishingly beautiful films I have ever seen.. The whole film, including the ironic tone of the narration [a feature considered 'needless' by the *Telegraph*] is a rare experience. It lasts for more than three hours, but once you have adjusted to the pace it becomes a marvellous antidote to the more conventional world of cinema entertainment.'

In contrast to those who found the film to be visually attractive but of little substance, Richard Combs in *Monthly Film Bulletin* concluded that 'for all the detached, meditative quality of its historiography and scene-painting, *Barry Lyndon* emerges as perhaps Kubrick's most intensely human spectacle, comparable to *Paths of Glory* in its tragic confrontations that seem to throw whole worlds into the balance with individual lives.' Penelope Houston reflected that 'working within a system which expects a large return for a large outlay,' Kubrick has 'acquired extraordinary authority not by the standard success method of delivering more of the same, but by having the will to surprise.'

Much of this, however, seemed to be lost on cinema audiences as the film was promoted as a 'prestige' production - guaranteed to put people off after a year spent watching *The Godfather* and *Jaws*. *Barry Lyndon* - with a cost finally set at $12 million, and despite Kubrick's over-optimistic prediction that it would 'gross in nine figures' - took just over $9 million at American box-offices, although it was more popular in Europe where, once again, Kubrick made every effort to ensure that it would be screened to its best advantage. Julian Senior recalls that the director had his assistants examine and equip 'two thirds of the principal cinemas in France and Germany [which] didn't have a 1:66 mask, something which cost no more than a few pounds.' Without this minor adjustment, he said, the projected image 'would overlap a little on the sides.'

At the year's US Academy Awards, *Barry Lyndon* became the most successful film of Stanley Kubrick's career in Oscar terms, winning four awards - Cinematography (John Alcott), Set Decoration (Ken Adam, Roy Walker), Costume Design (Britt Soderlund, Milena Canonero) and Original and/or Adapted Music Score (Leonard Rosenman) - and further gaining two personal nominations for Kubrick (as Director and Screenwriter) as well as a Best Picture citation. Those three categories all went to *One Flew Over the Cuckoo's Nest*, which became the first picture since Frank Capra's *It Happened One Night* (1934) to net all five major awards (film, director, actor, actress, screenplay).

Even with this success, however, *Barry Lyndon* today remains probably the most elusive of Kubrick's major films. Unavailable on home video in the UK for many years, and - no doubt due to its considerable running time of just over three hours - seldom seen on television, *Barry Lyndon* rivals *A Clockwork Orange* as the least visible of the director's works (discounting early shorts and the withdrawn *Fear and Desire*).

For the stars of the picture, *Barry Lyndon* did not mark any significant change of direction: Marisa Berenson returned to her New York apartment (perhaps taking too literally some of the publicity based comparisons with Greta Garbo) and was not seen again until the annoyingly-titled *Some Like it Cool* three years later. Only a handful of roles have followed, in films like *Killer Fish* and *Sex on the Run*, although in 1990 she appeared with Clint Eastwood in *White Hunter, Black Heart*. Ryan O'Neal had hoped that this film would enhance his screen image, but moved straight from *Barry Lyndon* to another light comedy - *Nickelodeon* - again co-starring his daughter Tatum and directed by Peter Bogdanovich. Nevertheless, he remained proud of his work on this picture, and revealed his fondest memory of the experience when, after struggling with a particular scene for some time, he finally hit the mark and Kubrick 'found a way to walk past me, giving instructions to the crew - "Let's move on to 32, move those lights into the foreground," and so on - but as he passed me, he grabbed my hand and squeezed it. It was the most beautiful and appreciated gesture in my life, the greatest moment in my career.'

---

* Some interesting names to be found in the credits at the end of *Barry Lyndon* included renowned beautician Barbara Daly as make-up artist, and professional stage conjuror David Berglas as 'gambling adviser.' Also among the crew was Assistant Director David Tomblin, co-creator of Patrick McGoohan's ambitious 1967 tv series *The Prisoner*, filmed at Portmeirion on the Welsh coast and MGM's Borehamwood Studios, with Bernard Williams (Associate Producer of both *A Clockwork Orange* and *Barry Lyndon*) as Production Manager.

1980

THE SHINING

The first epic horror film.
NEWSWEEK

Hawk Films/Peregrine Productions. (Warner Brothers)
Produced and directed by Stanley Kubrick.

Screenplay: Stanley Kubrick and Diane Johnson, based on the novel by Stephen King. Executive producer: Jan Harlan. Produced in association with The Producer Circle Company (Robert Fryer, Martin Richards, Mary Lea Johnson). Director of photography: John Alcott. Steadicam operator: Garrett Brown. Production designer: Roy Walker. Film editor: Ray Lovejoy. Assistant editors: Gill Smith, Gordon Stainforth. Art director: Les Tomkins. Assistant director: Brian Cook. Camera operators: Kelvin Pike, James Devis. Focus assistants: Douglas Milsome, Maurice Arnold. Camera assistants: Peter Robinson, Martin Kenzie, Danny Shelverdine. Costumes: Milena Canonero. Make-up: Tom Smith. Make-up artist: Barbara Daly. Personal assistant to the Director: Leon Vitali. Assistant to the producer: Andros Epaminondas. Music score: Wendy Carlos and Rachel Elkind ('The Shining', 'Rocky Mountains'), Gyorgy Ligeti (Lontano), Bela Bartok (Music for Strings, Percussion and Celesta), Krzysztof Penderecki (The Awakening of Jacob, De Natura Sonoris No. 2). Songs: 'Midnight, the Stars and You', performed by the Ray Noble Band with vocal by Al Bowlly, 'Home', performed by Henry Hall and the Gleneagles Hotel Band. Twenties music advisers: Brian Rust, John Wadley. Music editor: Gordon Stainforth (uncredited). Sound recording: Ivan Sharrock, Richard Daniel. Sound editors: Wyn Ryder, Dino Di Campo, Jack Knight. Dubbing mixer: Bill Rowe. Second unit photography: Douglas Milsome. Helicopter photography: MacGillivray Freeman Films. Production manager: Douglas Twiddy.

Cast:
Jack Nicholson (Jack Torrance); Shelley Duvall (Wendy Torrance); Danny Lloyd (Danny Torrance); Scatman Crothers (Dick Halloran); Barry Nelson (Stuart Ullman); Philip Stone (Delbert Grady); Joe Turkel (Lloyd); Anne Jackson (doctor); Tony Burton (Durkin); Lia Beldam (young woman in bathtub); Billie Gibson (old woman in bathtub); Barry Dennen (Watson); David Baxt, Manning Redwood (rangers); Lisa Burns, Louise Burns (Grady children); Robin Pappas (nurse); Allison Coleridge (secretary); Burnell Tucker (policeman); Jana Sheldon (stewardess); Kate Phelps (Receptionist); Norman Gay (injured hotel guest).

146 minutes (cut to 144 minutes, then 120 minutes). Colour.

The Torrance family on the long drive into the mountains and the Overlook Hotel
(Shelley Duvall, Danny Lloyd, Jack Nicholson).

Jack Torrance (Jack Nicholson), a struggling, out-of-work writer, is interviewed for the position of winter caretaker of the vast Overlook Hotel, high up in the Colorado mountains and due to close for the season.

Although he is successful, Jack is warned during the interview by hotel manager Stuart Ullman (Barry Nelson) that he and his family will be completely isolated once the guests and staff are gone and the hotel shuts its doors – roads leading up the mountain are often blocked during the winter months, and even the telephone wires can be brought down by heavy snowfalls. Jack, however, assures Ullman that solitude and isolation are exactly what he is looking for as he plans to complete his current writing project. Almost as an afterthought, Ullman adds that a previous caretaker had suffered a breakdown during the winter some years earlier – 'what the old-timers call cabin fever' – and murdered his entire family before killing himself. 'My wife will love that story,' says Jack cheerfully.

Meanwhile, at home, five-year-old Danny Torrance (Danny Lloyd) instinctively knows that his father has won the job, and tells his mother Wendy (Shelley Duvall) that his imaginary friend Tony has warned him

not to go there because of 'redrum'. Wendy dismisses this and, soon afterwards, the family head for the Overlook to take on the winter job, arriving on closing day as the hotel is being run down.

As he is showing Wendy around the huge kitchens, hotel chef Dick Halloran (Scatman Crothers) makes telepathic contact with Danny and, when they are alone later, explains that he had recognized immediately that the boy had the gift – what his old mother used to call 'shining'. When Danny tells him of Tony's warning not to come to the hotel, Halloran insists that there is nothing here that can hurt him, but that he should keep away from room number 237 in any case.

Left alone, Jack attempts to work on his play as Wendy and Danny occupy themselves in and around the hotel, including the huge maze in the grounds, but becomes increasingly short-tempered as his writing fails to progress. The first snowfall finds them cut off by telephone, with contact only possible by short-wave radio with the local rangers.

Danny, meanwhile, has seen two mysterious, silent young girls in various parts of the hotel, and once briefly sees them both, murdered with an axe. As Jack becomes increasingly withdrawn, he suffers a nightmare in which he has killed his family. When Danny – having entered the forbidden room 237 – appears with a badly bruised neck, Wendy accuses Jack of being responsible for his injuries.

Taking himself off to the hotel's deserted Gold Room, Jack sits at the bar, eventually striking up a conversation with the phantom bartender Lloyd (Joe Turkel) until Wendy rushes in to tell him that Danny has told her he was attacked by a mad woman in room 237.

Investigating the room, Jack discovers a young woman in the bath, but when she approaches him and he kisses her she becomes a wizened old hag whose rotting flesh comes away at the touch of his hand. Fleeing back to Wendy, he nevertheless tells her that the room was empty and that Danny must have put the bruises there himself. When she suggests that they should get away from the hotel, however, Jack loses his temper and tells her that she will not ruin his chance of making something of himself.

Making his way back to the Gold Room, Jack enters what appears to be a packed ballroom where Lloyd pours him a drink 'on the house', which is accidentally spilled by a waiter who, while cleaning Jack's coat, identifies himself as Delbert Grady (Philip Stone). When Jack challenges Grady to admit that he was actually the caretaker at the hotel and had killed his family, Grady replies that he has 'no recollection of that at all', and that Torrance has 'always been the caretaker. I should know, because I have always been here.'

At his home, hundreds of miles away, Halloran becomes aware that Danny is in danger and, when his attempts to contact the hotel fail, sets out to rescue him as Grady convinces Jack that his wife and son need to be 'corrected' as his two daughters had been. Wendy is forced to defend herself as she fears Jack's increasing madness, discovering that his writing consists only of one phrase repeated over and over – 'All work and no play makes Jack a dull boy.'

As Danny discovers the significance of 'redrum' – 'murder' spelt backwards, as in a mirror image – Wendy knocks Jack unconscious and drags him to one of the food storage rooms where she locks him in, only to find that he has previously disabled both the radio and the snowmobile and that she is now entirely cut off from the outside world. Released from the locked room – apparently by Grady – the completely deranged Jack breaks into the apartment with an axe, as Wendy lifts Danny out of a bathroom window to escape, though she is unable to squeeze through herself.

The 'shining' is on Dick Halloran (Scatman Crothers) as a message from Danny calls him back to a final confrontation with evil.

Hearing a snow-plough approaching outside, Jack abandons his attempt at cornering Wendy as Danny hides in the hotel kitchen. Ambushing Halloran as he enters the lobby, Jack kills him with his axe before going in search of his son, who has escaped into the icy, snow-filled maze outside. As Wendy encounters more phantom guests within the hotel, Danny covers up his tracks in the snow and hides, as Jack rushes past him along the impenetrable maze corridors.

Making his way back out again, Danny rejoins Wendy and they escape in Halloran's rented snow-plough as Jack aimlessly struggles through the maze, eventually collapsing through exhaustion and freezing to death in the snow.

Inside the deserted Overlook, the ghostly strains of a 1920s dance band drift through the corridors leading to the empty ballroom, as the smiling face of a youthful Jack Torrance stares down from a framed photograph labelled 'Overlook Hotel, July 4th Ball, 1921'.

* ✳ *

There would have been little point in looking over Kubrick's previously filmed subjects when attempting to guess what he might turn to next. Ever since the pair of crime-thrillers of 1955, his choice of stories had followed no logical pattern, other than that they were subjects which he 'just fell in love with.'

If there was a clue to be found anywhere, it was in a *New York Times* article published during the making of

'Here's Johnny!'

2001: A Space Odyssey, where the director had hinted at a number of possible, but so far unfocused, ideas for future projects. One bore a working title of *Blue Movie* and would tell the story of a film director with sufficient influence and power to make 'the ultimate pornographic film starring two well-known screen lovers'. Terry Southern, who was around Kubrick at the time, went on to write a novel of that title with a main character – the movie director – known simply as 'Boris', who does indeed secure backing for a professional porn movie. The story remains unfilmed.

The other main contender was 'the world's scariest movie, involving a series of episodes that would play upon the nightmare fears of the audience' and, 12 years later, Kubrick set about finding a suitable blueprint for his first deliberate excursion into the horror genre.

According to *American Film* magazine, Kubrick had bought a wide range of novels dealing with the supernatural, which he then methodically began to read in his office. If, after two or three pages, he found the book unconvincing or uninteresting, he would then 'fling it across the room against the wall' – a quite uncharacteristic response according to those who knew him. The report continued with Kubrick's unnamed secretary listening out for these regular thumps against the wall in her outside office, until 'one day [how long had this been going on for?] the thumps ceased' and the 'puzzled secretary went in. Kubrick said, 'This is it.' He was reading *The Shining*.'

Stephen King had been born in 1947 in Portland, Maine, where he later attended university and taught English. His first novel *Carrie* had been an immediate best-seller, dealing with the story of a misfit teenage girl bullied by her schoolmates, whose discovery that she has supernatural powers enables her to take revenge on her tormentors. It also became the first of King's works to be filmed – in 1976 by Brian de Palma, with Sissy Spacek in the title role – followed three years later by Tobe Hooper's version of *Salem's Lot*.

Not yet the one-man horror industry that he has since become, King had continued with a string of successful horror stories, including *The Shining*, first published in 1977 and soon afterwards sold to Warner Brothers, who also bought King's own screenplay. Stanley Kubrick, however, declined either to read the script which King had written, or to engage the author as co-writer on the film, favouring an approach which he had followed previously – that of taking the novel merely as a starting point without feeling bound to follow it slavishly.

Instead, Kubrick chose to work on the screenplay with American writer Diane Johnson, who he had first met in 1976 when he considered filming her own comic-novel *The Shadow Knows*. Long discussions took place before a single word of the script was put to paper, with Miss Johnson later recalling how 'Stanley uses the Socratic method: is the husband a nice man? Does his wife love him? What kind of clothes would she wear? In this way, Kubrick got to know and understand his characters before setting them in motion for themselves, calling on a variety of texts to help in this unravelling, including *Wuthering Heights, Jane Eyre*, Edgar Allan Poe, Sigmund Freud even Bruno Bettelheim's *The Uses of Enchantment*, a study of fairy tales.

The first official reported sign that Kubrick was again at work two years after the release of *Barry Lyndon*, was a short item in the June 1977 edition of *Screen International* which named the director as about to start shooting 'an occult terror story' with Jack Nicholson pencilled in as lead. The as yet unnamed project was to go into production at EMI Elstree, formerly the MGM studio where *Lolita* had been filmed 16 years earlier. So prestigious was a new Kubrick movie, that EMI's own *Death on the Nile*, an all-star Agatha Christie whodunit, was forced to move to Pinewood Studios at Iver Heath. Elstree studio head Andrew Mitchell explained that he had been in negotiation with Kubrick since December 1976 about making use of the lot, which had been standing idle for some months as the British film industry once again entered one of its regular periods of crisis. George Lucas had filmed *Star Wars* at Elstree in 18 weeks during 1976 but, apart from this, the company's outlook had seemed even more bleak than usual as cinemas closed down across the country. Mitchell commented that he had to 'keep the customers we're dealing with' as Kubrick undertook his first studio-made film since *2001: A Space Odyssey*.

Pre-production was to last a further 12 months, and shooting finally began on 1 May 1978. Jack Nicholson was by now confirmed as star, having known Kubrick for many years, and the director was clearly pleased to have him on board. 'I think that he's on almost everyone's first-choice list for any role that suits him,' he said, adding that 'Jack is particularly suited for roles which require intelligence. He is an intelligent and literate man, and these are qualities almost impossible to act.'

Nicholson's performance in the leading role of King's story – that of Jack Torrance, the struggling writer with a drink problem – was later criticized by some as an excuse for the actor to run amok with his characterization but, examined more closely, reveals a carefully structured, surprisingly subtle and entirely logical portrait of eternal frustration (much of it self-imposed) leading to an eventual, violently total breakdown. This was one of several points at which Kubrick's film began to depart from King's version, which pays great attention to Jack's previous problems, his accidental harming of Danny, the reason for his being fired from a previous teaching job and his relationship with Wendy. Much of this is only briefly suggested in the film, mostly passed over in one of the conversations with Lloyd the bartender.

Jack's encounters with the supernatural intrigued Kubrick more: is it all in his mind? Is Lloyd – a facially skeletal presence, thanks to the bar lighting in the Overlook ballroom – actually real? What of the women in Room 237? And Grady, the former caretaker? (The ice-cold, delightfully sinister Philip Stone, in his third consecutive film for Kubrick, once again, ought to have refuted the tabloid-friendly theory that actors will not work with Kubrick more than once. Apart from Stone, Joseph Turkel was recalled for his third appearance under the director, 25 years after *The Killing*). Although the director later said that 'A story of the supernatural cannot be taken apart and analysed too closely,' he felt that the story fooled its audience into thinking that everything would be explained in the end, and for much of the movie, we can pass these things off as simply Jack gradually losing his mind. That is, 'until Grady, the ghost of the former caretaker... slides open the bolt of the larder door, allowing Jack to escape [and] you are left with no other explanation but the supernatural.' 'We had to decide if these were actual ghosts,' Diane Johnson told the *New York Times* before filming began, 'or the projections of people's imaginations. Either way there are implications.' This took up much of the pre-production discussion as, she says, 'Stanley didn't know from the outset what kind of ghost he wanted, but the audience will know by the end.'

Other differences between the two versions included Kubrick's removal of both the wasps' nest episode, and the discovery in the basement of the scrapbook, which told Torrance the entire sordid history of the Overlook and its previous owners. Jack, in fact, spent little time in the basement during the film, as the decision to rewrite the ending made it possible to dispense with the significance of the hotel boiler's propensity to explode, since it would now have no real part to play in the story's finale. Also left out was the irrelevant flashback structure, which explained how Jack had been offered the job only at the insistence of an old drinking buddy who owed him a favour following a hit-and-run episode.

In contrast to the huge all-British cast of *Barry Lyndon*, the story of *The Shining* would require only four major casting decisions. Once Nicholson was signed, Kubrick chose Shelley Duvall as the suffering wife after seeing all of her previous films and admiring what he called 'her eccentric quality – the way she talks, the way she moves, the way her nervous system is put together.' Duvall would suffer most during the lengthy shooting period, being called on to maintain a sense of paranoia and hysteria seemingly endlessly. She later admitted to feeling something of an outsider within the company although, paradoxically, this discomfort would be put to good use in her performance as Wendy Torrance, which Kubrick had altered from that described in the novel. King's Wendy had been both attractive and resourceful, leading Kubrick to wonder 'why she has put up with Jack for so long.'

Unlikely as it seems, Scatman Crothers had supposedly never heard of Stanley Kubrick before being cast as Halloran, the Overlook Hotel chef who reveals to little Danny just what 'the shining' is. Crothers had already enjoyed a lengthy career as a song and dance man and actor – appearing previously with Nicholson in both *The King of Marvin Gardens* (1972) and *One Flew Over the Cuckoo's Nest* (1975) – but had clearly never been involved in anything like this before, nor had he previously encountered a director remotely like Kubrick. 'I had to get out of a Snow-Cat and walk across the street,' he later said. 'No dialogue. Forty takes... he always wants something new and he doesn't stop until he gets it.' Even with such demands being made on him, however, Crothers still insisted that 'Stanley's like a god. He sees everything and hears everything.'

The child actor required to play Danny Torrance would be more of a problem, as Kubrick specified certain characteristics which would make him a realistic child of the two leading actors. At Kubrick's instigation, local newspapers were chosen in Denver, Cincinnati and Chicago to carry Warner Brothers' ad requesting parents to submit photographs of their children for an unnamed project. The director's assistant Leon Vitali – last seen in *Barry Lyndon* as Lord Bullingdon – then selected and interviewed more than five thousand boys before choosing five who he felt would be suitable – 'actually not a bad average' said Kubrick. Video auditions of the most promising few were sent over to Kubrick, with the whole process taking approximately six months.

In March 1978, the *London Evening Standard* claimed that a child actor had finally been selected for the role, although he 'would not be named until the film was completed.' Whether this was ever the intention – to create further intrigue around a set already being described as one of 'excessive secrecy' – *Variety* revealed the name of the five-year-old, Illinois-born Danny Lloyd less than a month later. The son of a railway engineer with no previous theatrical experience or background, Danny Lloyd's contribution to the film would create inbuilt problems which further lengthened the shooting schedule. Kubrick confirmed that 'Danny always knew his lines... his performance was wonderful' but English law allows children to work for only 40 days in a year, and a limited number of hours each day – three, according to Kubrick, although John Alcott set the boy's hours as 'from nine in the morning until four in the afternoon'.

Alcott further revealed that 'if [Danny's] time ran out, we would suddenly have to abandon his shooting and go on to something else.' This inevitably created difficulties, as the original, half-completed scene may not be returned to until a week later 'because it would have been silly to come back and pick up just that one scene and then lose a day of his shooting time.'

The final major factor in the making of the film would be the appearance of the sinister, deserted Overlook Hotel itself. An amazing feat of set building, all exteriors of the vast frontage of the hotel were filmed at Elstree – the building recreated from photographs of an existing hotel in Oregon. The Timberline Lodge sits not far from Mount Hood, a dormant volcano which threatens to destroy the hotel and everything around it, should it ever decide to erupt. A further example of a deviation from the book, incidentally, was the renumbering of the sinister third floor room which Halloran warns Danny never to enter but to which he will inevitably be drawn. Though numbered 217 in King's novel, Kubrick – as a favour to Timberline Lodge – altered this as, although the Lodge did have a room 217, it did not have a room 237.

Kubrick, inevitably, did not visit Oregon to shoot or personally direct those opening scenes, in which Jack drives up through the stupendous mountain landscape on his way first to secure the caretaker job, and later as he takes his family on their momentous journey. This does not suggest, however, that he was at all willing to let this sequence get beyond his control – each and every scene in a Kubrick picture is as he insists it should be – so that, when a second-unit crew 'reported that the place wasn't interesting', he approached the footage they had sent back with some reluctance, only to find the results 'staggering. It was plain that the location was perfect but the crew had to be replaced.' An independent company – McGillivray Films – specializing in helicopter-shot footage was hired by the director – who evidently knew exactly who he needed in any given situation – to come up with 'some of the most beautiful mountain helicopter shots I've seen.' In these and later establishing shots, the Overlook clearly does not have a maze built in the grounds opposite the main entrance – a non-King plot device created at Elstree, and one which permeated the entire set, with the hotel interior itself featuring endless, sharply turning corridors and Wendy at one point describing the vast kitchen as maze-like: 'I'll have to leave a trail of breadcrumbs to find my way out.') One further minor point – these aerial shots stand alongside the opening of Charles Laughton's sole directorial effort, the magnificent *Night of the Hunter* (1955), in which the camera tracks above the sunlit open countryside to reveal the approaching, all-encompassing evil of Robert Mitchum as fake preacher Harry Powell.

What made the studio set appear even more real was the design of the lighting by Kubrick's now regular collaborator John Alcott, director of photography. Involved with the project ten months before shooting began, Alcott was able to suggest that all of the hotel lighting should be actually built into the set itself – each chandelier and wall bracket was a genuine working unit – and operated from a central control room, with 860 intricately arranged 1000-watt spotlights representing daylight flooding through the huge hotel lounge windows and capable of being rotated to simulate different hours of the day.

One of the most discussed technical aspects of the film was the generous use of the recently developed Steadicam, operated throughout by its designer/inventor Garrett Brown, who had been presented with a special Academy Award in 1978 for this remarkably innovative piece of equipment. This gliding camerawork following Danny through the hotel corridors or later in the snowy maze created a further, entirely unsettling look to the film.

Kubrick had seen a Steadicam test reel as early as 1974, and immediately cabled the Cinema Products Corporation responsible for Brown's invention, promising that 'You can count on me as a customer. It should revolutionize the way films are shot.' Brown later met Kubrick in 1977 as the first sets for *The Shining* were being designed by Roy Walker. Excited by what the Steadicam could do, Kubrick encouraged Walker to redesign the hotel and the newly-suggested maze, in order to accommodate some of the tricks which Brown's new gadget could handle. Sharp, right-angled corners, staircases, split-level rooms – normally these features of a set would create endless difficulties for a camera operator whose end results would inevitably show evidence of running, walking, climb-

Stanley Kubrick with long-time cameraman John Alcott on the EMI-Elstree set of *The Shining*.

ing, shakiness getting around corners or simply an inability to get at certain angles or tight spots. Brown assured Kubrick that his new mystery stabilizer could cope with all of these things without the need for tracking or dolly shots.

Kubrick finally insisted that Brown be hired as Steadicam operator on the film, since he clearly had greater experience with the device than anyone else. Brown was happy to agree because 'Kubrick is, let's face it, The Man. He is the one director working who commands absolute authority over his project from conception to release print. The ultimate technologist, but more, his technology serves a larger vision which is uniquely his own.'

John Alcott was deeply impressed by Brown's work on the picture, telling *American Cinematographer* that 'I have great admiration for Garrett. Being such a tall man he can go anywhere and he seems to be so fit, it's quite incredible. This particular film is a great showcase for the device because the story takes place in a very large hotel and one could only explain it being large and complex by travelling through it, and one could only travel through it the way one did by using the Steadicam. Otherwise, I don't know how we would have done it.'

After a full year spent working on *The Shining*, during which he 'realized by the afternoon of the first day... that the word 'reasonable' was not in Kubrick's vocabulary,' Brown enthused that 'He is a film-maker in the most pure sense of the word. I learned a great deal about the making of movies from simply being on hand for the stupefying number of discussions which sought to improve one aspect or another of the production.'

Uniquely – and, in an entirely different sense, just as revolutionary – Kubrick's daughter Vivian was following the proceedings with a less innovative 16mm camera, eventually completing a 33-minute documentary *The Making of The Shining* which provides the only record to date of her father at work on the set with his cast and crew. With unlimited access to the set and behind the scenes, the documentary shows much of the unglamorous aspect of film-making – make-up, rehearsing lines, setting up lighting, arranging extras and rewriting scenes as they progress (or don't).

Kubrick's mother Gertrude appears briefly in her granddaughter's film, as Jack Nicholson explains the system whereby new pages of script are copied on different coloured paper to identify them as rewrites. Nicholson eventually declares that he has given up on using his script, adding that 'I just take the ones they type up each day.' Kubrick is seen owlishly rattling away on a portable typewriter as Nicholson and Duvall rehearse their lines –separately and each with their own assistant. If there is a lingering impression of the director from this rare view of him, it is one of seeming eternal patience and quiet persuasion: at one point he calm-

ly instructs Nicholson on his reading of a particular line by warning him that it 'looks phoney', to which the actor later responds in a separately filmed interview 'When I disagree with a director, I want them to have control.'

A tearful Scatman Crothers is barely able to explain that he is actually shedding 'tears of joy. I thank the Lord I've been able to work with such beautiful people,' genuinely reflecting that 'I'll never forget this' – perhaps more understandably so when his next picture turned out to be *The Harlem Globetrotters on Gilligan's Island*. For Shelley Duvall, however, the filming often became a major ordeal. In ill-health, and suffering from the stress of being away from home for so long, she conceded that she felt some jealousy at the attention lavished on her co-star – well illustrated by a sequence where visitors to the set are clearly unimpressed by either Kubrick, Duvall or even James Mason in full Edwardian costume (having dropped by from a nearby production) as they make straight for the enigmatic star. 'People do tend to be a bit sycophantic around [Jack],' said Duvall, who confessed to initially feeling some resentment towards Kubrick too, 'because he pushed me and it hurt,' although she came to view this as a 'necessary turmoil – we just differed in our means.'

If – as logic might suggest – such a visible record of Kubrick at work would have the effect of laying to rest some of the extravagant and bizarre rumours surrounding his working methods and personal style, inevitably, this was not entirely the case. Although the film – produced by Eagle Films (another in the Kubrick tradition of bird of prey company names) – was screened on network television by the BBC to mark the opening of *The Shining* in the UK, it has been little seen since, leading as always to mis/reinterpretation. A 1996 *Sunday Times* article inaccurately referred back to the documentary, describing Kubrick's constant bullying of Shelley Duvall, with the director 'shouting and swearing at [her]' before he proclaims 'I have no sympathy with Shelley' and drags her back to work.'

In fact, having viewed *The Making of The Shining* quite recently, this scene actually shows an almost twinkling Kubrick – like some mischievous uncle – advising those around him in mock-serious tones 'Don't sympathize with Shelley,' before adding directly to his sniffing female star – victim of an English cold – 'It doesn't help you' (in her characterization); a quite different emphasis altogether, but one which would make him seem more human, so has no place in the article in which it was mis-reported ('Tinseltown Tyrant Returns to the Set').

Only once is the director seen to become irritated – when an elaborate set-up involving snow machines and tracking cameras outside the Overlook facade is spoiled by Duvall's missed cue – yet even here there are no hysterics, as he quietly confronts the star, and throughout the rest of the documentary he is seen calmly explaining or organizing what he wants. Perhaps this is the thing which most irritates others – his very calmness in the midst of everything. Film and music editor Gordon Stainforth confirmed to me that Kubrick is 'not prone to hysterics or tantrums at all,' and sees the director as 'a very emotionally controlled person [whose] rather naughty sense of humour is likely to come out when others are losing their tempers. He seems to rather relish seeing other people losing it, I think!'

Despite her discomfort during the shoot, Duvall nevertheless told the unseen interviewer that Kubrick's 'volley of ideas and butting of heads' had brought out more than she knew she had in her. 'I really like him as a director and as a person,' she said finally. 'He taught me more than any of the other pictures I've done' – a view seemingly confirmed when she reported for her next role – Olive Oyl in *Popeye* – to be described by director Robert Altman as 'a changed artist.'

Jack Nicholson, meanwhile, revealed that, although there was always intense, constant pressure on any movie set, 'Stanley doesn't relate to it. He just deals with what has to be done.' As for his directing style, as others had remarked previously, Kubrick was clearly looking for something different from his cast – after Nicholson had spoken of his years of attempting to perfect what he considered a real performance, Kubrick demolished this with 'Yes, it's real but it's not interesting.'

Nearing completion – with an estimated one month still remaining – and with a shooting schedule which had stretched into February 1979, there came a further delay when one major set was destroyed by a fire which started one evening after Kubrick and his crew had left for the day. Although Warner Brothers noted that 'any lesser director would have simply cut the scene short,' Kubrick insisted on the set being rebuilt at a reported – but unconfirmed – cost of £100,000. The film finally wrapped in April after 46 weeks of shooting, with editing and dubbing taking a further 12 months.

Kubrick's choice of music for the film was as eclectic as ever, ranging from electronic treatments of classics (the menacing main title adapted by Wendy – formerly Walter – Carlos and producer Rachel Elkind) to Bela Bartok and the avant-garde tones of Krzysztof Penderecki, with authentic dance band music of the 1930s heard during the phantom ballroom sequences – despite the setting of the story, Kubrick chose a recording of British dance bands as opposed to American, for the simple reason that it worked best in the scene.

Although uncredited, Gordon Stainforth remains justly proud of his work as music editor on *The Shining* – a score so well-loved that it even has its own web-site! 'In this area I think I did make a considerable artistic input to the film,' he says. 'I know that Stanley was very happy with it.' As usual, Kubrick had a list of pieces of music he felt might work well in the movie, which he presented to Stainforth, who then 'spent hours listening to it, searching for moments/music cues which I thought might work.' Having selected suitable extracts from the recordings, and in order to achieve the precise effect necessary – i.e. to have a musical cue match exactly the images on the screen – Stainforth would on a few occasions ask film editor Ray Lovejoy to make small changes to the scene, even such minimal alterations as the removal or addition of just two or three frames of film whenever it proved impractical or unacceptable to edit the music itself. 'There was enormous trial and error on my part,' he says, although he recalls that 'Stanley gave me an enormous amount of leeway' – even to the extent of allowing Stainforth to add music to sequences which he had originally conceived as 'silent'. On other occasions – notably the washroom sequence between Jack and the icily enigmatic Delbert Grady – 'Stanley simply told me to keep the band music playing throughout in the background, and he left it to me to use whatever worked best from a short-list of favourites previously agreed.'

Of any further lengthy debate on the creation of the score, Stainforth says that he simply has 'absolutely no memories of any very long discussions, because there was this strong understanding between us as to how the music should work in the film. I'm sure if he'd disliked or disagreed with what I was doing, I'd have much stronger memories of his direction! That I think is my most abiding memory: that he quite definitely entrusted it to me.'

Originally called to the set in May 1979 to help edit Vivian Kubrick's documentary, by August Stainforth had moved into the cutting rooms as assistant editor on *The Shining* itself as Vivian considered how best to proceed with *The Making...* In early January, Ray Lovejoy fell ill and, with first assistant Gill Smith away from the production for one weekend and the final 40 minutes of the picture still to be cut, Stainforth was 'just putting on my motorcycle helmet to go home, when there was a message on the Tannoy system – "If Gordon is still here, Stanley would like you to come and cut some film!"'

Stainforth gives a rare and interesting insight into Kubrick's method of working as, although Kubrick did allow himself a screen credit as film editor since *Killer's Kiss* in 1955, 'I think it would be fair to say that Stanley was the true editor,' he says. 'He had absolute creative control, but at the same time he wanted maximum input from his technicians – he was always open to suggestions, if they were good enough.' Stainforth recalls that 'on the very first day I worked with him, we were cutting the scene of Jack axing the first door, and I suggested improving a cut we had done earlier.' Popular mythology would at this

Jack (Jack Nicholson) on the prowl in the Overlook maze. 'I ain't gonna hurt ya, Dan.'

point have the megalomaniacal director exploding into a fury, but in reality 'Kubrick said "OK, try it," and he saw at a glance that it was better. "OK, good," he said, and on we went.'

Editing continued at an increasingly hectic pace – Stainforth's diary reveals the lengthening hours spent cutting the picture with the director, on average at least 12 hours each day and at one point working for 48 consecutive days without a break. Dubbing had been completed 'working more or less round the clock, in about two and a half weeks in May – still very fast for a big feature – because the film was by then very behind schedule.' Typical of his final mammoth sessions as music editor during the second half of May were 14th-15th May 10 am to 6.30 am, 18th-19th May 9 am to 3.30 am, 22nd-23rd May 9 am to 5.30 am, often without lunch breaks. With the film completed, Stainforth returned to Vivian Kubrick's documentary, and worked with her throughout the summer, again with few breaks and even including 'on 27th-28th September a 34-hour day with no lunch break on the Saturday and no breakfast on the Sunday.' Working with the Kubricks, Stainforth concluded, 'is *hard* work!'

Stephen King had maintained what he called 'a considerate distance' from the set, apart from one visit where Kubrick mentioned a proposed new ending to the story. He had found the close of the novel to be 'a bit hackneyed and not very interesting,' and suggested that Jack, Wendy and Danny should be seen back in the hotel lobby on reopening day as Ullman greets another new caretaker and his young family. As they pass by, it becomes clear that no one else can see the Torrances – the latest ghosts to occupy the Overlook. When asked his opinion, King unpromisingly remarked that he thought 'audiences would feel cheated.' Whether as a result of this or not, Kubrick completely reworked the ending to feature the impenetrable maze which had replaced the sinister living topiary animals of the original novel – impossible to create satisfactorily on screen at that time.

Probably none of Kubrick's films has divided audiences quite so much as *The Shining* did – those who admire it do so for its mounting sense of unease, the performance of Jack Nicholson, the technical perfection of the sets and camerawork and the hugely disturbing emptiness of the Overlook Hotel, with its effect on an already vulnerable family – without resorting to schlock-horror tactics. Those disappointed by the film were almost all King fans aghast that Kubrick should change the novel at all. The author himself later admitted that, although 'I love the movies, and it's immensely flattering to have somebody want to turn a book into a movie,' he still had some reservations about the whole process, and whether he ought to take an active role in it or not. 'John Updike used to say it's the best of all possible worlds,' King said, 'when they pay you a lot of money and don't make the movie.'

His friend Chris Chesley thought after seeing the film with King that 'he didn't say so in so many words [but] he liked what the director had done, [although] the supernatural side of it had been excised,' despite which King's published comment at the time was that it was 'a beautiful film. It's like this great big gorgeous car with no engine in it – that's all.' In 1998 – making his first visit to England in 20 years – the writer addressed a packed Royal Festival Hall in London to discuss his career and reportedly declined to comment on Kubrick's film due to an unspecified 'contractual stipulation, but still made it clear he hated it.'

If so, then surely a 1996 television version boasting a screenplay by the author, who also acted as executive producer, would unquestionably give us the definitive account of *The Shining*? Directed by Mick Garris, the five-hour production starred Rebecca De Mornay and Steven Weber as the clean-cut couple among a gallery of made-up grotesques, slobbering and rotting visages. The much discussed hedge animals – absent from Kubrick's version – were (briefly) there, as were most other elements of the story – the hotel's chequered history and mob involvement, the steaming boiler, the wasps, the priggish characterization of manager Ullman (played by Elliott Gould) forced to recruit Jack against his wishes. Indeed, in five hours, it is not surprising that King could include most of the story's sub-plots and flashbacks and finally, yes, the hotel did go up in a huge fireball as in the book, with the resourceful Halloran, Wendy and Danny fleeing to safety – (almost) faithful to the original.

Elsewhere, the mini-series version deviated sharply even from King's own original, with the enigmatic Lloyd disappearing altogether to be replaced by Delbert Grady as a composite bartender/caretaker joining forces with a whole army of chalky-faced ghosts from the Overlook's past to gain control of the boy as if this were yet another episode of *The Omen*. The hotel itself assumes the persona of one of those things that go bump in the night, with moving furniture, flying chairs and extinguished fires which suddenly burst into flames in the grate. At other times, the screenplay even seemed to follow Kubrick's version more closely than King's novel, with Weber – whose descent into madness manifests itself in the appearance of a few pimples and bad

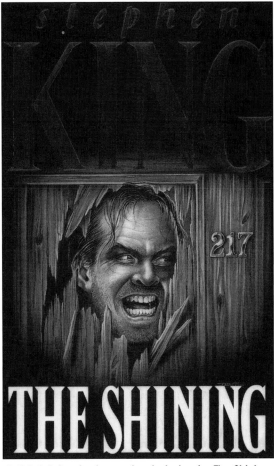

A Kubrick-inspired paperback design for *The Shining*.

teeth – apparently unable to resist a few sub-Nicholsonisms, as when he presses his face through the shattered apartment door and calls out 'Boo!' Jack Nicholson claimed that it had been at his suggestion that the much-imitated 'Here's Johnny!' had been included – a manic corruption of the regular opening to Johnny Carson's wholesome and long-running US television show *Tonight*. He further claimed that Kubrick had been away from America so long that he didn't understand the joke – unconvincing, since Kubrick famously received videotapes of American football games at his home on a regular basis and – even after 35 years – maintained links with the US media.

The television adaptation utterly destroyed the intrigue of the phantom ballroom scenes – so carefully established and maintained in Kubrick's adaptation – by inserting cutaway shots a couple of times to reveal that Jack is indeed alone and simply imagining things, but surely the most disappointing aspect of the King-written version was the cringingly awful closing scene in which we see a late-teenage Danny graduating from college some ten years later. The brave Wendy – fully recovered despite being hit repeatedly with a croquet mallet, and looking not a day older than the day she first set foot in the Overlook – sits proudly in the audience alongside Halloran, as Jack's immaculately tailored ghost makes a special appearance on stage to toe-curlingly reassure his boy 'I love you, Doc.' The charmlessly played Halloran wisely informs the boy's mom – unable to see what the two shiners can see – 'It's okay precious – all's well that ends well,' before Jack mercifully vanishes like some Nosferatu caught in the sunlight. Not in the novel, this embarrassing finale becomes inevitable following the previously botched sequence, in which a semi-lucid Jack nobly and self-sacrificingly fights off the ghosts of Grady and Howard Derwent to deliberately overheat the boiler and send the Overlook into the stratosphere. Such a sentimental ending is sadly all too familiar in several of King's other stories put on television, in which God, Love, the Family and the All-American Way are seen to conquer all of the evils in the world – and the undead world – in increasingly syrupy fashion. If the intention is to give audiences cosy reassurance, then the true effect is merely to diminish all that has gone before – in the process creating an entirely different vision than that which Kubrick intended, which was one of unease, and not altogether explainable. The final shot of Kubrick's *The Shining*, with the smiling face of Jack Torrance central amongst a group of 1921 hotel guests, is more unsettling than anything offered by the so-called 'real' version – and entirely consistent with what Diane Johnson had hoped: that the ending of the story would have 'the artistic satisfaction of a fairy-tale.' Kubrick's own litmus-test of the film's success was that it should be 'good enough to raise the hairs on the back of your neck... I hope the audience has had a good fright, has believed the film while they were watching it, and retains some sense of it.'

Mystifyingly, critics gave *The Shining* a deeply unfavourable welcome on its initial release, especially in the UK national press (the film was premiered in New York in May 1980, and opened in Britain just before Christmas). The *Daily Star* dismissed it as 'the biggest non-event of the year. It's not even scary,' while the *Financial Times* thought 'Kubrick's $18 million horror epic offers considerable boredom, laced with just a few effectively chilling moments.' Admitting that the hotel set 'looks absolutely splendid,' and the film itself was 'meticulously crafted,' they still found it 'cold and unengaging; the question mark that hung around Kubrick after the immaculate but calcified *Barry Lyndon* refuses to go away.'

Richard Combs in the respected serious journal *Monthly Film Bulletin* feared that 'The Kubrick magic for holding both audiences and critics in thrall seems to have come unstuck... *The Shining* confirms what *Barry*

Lyndon suggested; the seclusion has taken its toll,' as the director found himself out of step with fashion. Combs nevertheless concluded that '*The Shining* is an iceberg that may in time prove to be one of the great Kubricks (with *Paths of Glory*, *Lolita* and *Barry Lyndon*), or may be the start of a whole new Kubrick.'

Films in Review – as ever, not among the director's biggest fans – considered the film worthy of *two* reviews – the first declaring that 'the real horror of *The Shining* is in suffering two and a half hours of pablum', a statement guaranteed to send readers off in search of their nearest dictionary. My *Oxford English* gives four definitions of the word 'pabulum' as opposed to 'pablum' (which is listed as a proprietary brand of children's breakfast cereal – an unlikely parallel in the circumstances). Reviewer Pat Anderson may, unintentionally, have used the word in its context as 'that which nourishes and sustains the mind', but judging from the tone of the remainder of the review, seems more likely to have intended it as 'bland intellectual fare; an insipid or undemanding diet of entertainment,' as she further complained that the 'film looks static... everything is telegraphed long before it occurs.'

Their second – less fierce – opinion was that 'Kubrick may be out of touch, but he hasn't lost *the* touch,' despite his 'beginning to look like the least innovative director working today.' Jeffrey Wells thought that '*The Shining* may be a masterpiece, very predictable or very funny... Or maybe all three – or maybe none of the above.' Both reviews, however, considered Jack Nicholson – with Kubrick's assistance – to be guilty of 'mug[ging] all over the place... seems really to have lost control [and] in one sequence looks more like Harpo Marx' (though not in any Marx Brothers film that I can recall...).

By the time of these hatchet jobs (August/September 1980), the film had already been reviewed and released in the US, where the public clearly enjoyed it more than the British critics. *The Shining* had broken all opening box-office records in both New York and Los Angeles in June, yet Kubrick again recalled the picture – as he had with *2001: A Space Odyssey* – and cut its length by almost 26 minutes, in the process eliminating some minor characters altogether (a doctor and nurse in a completely deleted scene in which Danny is examined, and Tony Burton as 'Durkin', the garage owner who rents his snow plough to Halloran). Confusingly, all of these unseen characters remained in the film's end credits but were not seen in the UK until a print of the complete, full-length version surfaced on television in December 1989, although the shorter version remains most common, available on home video.

US reviewers had been generally more sympathetic to the picture, although *Variety* complained that 'With everything to play with, director Stanley Kubrick has teamed with jumpy Jack Nicholson to destroy all that was so terrifying about Stephen King's best-seller.' Richard Schickel in *Time* was more analytical, urging, 'it is impossible not to admire Kubrick for flouting conventional expectations of his horror film just as he did those of the sci-fi tale in *2001*.' Schickel hailed the film as 'daring', with Jack Nicholson managing to 'sustain attention in a hugely unsympathetic role... with a brilliantly crazed performance'. The review ended by suggesting that 'only those who find Stanley Kubrick to be one of the world's great living film artists will respond to [this film].'

Despite the public approval for the film as evidenced by the impressive box-office receipts, critical opinion appeared to be upheld when *The Shining* became the first Stanley Kubrick picture not to receive a single nomination at the American Academy Awards since *Paths of Glory* 23 years earlier. Such a snub must have rankled with both Kubrick and Warner Brothers, although the studio would have been happy with the picture turning a profit of more than $12 million on North American rentals alone, and *The Shining* was one of the ten most popular films in a year dominated by George Lucas' *The Empire Strikes Back*. (Other major box-office successes were *Stir Crazy, Airplane!, Any Which Way You Can* and *Smokey and the Bandit II*). *The Shining*, however, was still listed in the top 50 grossing films of the decade (1971–80).

Kubrick's horror film, however, has since been periodically reappraised – although it still divides audiences and critics alike, depending on your opinion of Stephen King's work as sacrosanct. The portrait of Jack Nicholson's leering face pushed through a splintered door panel has become one of cinema's iconic images –

more so, certainly, than any of the slew of horror slash movies prevalent at that time and which spawned – and I do mean spawned – increasingly awful sequels: *Halloween* (1978), *The Amityvile Horror* (1979) and the seemingly endless *Friday the 13th* (1980).

Australian journal *Cinema Papers* recognized this when they wrote 'In the context of the grotesque, it isn't usual to speak of nobility, but Kubrick's spirited exploration of some inner and outer limits may justify it.' Highlighting some of the film's bravura moments – 'when Jack's frustration brings a table maze to life' (a remarkable special effects shot) – the review picked out 'a scene in which Jack pursues Wendy up the Overlook's main stairway [which] brings the action right into our midst... Kubrick knows how to tease the audience in the sense that a maze teases.' Anticipating that there would be no *Shining II*, they correctly noted that 'Kubrick apparently wanted no survivors at the Overlook Hotel.'

What might have been the beginnings of a profitable – and artistically indefensible – series became, in Kubrick's hands, something considerably more than just another haunted house yarn, largely as a result of the director's own view of ghost stories, as he explained in an interview with *Newsweek* in May 1980. 'There's something inherently wrong with the human personality,' he said. 'There's an evil side to it. One of the things that horror stories can do is to show us... the dark side, without having to confront it directly.' Kubrick's analysis of the appeal of such tales continued with the theory that, 'If you can be afraid of a ghost, then you have to believe that a ghost may exist. And if a ghost exists, then oblivion might not be the end.'

---

* Despite his fine performance in *The Shining*, little was subsequently heard or seen of Danny Lloyd, other than an appearance as 'Young Liddy' in the 1982 *Autobiography of G. Gordon Liddy* – the everyday tale of a Nixon campaign fundraiser sentenced to four years in prison for his part in the Watergate scandal, but now a top radio talk-show host and sometime actor. Crime, it seems, does not pay – not as much as *The Oprah Winfrey Show*, anyway.

1987
FULL METAL JACKET

Vietnam can kill me, but it can't make me care.
TAG LINE FOR THE FILM

Natant Films. (Warner Brothers)
Produced and directed by Stanley Kubrick.

Screenplay: Stanley Kubrick, Michael Herr and Gustav Hasford, based on the novel *The Short-Timers* by Gustav Hasford. Executive producer: Jan Harlan. Co-Producer: Philip Hobbs. Associate producer: Michael Herr. Assistant to the director: Leon Vitali. Lighting cameraman: Douglas Milsome. Production designer: Anton Furst. Editor: Martin Hunter. Original music score: Abigail Mead. Songs: 'Hello Vietnam' (Tom T. Hall, performed by Johnny Wright); 'These Boots Are Made For Walking' (Lee Hazlewood, performed by Nancy Sinatra); 'Woolly Bully' (Domingo Samudio, performed by Sam the Sham and the Pharaohs); 'Surfin' Bird' (A. Frazier, C. White, T. Wilson Jr, J. Harris, performed by The Trashmen); 'The Marines Hymn' (Traditional, performed by The Goldman Band); 'Chapel Of Love' (Jeff Barry, Ellie Greenwich, Phil Spector, performed by The Dixie Cups); 'Paint It, Black' (Mick Jagger, Keith Richard, performed by The Rolling Stones). Sound recording: Edward Tise. Sound editors: Nigel Galt, Edward Tise. Dubbing mixers: Andy Nelson, Mike Dowson. Steadicam operators: John Ward, Jean-Marc Bringuier. Aerial photography: Ken Arlidge, Samuelsons Australia. Casting: Leon Vitali, Mike Fenton, Jane Feinberg, Marion Dougherty, Dan Tran, Nguyen Thi My Chau. Assistant directors: Terry Needham, Christopher Thompson. Production manager: Phil Kohler. Make-up: Jennifer Boost, Christine Allsop. Art directors: Rod Stratfold, Les Tomkins, Keith Pain. Technical adviser: Lee Ermey. Armourers: Hills Small Arms Ltd., Robert Hills, John Oxlade.

Cast:
Matthew Modine (William Doolittle/Private Joker); Adam Baldwin (Animal Mother); Vincent D'Onofrio (Leonard Lawrence/Private Gomer Pyle); Lee Ermey (Gunnery Sergeant Hartman); Dorian Harewood (Eightball); Arliss Howard (Private Cowboy); Kevyn Major Howard (Rafterman); Ed O'Ross (Walter J. Schnioski/Lieutenant Touchdown); John Terry (Lieutenant Lockhart); Kieron Jecchinis (Crazy Earl); Bruce Boa (Poge Colonel); Kirk Taylor (Payback); John Stafford (Doc Jay); Tim Colceri (doorgunner); Ian Tyler (Lieutenant Clives); Gary Landon Mills (Donlon); Sal Lopez (T. H. E. Rock); Papillon Soo Soo (Da Nang hooker); Ngoc Le (Vietcong sniper); Peter Edmund (Snowball); Tan Hung Francione (ARVN pimp); Leanne Hong (motorbike hooker); Marcus D'Amico (Hand Job); Costas Dino Chimona (Chili); Gil Kopel (Stork); Keith Hodiak (Daddy Da); Peter Merrill (TV journalist); Herbert Norville (Daytona Dave); Nguyen Hue Phong (camera thief); Duc Hu Ta (dead NVA).
With: 70 credited actors as the Parris Island recruits and Vietnam Platoon.

116 minutes. Colour.

The astonishing Lee Ermey as Gunnery Sergeant Hartman in *Full Metal Jacket* demonstrates his contempt for the presence of a jelly doughnut in his spotlessly clean barracks dormitory.

At the Parris Island Marine Corps Depot, a new batch of raw recruits begins training, which will turn them from inexperienced individuals into hardened marines – 'Ministers of Death, praying for war' – ready for duty in Vietnam when called.

Under the control of Gunnery Sergeant Hartman (Lee Ermey) – a brutal and inflexible monster of a commander - the young men gradually fall into an accepted routine designed to make them 'good marines'. Among the recruits – many of them renamed by Hartman as a means of enforcing his superiority over them and diminishing their own individuality – is the unconventional, comical Private 'Joker' (Matthew Modine), Private 'Cowboy' (Arliss Howard) – so named because he comes from Texas – and Leonard Lawrence (Vincent D'Onofrio), an overweight, childlike figure who Hartman immediately christens Private 'Gomer Pyle' and sets about singling out for special attention at every opportunity.

The relentless bullying of the recruits is borne by the majority, although the victimization of Leonard takes its toll as he fails at successive tasks and is unable to meet the physical demands of the training ground.

When Joker is promoted to squadron leader, in place of the negro Private Snowball (Peter Edmund), he assumes responsibility for Leonard, helping him through the rigorous training until he becomes an efficient member of the squad. At inspection, however, Hartman discovers that Leonard has hidden a doughnut in his foot locker and announces that, as the company has let him down, he will in future punish them all for Private Pyle's mistakes.

Soon afterwards, Leonard tells Joker that he feels everybody now hates him and, although Joker offers reassurance, the rest of the dormitory attack Leonard that night in his bunk, beating him with bars of soap wrapped in towels. Joker is coerced into taking part and, both intimidated and eager to be one of the group, beats Leonard more viciously than any of the others.

From then on, Leonard becomes increasingly withdrawn, although he still manages to complete his training, becoming in the process an expert marksman. The training finally ended, on their last day at Parris Island the new Marines are given their future assignments: Joker – who had once worked on his

The duality of human nature: Private Joker (Matthew Modine) in 'Born to Kill'/'Ban the Bomb' mode, followed into battle by Animal Mother (Adam Baldwin, left) whose own headgear pronounces 'I am Become Death.'

local newspaper – will become a war correspondent, while Cowboy and Pyle will join the 0300 Infantry in Vietnam. Leonard greets the news without emotion and, later, when Joker is patrolling the barracks, he discovers him, in the latrines, loading his rifle with a full magazine of live ammunition. Hartman confronts the deranged private, ordering him to put the gun down, only for Leonard to shoot him dead before turning the rifle on himself. He has achieved the destiny which Hartman had promised them all – to become a Minister of Death.

Some months later (January 1968) in Vietnam, Joker is working on the US military newspaper, *Stars and Stripes*, with photographer Rafterman (Kevyn Major Howard), covering mostly dull stories which are in

any case being censored to give an acceptable view of the war. There are only two kinds of story required: heart-warming human interest where US soldiers take pity on Vietnamese refugees, or combat reports which include the killing of significant numbers of the enemy. When Joker answers that he has not seen anybody killed, he is told to 'make it up'.

During the Tet holiday cease-fire, the Vietcong and North Vietnamese stage surprise attacks with devastating results. Joker's attitude towards the news singles him out, and he is sent by the editor to cover the action close to the front line. Eventually, he and Rafterman meet up with Cowboy's Marine regiment and join them as they advance on Hue.

During the march, the platoon's commander is killed by a volley of machine gun fire, and the remainder are sent on to scout ahead. When next-in-line Crazy Earl (Keiron Jecchinis) is killed by a booby trap, Cowboy takes uncertain command and the platoon find themselves lost among the rubble of a shattered town. As Eightball (Dorian Harewood) is cut down by a sniper while crossing an open space, Cowboy is unable to control his remaining men, and Doc Jay (John Stafford) – attempting to help his comrade – is also shot by the unseen sniper. Animal Mother (Adam Baldwin) defies Cowboy's order to retreat, and heads out to see what he can do, discovering that both Eightball and Doc Jay are dead, but finding the sniper's range, he signals to Cowboy, who – with Joker, Rafterman and a few others – runs across to him to decide on their next move.

As they shelter behind the corner of a building, however, the sniper picks off Cowboy through a hole which has been blown in the wall, and he dies in Joker's arms. Animal Mother and Joker determine to locate the sniper and, under cover of a smokescreen, they enter the artillery-blasted buildings. Joker eventually discovers the sniper but, as he prepares to shoot, his rifle jams, allowing the assassin to turn on him instead. As the sniper is revealed as a young Vietnamese girl, Rafterman opens fire, mortally wounding her. When Animal Mother orders that they should move on, Joker insists that they cannot leave the girl to die in agony. Eventually it falls to him to shoot her as she begs for an end to her suffering.

As the platoon march on towards the river under cover of night, lit only by the blazing remains of the town they have just passed through, Joker declares that he is 'glad to be alive... and I am not afraid.' He has made his first kill.

The Green Berets (1968) had been the first major film to deal with what was still being described as American 'involvement' in Vietnam, but remained little more than an ill-conceived vehicle for its director John Wayne to demonstrate his patriotic support for the war under the pretext of showing 'what our boys are going through out there.' Critics rightly described the film as more akin to a Second World War movie, with the Americans still assuredly the 'good guys' though in an utterly unfamiliar situation. That this remained cinema's only comment on the war – and, it is worth noting, a hugely popular one at the box office

– for more than a decade illustrates America's continuing unease with the subject.

In 1979, Francis Ford Coppola had taken Vietnam as the setting for a loose adaptation of Joseph Conrad's short novel Heart of Darkness – also incorporating the little-known true-but-denied-by-the-US-government story of Anthony Poshepny, unofficially sent into Laos under cover in 1961 to recruit a secret army from rebels in the Vietnam hills. Within months, Poshepny was commander of 10,000 militants, who – as with Colonel Kurtz in the Conrad story – accepted his orders without question, and he remained there until 1973, despite being several times ordered home by the US military – who, he claims, also sent an agent out there to assassinate him as an embarrassment to the government.

Apocalypse Now (1979), famously shot on location in the Philippines at a staggering (for its time) $40 million – had been originally budgeted at $12 million and took four years to complete due to illness (Martin Sheen – hired to replace Harvey Keitel when the latter was dismissed by Coppola – suffered a heart attack during filming), increasingly impossible weather conditions and natural disasters in the form of an earthquake which demolished $1 million worth of sets.

During Coppola's production period, Michael Cimino released The Deer Hunter (1978) – another Vietnam-based drama, though one which sought epic status on a different level as, Variety noted, 'various ceremonies and cultural rituals are explored, compared and juxtaposed – the wedding, the game [a forced round of Russian roulette at the hands of the Vietcong] and the deer hunt. It is up to the viewer to decide how these rituals fit together, and it is a big comprehension demand.'

Both The Deer Hunter and Apocalypse Now – the first mainstream picture to suggest that Americans had been guilty of anything other than honourable behaviour in Cambodia – were huge hits and Oscar-winners in various categories, but this did not lead to a sudden explosion of Vietnam war movies – at least not immediately, although by the time that Stanley Kubrick's next movie – his own take on the war – finally arrived on cinema screens, a full seven years after The Shining, it would be in almost direct competition with a handful of other films on the same subject.

The novel which eventually became Full Metal Jacket had been published in 1979 as The Short-Timers by Gustav Hasford – a former combat correspondent with the US Marine Corps in Vietnam. The title of the book refers to what was called 'a short-time' (385 days) tour of duty in Vietnam following training at the Parris Island base. Hasford – who denies that the book is autobiographical, although he did indeed serve with the same Division as Joker in the story and was involved in the Tet offensive – had spent seven years writing this, his first novel, which was then turned down by a number of publishers over a three year period.

The brutal horror of war has seldom looked so appallingly grim as in *Full Metal Jacket*.
Eightball (Dorian Harewood) becomes the second victim of the unseen sniper
as he attempts to retrieve his wounded comrade.

The author later explained to *Cinema Papers* his motivation for writing *The Short-Timers*, since 'the image of the Vietnam veteran as a cold-blooded psychotic is something the US government started when men were coming back saying "The war is wrong – we shouldn't be there".' Since the government line was that 'US servicemen don't say that sort of thing!' this made it necessary to concoct the theory that 'we were traumatized from seeing our friends blown up and didn't know what we were saying.'

Kubrick had come across the book in late 1983, and the following January it was announced as the first of a new three-picture deal the director had signed with Warner Brothers. The title would be changed to *Full Metal Jacket* because, Kubrick said, few civilians would be aware that 'Short-Timers' referred to the length of a Vietnam tour of duty. In fact, probably just as few would have known prior to this that the 'Full Metal Jacket' was an ammunition design – a lead bullet within a copper case designed to prevent the bullet from expanding or exploding on impact. Kubrick explained that this was called for by the Geneva Convention as a 'more humane' form of combat.

For the first time in almost 20 years – since *Dr Strangelove* in 1963 – Kubrick asked the author of the original novel to collaborate with him on the screen-play, with further contributions coming from journalist Michael Herr, who had also previously worked on *Apocalypse Now*, writing the narration voiced by Martin Sheen. Herr had covered the conflict most notably in *Dispatches*, published in 1978, in which he had stated that 'Vietnam was what young men had instead of a childhood,' and was said to have regarded the war almost like a movie – 'Not *The Green Berets* but *The Quiet American* or better still *Catch-22*.' Herr continued by pointing out that, 'For those who had been brought up on the powerful images of John Wayne's mythic heroism there was much that had to be unlearned if one was to understand what the war was about and thus stay alive,' and the resulting film would be about as far from the John Wayne-style war movie as it was possible to get.'

Kubrick's first act in setting the casting process in motion was to dispense entirely with the usual round of casting agencies and directors. Instead, he requested that video-tape auditions be sent direct to him via Warner Brothers' office in London. Determined not to sign a major star simply for box-office reasons, Kubrick told reporters that 'the average age of American marines was only eighteen. This is not going to be one of those films where ages are adjusted to accommodate Hollywood stars.'

This unconventional approach would at least have the advantage of Kubrick and his assistant, Leon Vitali, seeing 'each applicant personally' – in a three minute scene in which they were told to 'Wear a T-shirt and pants. Do a close-up and full length shot of yourself from the front, and a left and right profile' while giving a brief description of themselves – although this was also gleefully interpreted by the 'Kubrick-as-hermit/recluse' brigade as further proof of the allegedly eccentric director's fear of meeting new people. It also caused some resentment – unsurprisingly – from casting agencies, who complained of a somewhat disproportionate loss of business from this single production, warning that 'it's unlikely that a nice unknown American boy can afford to make a video.' Further insisting that 'We can provide unknowns,' the agency spokesman added that Kubrick 'certainly won't have the choice he would have had if he had used a casting director,' but finished by voicing the opinion 'I think he's very brave' – evidently resisting the obvious temptation to use the word 'foolhardy.'

Behind the camera, the reassembling of Kubrick's regular crew would be more difficult after a break of some four or five years. Among those few members of personnel available again were art director Les Tomkins, and Kubrick's brother-in-law Jan Harlan as executive producer. Most significantly, though, cameraman John Alcott here ended his association with the director, which had stretched back almost 20 years to *2001: A Space Odyssey.*

Although he had previously made himself available whenever a new Kubrick project was set in motion, Alcott had been settled permanently in America since 1983, where he was now a much in-demand cameraman. His wife Sue later told *American Cinematographer* that, despite the extraordinary demands involved with working with Kubrick, this had always been 'a labour of love for John because he knew he was learning so much. God knows how many cinematographers would love to have been in John's shoes, to have gone though the experiences he went through with Stanley. I think it was the highlight of his life to work with him, and one of the virtues Stanley saw in John was his insurmountable patience to want to get it right.'

Alcott himself had told *Newsweek* following the release of *The Shining* that 'If Stanley was a cinematographer he'd be the most sought after one in the world.' Crediting the director with having made him a cameraman in the first place, he added that 'For many films after I've worked on a Kubrick film, I'm using ideas he gave me.' Nevertheless, at the time of the preproduction for *Full Metal Jacket*, Alcott opted not to join the team this time around, saying that he 'wanted a break from Kubrick's demanding schedules.' He

remained instead in Hollywood where, in 1986, he photographed his last picture, *No Way Out* – a remake of *The Big Clock* (1947) directed by Roger Donaldson and starring Kevin Costner and Gene Hackman. Shortly before Kubrick's *Full Metal Jacket* was finally due to open the following year, the cameraman had been in discussion with David Lean over a planned version of Joseph Conrad's *Nostromo* but, two weeks later on holiday in Cannes with his wife, he was dead following a massive heart attack. (*Nostromo* was seemingly doomed never to materialize, since Lean himself died without ever getting it into production.)

Alcott's replacement on the Kubrick set was to be Douglas Milsome who, like his predecessor, had come up 'through the ranks', having been focus-puller on both *A Clockwork Orange* and *Barry Lyndon*, and then second-unit director on *The Shining*. He also shot some first-unit footage on that film when Alcott was called to work on another production as Kubrick's schedule lengthened. 'I'd like to carry on where John left off,' remarked Milsome. 'I learned a lot from him working with Stanley. I use the Alcott System all the time now. He lit like no other cameraman, so effectively with little or no light... that's what I like and it's what Stanley likes too.'

Further unconventional aspects of the production followed when Kubrick – who, clearly, was unlikely to decide to shoot the picture in Vietnam itself, nor risk the unpredictability of the Philippines as Coppola had done – found what he decided were all of the suitable locations for *Full Metal Jacket* within 30 miles of each other in the North-east area of London. The exteriors and training grounds of Parris Island military camp were actually filmed at a genuine army base at Basingstoke, although interiors were built at Enfield, with the vast barrack set recalling the similarly huge kitchen of *The Shining* both in size and in glistening, spotlessly anonymous decor.

For the second part of the picture, set in Vietnam itself, the city of Hue was recreated on disused land owned by British Gas in London's Docklands, with buildings already in the process of being demolished further attacked with explosives and a wrecking ball – 'with the art director telling the operator which hole to knock in which building' – to give an accurate sense of a war-zone still under relentless bombardment. This was no easy transformation: Kubrick had studied still photographs of Hue from the relevant period (1968) before settling on a square-mile area of the British Gas site which had 'the same 1930s functional architecture... not every bit of it was right, but some of the buildings were absolute carbon copies of the outer industrial areas of Hue.'

Unlike the increasing number of other films dealing with Vietnam – where an obligatory jungle setting was apparently everything – Kubrick had chosen to

Stanley Kubrick examines a video playback in London's Docklands during the filming of *Full Metal Jacket*.

show an entirely different and unexpected profile of the country, and one which not all reviewers and critics would appreciate – one sniffily remarking that 'the light quality was obviously not right for Vietnam,' for the benefit of the majority of his readers who had never actually seen Vietnam (which, presumably, the writer had, and which was no doubt the entire point of the comment). The director, however, remained enthusiastic about what he called 'a tremendous set dressing and rubble job,' explaining that 'you couldn't build [a set like] that if you spent $80 million and had five years to do it. You couldn't duplicate all those twisted bits of reinforcements. And... you'd have to find some real rubble and copy it... no one can make up a rock.' This attention to detail had scarcely been exercised before, with most earlier productions content to decorate a landscape with polystyrene rocks tied down to prevent them from blowing away or being displaced by actors brushing against them. Kubrick had intriguingly discovered, while making *Paths of Glory* 30 years earlier, that 'every rock has an inherent logic you're not aware of until you see a fake rock.'

To fill out the set, an estimated 100,000 artificial tropical plants were ordered, together with genuine North African palm trees brought in from Spain by Anne Edwards of Berkeley Nurseries, described as 'an up-market office plant company' but, as a result of their involvement with *Full Metal Jacket*, launched on an entirely new career as supplier of exotic foliage for film-makers from their base at Heathrow, within strik-

ing distance of the major British studios Shepperton, Bray, Elstree and Pinewood. Kubrick had phoned Edwards in April 1985 to enquire as to the likelihood of securing 60 palm trees, for which the specialist quickly guaranteed delivery. Edwards then flew to Spain and photographed 300 trees for the director to choose from – the selected, 40-year-old trees soon uprooted and sent to England, with Kubrick apparently paying export duty of £1,000 per tree before he was able to take delivery. Edwards later defended the ethics of supplying comparatively rare trees in such a way by pointing out that the location filming of *Apocalypse Now* had resulted in 'probably thirty acres of natural palm forest [being] completely razed.' At least some of the palms in Kubrick's picture survived the experience.

Yet more logistical problems involved the use of US military tanks and equipment in the picture. After exhausting the traditional routes, Kubrick eventually advertised in a war fan magazine, receiving a response from a Belgian lieutenant colonel – who also happened to be a Stanley Kubrick fan – with an offer to take six US M47 tanks out of service from the Belgian army and ship them across to Britain. (Inevitably, when the film was completed, the director was faced with the dilemma of being left with a considerable arsenal of rifles, mortars and military supplies, and was forced to hire an international arms dealer to dispose of these surplus items.)

With a cast of virtual unknowns – Vincent D'Onofrio with only one movie to his credit (*The First*

Turn On, released in 1983), and original Joker Anthony Michael Hall replaced by the equally unfamiliar Matthew Modine – the film began shooting in August 1985 and, although the actual schedule was set for around six months, was not finished until September 1986 – the production being shut down for almost five months following injuries to some of the major players, though not all of these were entirely connected with the shooting itself. Modine broke an arm rehearsing one scene, but the longest delay was caused by a near-fatal car crash involving Lee Ermey, who came off the road driving through Epping Forest at one o'clock in the morning and, according to Kubrick, 'broke all his ribs on one side... tremendous injuries, and he would probably have died except he was conscious and kept flashing his lights [until] a motorist stopped... Lee was out for four and a half months.' (Interesting to note here that Kubrick kept faith with Ermey – despite such a delay and the resulting cost – rather than replace him. Those who speak less well of the director's relations with his actors may wish to reflect on this.)

The six months actually spent shooting the film would still be considered a lengthy period by many other film-makers, but Douglas Milsome later explained to *American Cinematographer* that the time spent on a Kubrick picture was certainly not the result of any slacking on the director's part, since 'he loves to do things quite differently than what's ever been done before... and you work very hard to make something which bears his mark.' This experience could be both difficult and rewarding for the cameraman, who revealed 'I've actually had a lot harder time working for a lot less talented people than Stanley. He's a drain because he saps you dry, but he works damn hard himself and expects everybody else to.'

There may have been some who questioned Kubrick's credentials to make a film on the Vietnam war, since he had been in England throughout most of the sixties when the conflict was at its most intense. By the time *Full Metal Jacket* was ready for release, *Platoon* (1986) had already won Oscars for Best Picture, Director, Editing and Sound Recording, with much of the film's allegedly 'authentic' flavour credited to director Oliver Stone's status as a genuine Vietnam veteran. *Variety* noted that Stone 'obviously had urgent personal reasons for making this picture,' and the director would return to the subject again two years later with *Born on the Fourth of July* (1989) starring Tom Cruise as paralysed Vietnam veteran-turned-activist Ron Kovic.

Platoon, coincidentally or otherwise, dealt with the same incident of the war as did *Full Metal Jacket* – the so-called Tet Offensive, which became a major turning point in the public response to the conflict. With the first US advisers being sent to Vietnam in 1959, by 1967 there were half a million Americans in the country charged with helping the pro-West South Vietnamese government resist what was seen as a potential Communist take-over of South East Asia, led by the Vietcong of North Vietnam. While the American public were assured by news reports that the war would soon be over, the US military had been warned that a major offensive was about to be launched by the Vietcong during the unofficial cease-fire marking the Buddhist New Year Festival of Tet at the end of January 1968, when many south Vietnamese soldiers would be allowed home on passes to visit their families.

With the embassy at Saigon overrun on the morning of the 31st, and US Marines ambushed at Hue, the ensuing battle lasted for 26 days before the Americans regained control of the two cities, losing more than 1,500 dead in the process. With no territorial advances made by the Vietcong, who suffered casualties of over 40,000 during the offensive, this could still have been claimed a US victory – on paper, at least – but, instead, led to the American public questioning why there had been calls for so many reinforcements, why it was claimed that the US embassy had not been entered when there was firm evidence to the contrary, and why the supposedly all-but defeated Vietnamese had been able to inflict so much damage and injury. Student demonstrations and marches outside the White House would become a familiar sight from now on, as the conflict lingered on until, in 1973, a new president – ironically, the later disgraced Richard Nixon – ordered the withdrawal of US troops from a war they obviously would never be able to win. By 1975, South Vietnam had been absorbed by the Communist North.

Unlike *Platoon* and *Born on the Fourth of July*, *Full Metal Jacket* began well away from Vietnam, at the Parris Island training camp where young recruits are shorn of all individuality – symbolically, we see each of them having their heads shaved during the opening credits sequence – and brutally moulded into killing machines in an 'eight week college for the phoney-tough and the crazy-brave.' The dehumanizing, humiliating treatment of the men had never been so graphically portrayed as here, and much of the credit for this must go to Lee Ermey, himself a former Parris Island drill instructor who had originally been engaged as technical adviser to the production following similar assignments on *Apocalypse Now*, *The Boys in Company C* (1977) and *Purple Hearts* (in 1984, also acting in each movie – predictably as a drill instructor, although as an uncredited helicopter pilot in *Apocalypse*). 'I wanted that role so much,' he said later of his call to the Kubrick set, 'I stole it.'

Another actor had been originally cast as Sergeant Hartman but, according to Ermey, 'I turned up in my old Smokey Bear uniform and got my boys doing push-ups. I think I made quite an impression.' Ermey in fact came to *Full Metal Jacket* prepared with a tape recorded, non-stop barrage of verbal abuse which, Kubrick later claimed, ran to some 240 transcribed pages – a far cry from the overly sentimental approach towards drill sergeants in most movies. Kubrick compared Ermey's performance with that of Lou Gosset in *An Officer and a Gentleman* (1982), a 'film [which] clearly wants to ingratiate itself with the audience. So many films do that.' Hartman was never going to evolve into the 'drill instructor [with] a heart of gold – the mandatory scene where he sits in his office, eyes swimming with pride about the boys and so forth... sentimental bullshit'. *Full Metal Jacket's* sergeant may be a brute, with the ceaseless abuse harbouring a basic truth – 'A rifle is only a tool – it's a hard heart that kills' – even if it is sometimes unconventionally presented, as when – with apparent sincerity – he lists Lee Harvey Oswald as a suitable role model for his men by virtue of his Marine training: What one motivated marine and his rifle can do.' Of the sergeant's complex personality, Kubrick continued, 'Unless you're living in a world that doesn't need fighting men, you can't fault him – except maybe for a certain lack of subtlety.'

Ermey claimed to have written his own opening speech in the film 'with Kubrick. Then we just oiled the camera wheels, did a walk-around test and had it in the can in three takes,' although cameraman Douglas Milsome remembers the events somewhat differently, with at least 25 takes involved. Shortly afterwards, however, the actor suffered his car accident, which shut down the production for several weeks. By the time Ermey returned to the set, Milsome says, 'He'd improved no end as an actor. I think he polished up his part quite well, so we did that particular scene again. It was well worth it because he was so much better.'

Kubrick was clearly impressed by Ermey's range – and not simply as an actor, although he gives an ultimately astonishing performance in the film, and one which opened up a whole new career for the instructor-turned-adviser-turned-actor, later cast in many big-budget Hollywood movies including *Mississippi Burning, Sommersby, Se7en* and *Dead Man Walking*. Kubrick had been equally struck by Ermey as a character in his own right, grimly admiring what he described as 'the greatest collection of off-the-wall insults we have heard.' Some of the few printable comments as he surveys his recruits for the first time – 'Did your parents have any children that lived? You're so ugly you could be a modern art masterpiece' – are indeed great comic one-liners, yet buried amid such a wealth of obscenity that even this eventually has little effect. Hasford later revealed that he had received complaints over the language in the book, but insisted that he had actually toned this down. 'Everything a Marine says is dirty,' he added.

This opening 40 minutes set at Parris Island is superbly sustained by the director, switching from the in-barracks barracking of the men – 'I am fair... To me

you are all equally worthless' – to the physical aspect of training out on the parade ground and obstacle course. Seldom are any of the raw recruits allowed any sign of individuality, although the voice-over suggests that Joker at least has retained something of his innate cynicism. The sole outwardly individual member of the troop is Leonard Lawrence – renamed by Hartman as Gomer Pyle (gormless leading character of a mid-sixties US television comedy series) – who stands apart from the rest for all of the wrong reasons. Leonard is slow-witted, physically unfit and, to someone like Hartman, a born victim who instantly becomes the prime target for the worst of his abuse, both verbal and physical. Unable to tell his left from his right, Pyle is next seen being forced to march behind the orderly rows of men with his trousers around his ankle and sucking his thumb – something which admirers of the Marine training programme insist would never be allowed to happen. Kubrick – with the first-hand knowledge of Lee Ermey as his back-up – merely responded 'They always say that.'

Such an impact does Ermey make while on-screen that his disappearance at the end of the Parris Island scenes renders the remainder of the film slightly flat. That death scene is terrifyingly set up, with the now-deranged Lawrence/Pyle an expert with his rifle – Hartman's greatest success story, in fact – out to fulfil his destiny by claiming the first kill of the platoon. The extraordinary look on Vincent D'Onofrio's face, says Douglas Milsome, was apparently described during shooting as the 'Kubrick crazy stare.' The cameraman explains: 'Stanley has a stare like that which is very penetrating and frightens the hell out of you sometimes.' By whatever means, Milsome continues, 'he is able to inject that into his actors as well.' Scary...

As the film enters the Vietnam war, the story becomes episodic and, by turns uneventful and devastatingly horrific. The civilian population consists only of prostitutes and their pimps, all of them thieves. The boredom of life away from the front line tells on Joker, who has allowed his cynical attitude to surface away from Parris Island, never more so than when he is instructed as to the two acceptable types of story he must report. Kubrick summed up this attitude by claiming that, 'The Americans in Vietnam were encouraged to lie. If a couple of shots were fired on patrol it was good to say that you'd killed two gooks, and if you said two somebody would make it eight.'

Joker's equivocal stance in the midst of all of this is demonstrated by his cloth helmet camouflage bearing the legend 'Born to Kill' while, on his tunic, he wears a badge carrying the CND peace symbol. Challenged by a general, he claims that it is meant to represent the 'duality of human nature' – an instant off-the-cuff explanation. Amidst a new platoon including 'Animal Mother' (Adam Baldwin), whose own headgear states

'I am Become Death' (see the opening of the chapter on *Dr Strangelove* for the relevance of this phrase), Joker is thrown into combat without any real warning, in the process watching his fellow recruit Cowboy killed, as well as two other platoon members, all of them cut down by the same sniper.

The revelation that the sniper is in fact a young Vietnamese girl is, in truth, not such a shock as Kubrick probably intended it to be, although the scene of her own death is immensely powerful. Wounded by Rafterman as she was about to shoot Joker, she is clearly dying, with the unforgiving Animal Mother suggesting they leave her there to rot. It is only the remains of any humanitarianism left within Joker which argues that she cannot be left to die.

There follows one of those infrequently occurring moments in Kubrick's films – the second in this particular film – in which a character is faced with a moral dilemma and forced to act against his nature in order to follow the required course of action: as far back as *The Killing*, Timothy Carey – after engaging in friendly conversation with an appreciative black car park attendant – had been forced to resort to racist abuse, as a means of gaining the necessary uninterrupted moments to carry out his part of the plan. In *2001: A Space Odyssey*, Bowman is forced to release Poole's body into space as he looks for a way of re-entering the spaceship Discovery. Spartacus must kill Antoninus, who he loves as a brother, to spare him from being crucified.

Now, in *Full Metal Jacket*, Joker is forced a second time to act as his comrades expect him to, to prove that he is 'one of them.' Earlier, at Parris Island, as the recruits attack Leonard in his bunk, beating him as retribution for their being punished in his place by Hartman, Joker (up until that point, Leonard's support and defender) is goaded into joining in and, after a moment's hesitation, beats him more enthusiastically than the rest. This is the turning point for Leonard who, from then onwards, begins to lose himself in his muddled determination to escape being either a failure as a Marine or hated by his group, talking to his rifle and eventually killing the two men who have brought him to this insanity – Hartman and himself.

At the film's climax, Joker is now faced with the dilemma of leaving the Vietnamese girl sniper to die or else, as Animal Mother eventually relents, 'finish her off here and now' as she begs for someone to shoot her dead. In an agonizingly long close-up on Joker's face – estimated by Kubrick to be over a minute and a half – he finally pulls the trigger and watches as his first kill becomes a sickening reality. This event has finally hardened Joker, who is next – and finally – seen joining the rest of the platoon as they march away from Hue, singing 'The Mickey Mouse Song' as they go.

The irony of the song is typical of Kubrick – recall

'We'll Meet Again' from *Dr Strangelove* – but overall, music plays a less noticeable part in *Full Metal Jacket*, although those selections included still provide some surprises. Most other Vietnam movies appear to suggest that Marines listened to a non-stop backdrop of Jimi Hendrix, The Doors and Jefferson Airplane – fashionable in retrospect, but actually seldom heard on mainstream radio in 1966–8, and probably more a reflection of the individual directors' preferences than of the authentic listening of the period: not all Marines were as turned-on as the pre-Woodstock hippie generation they left back home.

Kubrick later recalled that he had 'checked through Billboard's list of Top 100 hits for each year from 1962 to 1968' so as to avoid any anachronisms, but also looked out for songs which 'played well with a scene.' In particular, he cited the use of 'Surfin' Bird' by The Trashmen, which 'suggests postcombat euphoria – which you see in the marine's face... the pleasure one has read described in so many accounts of combat.' Other music included the bland country-and-western 'Hello Vietnam' which opened the film as the young recruits' heads are roughly shaved, transformed by their later experiences to the closing 'Paint It, Black' by The Rolling Stones over the end credits. Very little original music appeared in the film, with what there was supplied by Kubrick's daughter Vivian – the child in *2001* and later director of the *Shining* documentary. Here she was anonymously credited under the name of Abigail Mead but identified by reviewers almost immediately. Her contribution to *Full Metal Jacket* consisted of a heavily percussive sequence during the Marines' training – strongly reminiscent of Alex North's music for the corresponding section in *Spartacus* – some further avant-garde style pieces which cleverly segue from and complement sounds of either gunfire or machinery (note particularly the use of creaking, swinging iron which leads into a music track) and the menacingly moody electronic atmosphere reflecting Pyle's mental torment as he prepares to shoot Hartman, reprized later as Joker takes the decision to make his first kill.

Some reviews – with some justification – have accused Kubrick's films of being misogynistic, and clearly women play little central part in the majority of his movies. Discounting the pre-written *Spartacus* and the unavoidably female presence of *Lolita*, there have been few significant women in Kubrick's oeuvre – in *Full Metal Jacket*, the only women seen are either Vietnamese prostitutes or the young sniper – and Australia's *Cinema Papers* took the theme of this latest Kubrick movie to be 'that men destroy each other when they deny the female in themselves,' although the review never fully explored the theory other than to recount that 'the only references to women are obscene' – mainly in the drill hall sequences where Hartman leads the recruits in a series of singalongs of varying sexual explicitness. Several articles also noted that exactly 30 years had separated *Full Metal Jacket* and *Paths of Glory*, and looked to Kubrick's use of the lone woman amid a group of fighting men at the end of each picture – the innocent peasant girl in the earlier film compared to the cold-blooded assassin later. Questioned on the significance of this, Kubrick was dismissive: 'That resonance is an accident,' he said, adding that 'the scene comes straight out of Gustav Hasford's book.'

The virtual absence of women in *Full Metal Jacket* – and the dubious nature of those few who do appear – does not necessarily imply a misogynistic attitude. We do not come away from the film having seen women exploited in the same sense that they have graphically been abused in, say, *Casualties of War* (1989) or *Platoon* (1986). Prostitution has become an integral part of any war – and, consequently, any war film – and the ambiguity of Joker's feelings about the sniper are equally felt by the audience: she has murdered his friends in cold-blood, but she is still only a girl. What would a gentleman do – except that there are no gentlemen among the marines in Vietnam.

While *Paths of Glory* had been hailed as one of the greatest anti-war films ever made, *Full Metal Jacket* found itself drawing the same comment from those reviewers who recognized that this was not just 'another Vietnam war movie' at a time when *Hamburger Hill* and *Good Morning Vietnam* were about to reach the public in the same year, soon to be followed by *Casualties of War*, taking its place alongside the lengthening roll of movies portraying American soldiers' atrocities in some seemingly concerted effort to atone for the atrocities themselves – as though by admitting their sins, they could be wiped clean – or else making some political statement.

Kubrick's film stands with and apart from these others. Without dwelling on the behaviour of the Marines and on any brutal ill-treatment of the mostly unseen Vietnamese, Kubrick deals, instead, with the dehumanizing process of what military preparations for war do to the minds and sensibilities of young men. There may have been similarities with *Paths of Glory* in the film's determined anti-war stance, but there was also the sense – as had been made clear by the narrator to *Fear and Desire* – that this was also about any war which in this case just happened to be in Vietnam.

Kubrick and Douglas Milsome had aimed for an almost documentary visual style, achieving a 'desaturated, grainy look' by the use of a high speed film set at an extra high speed which, the cameraman explained, 'we were pushing a little beyond where it would've given us a really solid black.' The presentation of a realistic style of war footage was also later a significant factor in the effectiveness of Steven Spielberg's much-praised re-creation of the D-Day landings during the opening half hour of *Saving Private Ryan* (1998) with, again, muted colour and a grainy, harsh look to the film. Spielberg – who is and seems likely to remain one of the most popular and successful film-makers in the history of the cinema – nevertheless appears unable to resist the sometimes distracting and inappropriate streak of sentimentality which runs through all of his films – *Schindler's List* (1993) and *Saving Private Ryan* included. Where Kubrick differed from not only Spielberg but virtually every other director was in his willingness to deny his audience an easy ride. *Full Metal Jacket* makes no attempt at being likeable or comfortable to watch, with an ending described by *American Cinematographer* as 'the most disturbing, despairing and cynical of any Kubrick film. In the 30 years since *Paths of Glory*, the brilliant but naive young film-maker has apparently lost whatever faith he had in the humanity of the human race. At the end of *Paths of Glory*, Kubrick's soldiers are able to rediscover their souls, but in *Full Metal Jacket* they have lost theirs irretrievably.'

Such a dark, discouraging story – one which would have been labelled as 'too downbeat' for studios in an earlier decade – cannot simply be dismissed as such; Kubrick's skill is far too great for that, although some reviewers still found their expectations disappointed. The normally supportive Richard Combs in *Monthly Film Bulletin* thought Kubrick's career 'beginning to loop a predestined loop [and] *Full Metal Jacket*... full of echoes of just about every other Kubrick movie.' Accurately drawing comparison to *Spartacus* in that 'it begins with a training programme, climaxed with a murderous assault on the drill instructor, before the processed but humanly unformed hero is launched into the world,' Combs still found 'Kubrick, unable to turn it into a rattling good yarn [and] unsure how to make it one of his subject films,' finally dismissing the ending – with its 'enigma about the co-existence of destructive and compassionate instincts in man' – as 'not only unresolvable, it fails even to be an interesting question.'

The *Morning Star* recognized that 'there have been so many films made about the Vietnam war, ranging from the jingoistic to the sentimental,' but that 'Hot on the heels of *Platoon* comes Stanley Kubrick's *Full Metal Jacket*, which is neither.' The director, they said, 'has made a powerful and disturbing film which brings forward a new slant on familiar material,' while Tom Hutchinson in the *Mail on Sunday* considered that, 'if you think you have been here before, think again. It is the genius of Kubrick to make us look afresh and appalled at the conflict of war – and to make it a vision of enlightened truth.' Hutchinson boldly hailed the movie as 'one of the best films of the year' while, in *The Scotsman*, William Parente found Kubrick's latest effort 'less perfect than *2001*; less imaginative than *Dr Strangelove*; less ambitious than *Barry Lyndon*. But the man cannot make an uninteresting film, and for insight and perception it knocks its competitors for six. If you must see a film about Vietnam, this is the one.' *Cinema Papers* summed up their feelings on the film's closing sequence by noting that 'as the Marines stride to perdition with the sounds of Walt Disney on their lips and the thought that the dead know only that it is better to be alive... Kubrick offers only the despair of a latter-day Conrad.'

Brian Baxter in *Films and Filming* noted that Kubrick had 'made few direct political points' – a distinct and welcome change from the constant railing of Oliver Stone, who also highlighted a high level of drug misuse among US troops; something which Kubrick considered irrelevant – but that its seemingly negative virtues: 'harsh, unrelenting, passionless (on the surface), pessimistic, painfully realistic,' conversely made it the best film of 1987. 'It's about relationships,' he continued, 'special forms of madness, about the ill-treatment of women (as sex objects) and about war – its idiocies and atrocities. It concerns itself less with the politics of the war than with its dreadful inconsequences.' Perhaps that is the coldest thing about *Full Metal Jacket* – wrongly attributed to its director – and ultimately about war itself: that whatever happens in these isolated incidents, nothing really changes. The death of the three Marines, the killing of the sniper, the death of the entire platoon afterwards if it should come to that (as, indeed, it might) will have no overall effect on the war, as any similar incidents will not change any other war. War itself is the brutal, heartless entity which dehumanizes and makes men cold. Kubrick – a non-participant in the war or in the military – merely observes and illustrates this from the position of an artist.

Full Metal Jacket was a major box-office success, easily recouping its $17 million cost and – following the shunning of *The Shining* at the Academy Awards – receiving an Oscar nomination in the Best Screenplay based on material from another medium category. Douglas Milsome's work behind the camera was regrettably overlooked, as was Kubrick's as director. In an unexpected result, however, the 'US campaigners against screen violence' picked *Full Metal Jacket* as one of the best releases of the year, explaining that 'the action-packed film portrays violence realistically as a human tragedy'.

Films and Filming warned that the film 'demands concentration and a form of stamina alien to audiences in these days of pap and cinematic trash,' but insisted that 'the excitement [which Kubrick] brings to each genre he tackles' made it even more desirable that he produce work more often. 'It is a sad indictment that we have waited seven years since his last film,' Baxter wrote, 'and a further five since *Barry Lyndon*. Let's hope that the gap is shorter next time.'

PART 4
SWANSONG

1999
EYES WIDE SHUT

No comment.
HARVEY KEITEL

(Warner Brothers)

Produced and directed by Stanley Kubrick.

Screenplay: Stanley Kubrick and Frederick Raphael, inspired by the book *Traumnovelle (Rhapsody: A Dream Novel)* by Arthur Schnitzler.

Cast: Tom Cruise; Nicole Kidman; Sydney Pollack; Marie Richardson; Todd Field; Alan Cumming; Thomas Gibson; Tres Hanley; Vinessa Shaw; Leelee Sobieski.

151 minutes. Colour.

So what was Stanley Kubrick doing for 12 years? With the appearance of *Full Metal Jacket* in 1987, past experience suggested that a new project might be announced - or at least rumoured - within a couple of years, as indeed it was.

In August 1989, the *Independent* reported that *Napoleon* was once more on the starting blocks, even though Kubrick had earlier been quoted as saying he doubted that he could do justice to the story in just three hours. Now, however, he was said to be budgeting for a call sheet requiring 40,000 infantry and 10,000 cavalrymen, and telling US writer Joseph Gelmis 'I think it's extremely important to communicate the essence of these battles for the viewer, because they all had an aesthetic brilliance that it doesn't require a military mind to appreciate.' To suggest that any war might be described as 'aesthetic' was bold enough, and Kubrick further - tellingly - noted 'it's almost like a great piece of music or the purity of a mathematical formula.' Within weeks, however, *Napoleon* had once more ground to a halt, to be replaced by an entirely new project.

Writer Brian Aldiss' 1974 book *Billion Dollar Year Spree* (a history of science fiction), had named Stanley Kubrick as 'our greatest science-fiction writer.' Over lunch, the two men discussed possible projects, until Kubrick suggested that they come up with an original story which would 'gross as much as *Star Wars*.' Easier said than done, it seemed, as nothing further came of that idea.

In 1982, Kubrick bought the rights to Aldiss's late sixties tale *Super-Toys Last All Summer Long*, the story of a five year old boy who - unaware that he is in fact an android - cannot understand why his mother does not love him. Despite Aldiss's protests that the 2000 word piece was too short to form the basis of a movie, Kubrick reminded him that he had done just that with Arthur C. Clarke's *The Sentinel* (basis of *2001: A Space Odyssey*). According to the writer, 'One of the many sensible and perceptive comments [Stanley] made over the years was that a movie consists of, at most, sixty scenes, whereas a book can have countless scenes [which were] very difficult to boil down to make a film. Much easier to take a short story and turn it into a major movie.'

Super-Toys remained on the shelf, however, while *Full Metal Jacket* went before the cameras. Then, in 1988/89, Aldiss was asked to collaborate on a screenplay to be called *A.I.* - short for 'Artificial Intelligence' - and spent six months working 'ten hours a day, eyeball to eyeball' with Kubrick although, by the end of that time and having 'written the equivalent of three novels' they were still getting nowhere as 'Stanley kept having more and more ideas' and the story moved on in ever changing directions. 'My favourite was when David and Teddy got exiled to Tin City,' said Aldiss, 'a place where the old model robots, like old cars, were living out their days.'

Aldiss's involvement with *A.I.* ended when he took a two-week break in Florida and, he says, was told on his return that he had violated his contract, which included 'an undertaking that I wouldn't go abroad while I was working with Stanley Kubrick.' In his defence, Aldiss noted 'I sent him a postcard didn't I!' and still expressed the - unlikely - hope that he would be able to work again with Kubrick, who he 'remember[ed] with great affection.'

Kubrick persevered with the story - first with a science-fiction writer called Bob Shaw, then with Ian Watson and even at one point calling in Arthur C. Clarke to provide a scenario - only for the project to stall in the early 1990s when 'technological difficulties' made it impossible for the picture to continue - the best special effects available were simply not good enough for what Kubrick had in mind, although an unnamed source promised that 'it is an enormous project that is on the back burner for a while.'

In 1991, a select few managed to see a new Stanley Kubrick film when a 10-15 minute home movie was presented during a civil court action brought by the director against a neighbour for the cutting down of some 68 trees bordering the Childwickbury estate - two dozen of them carrying preservation orders. Kubrick did not attend the court hearing, but was described to the press by Julian Senior as being 'Green before anyone knew the word. Stanley's major concern is the fact that there is not much woodland left,' with his own land said to be a 'sanctuary for foxes, kestrels and other wildlife.' The claim for damages - £40,000 - was successful.

On to April 1993, and *Variety* headlined with 'Kubrick's got his next pic,' confidently announcing that the 'enigmatic director' was to 'begin filming this summer on his first film in more than six years.' The untitled project was 'set during the aftermath of the fall

**Stanley Kubrick on the Pinewood set
of *Eyes Wide Shut***

of the Berlin Wall, and centers on a boy and a young woman on the road in Eastern Europe.' Joseph Mazzello - child actor soon to be seen in *Jurassic Park* - was to play the boy opposite either Uma Thurman (denied by her agent) or Julia Roberts ('possible'). What made the story more intriguing - and at the same time more improbable - was the suggestion that Kubrick intended to shoot the film far outside of the UK in Eastern Europe, with locations reportedly already chosen in Poland, Hungary and Slovakia.

Sight and Sound were clearly less impressed by what they considered to be Kubrick's 'notoriously inflated ego,' concluding that 'going on past form, [that] is more or less all that anyone is likely to know about the film until it premieres.' The title of the mystery project was leaked as *Aryan Papers*, based on the novel *Wartime Lies* by Louis Begley and dealing not with the comparatively recent events in Germany, but the World War Two Holocaust.

A unit was duly despatched to Potsdam, sending back 'hundreds of photographs of the location which Kubrick then analysed and sent back his instructions', according to the *Guardian*, although their source ultimately claimed that the production had never reached the casting stage, and that Kubrick had simply 'pulled the plug.' What seems likely - as James B. Harris confirmed to me - is that the subject matter of the film was proving to be just a little too close in subject matter to Steven Spielberg's monumental *Schindler's List*, in production at roughly the same time. Having been accused in some quarters of producing *Full Metal Jacket* at a time when Vietnam pictures were suddenly 'fashionable' (actually an unsustainable argument given that his picture had been in production two years before either *Platoon* or *Hamburger Hill*), Kubrick had probably decided not to chance the same unfounded criticism again.

If Spielberg's holocaust picture had caused him to abandon *Aryan Papers* then, ironically, it was the release of *Jurassic Park* with its groundbreaking special effects and computer-generated images which rekindled Kubrick's interest in *A.I.* - reported in November 1993 by the *Los Angeles Times* as 'definitely' in production.

A brief outline of the story - considerably removed by this time from *Super-Toys* - set the picture in a postgreenhouse effect world in which a flooded New York has all but disappeared, and is run by androids who have developed the ability to think and age as humans. A pre-*Titanic* James Cameron - with effects-heavy productions *The Terminator* (1984) , *Aliens* (1986) and *The Abyss* (1989) behind him - was among those invited to St Albans to discuss special effects following the release of his own 1994 movie *True Lies*, later telling *Wired* that Kubrick 'showed me some of the artwork for *A.I.* There was a lot of water interaction stuff - very difficult.' Cameron confessed to being 'really honored' by the invitation, although he later said 'it turns out he does this with everybody. He's like a brain vampire. He likes to get people and suck what they're doing out of their heads.'

Also consulted was Dennis Muren, effects supervisor for the famed Industrial Light and Magic workshop (who had worked on *Jurassic Park*), only for Kubrick to then decide to create the effects himself at his home workshop - or perhaps not, as *Wired* noted that Muren had again been approached to work on the movie, but was by then involved with Spielberg's *Jurassic Park* sequel, *The Lost World* (1997). Brian Aldiss, meanwhile - despite his likely exclusion from further involvement with the production - still felt that 'Stanley definitely had the ambition to make another big science-fiction movie,' although he also felt the director 'hasn't got the dashing confidence of youth - but, of course, with age, you acquire a different sort of confidence.'

Not content with this, an internet rumours site revealed that the story had been secretly filming 'for two months every five years, using a young actor (again rumoured to be Joseph Mazzello) and filming his progress as he grows older.' Fascinating stuff, although it does sound rather more like Michael Apted's admirable *7-Up* etc. ongoing television documentary series than any feasible idea for a movie. What about the rest of the cast? What about retakes? The rumour-monger nevertheless boldly announced that 'So far Kubrick has filmed four months/ten years.'

A Warner Bros press release dated 15 December 1995 finally announced that 'Stanley Kubrick's next film will be *Eyes Wide Shut*, a story of jealousy and sexual obsession, starring Tom Cruise and Nicole Kidman. Filming is planned to start in London in the summer of 1996.' The statement further said that '*A.I.* - believed to be one of the most technically challenging and innovative special effects films yet attempted - is in the final stages of set design and special effects development, and will follow *Eyes Wide Shut*.' Was it at all likely after a decade away from active movie-making that Kubrick would embark on two major productions virtually back-to-back? The prospect was indeed mouth-watering, with further rumours posted daily, including the unconfirmed suggestion that Warner Bros had prevailed on the director to first complete *Eyes Wide Shut* with the highly bankable Cruise/Kidman team before embarking on the mammoth - and no doubt costly - science-fiction spectacle which *A.I.* was likely to prove.

It was mid-1996 before any apparently reliable information was forthcoming on Kubrick's return to filming, with Douglas Milsome telling the *Guardian* that he had 'talked with Stanley many times recently. I start probably about mid-June, I'd say.' Following his work on *Full Metal Jacket*, the cameraman had worked on a handful of big budget movies - *The Beast* (1988), a remake of *The Desperate Hours* (1990) and the hugely successful *Robin Hood: Prince of Thieves* (1991) - but was to be found at other times locked into the endless treadmill of mini-series' for American television. Respectable productions of *Great Expectations*, *The Old Curiosity Shop* and the epic western saga *Lonesome Dove* were nevertheless followed by the dross of *Diana: Her True Story* and *Liz: The Elizabeth Taylor Story* - Milsome's most recent assignment had been a feature-length revival of much-unmissed seventies series *Hart to Hart*. Of the upcoming Kubrick project, he declared himself 'very honoured when [Stanley] asked me to come back, and very proud to accept. I don't like to say much more - in fact, I don't know much more.'

Novelist and screenwriter Frederic Raphael (Oscar-winner for *Darling* in 1965) revealed that he had worked with Kubrick on what could well be the screenplay to the new film, although the writer's agent claimed not to know even the title of the work. Raphael meanwhile offered an opinion of his co-writer as 'a hard master to please, but among the charlatans in the business he is one worth pleasing.'

The Sunday Times celebrated the news of Kubrick's teaming with Cruise and Kidman on *Eyes Wide Open* [sic] as 'an encounter of the beauties and the beast' in an astonishing - and shamelessly padded - article dismissing Kubrick as a 'brilliant bully.' Un-named 'friends' expressed themselves fearful of the two young stars' sanity during their tenure with 'the most feared director in Britain,' as the ill-informed piece - devoid of any direct recent quotes - recycled the same old, unsubstantiated stories, mostly drawn from Kubrick's most recent - and typically ill-serving - unofficial biographer. To spice things up further, the story inaccurately added that the to-follow *A.I.* would be 'based on an Isaac Asimov short story about sex between computers.'

Even by Kubrick standards, however, the news blackout on *Eyes Wide Shut* was total, so that - as late as February 1998 - Julian Senior, Kubrick's virtual 'spokesman' at Warner Brothers and, officially, Senior Vice President in charge of European Advertising and Publicity, would only confirm 'the information that you have is all we have at this stage. This is par for the course with Mr Kubrick... He will not be making himself available for interviews, with a possible exception of a selected group of major magazines and newspapers. His work ethos is very pragmatic. The interviews will be aimed at supporting the release of the film.'

Rumours continued to surface on the internet - a source which had been virtually non-existent during the making of Kubrick's last picture. Some stories were more convincing than others - a few were even true: Harvey Keitel and Jennifer Jason Leigh were among the cast by the time shooting began in November 1996, although Keitel was to be replaced a few months later by Sydney Pollack, who - although he and Kubrick had never actually met face to face - had been in regular phone contact with him over the years, and was considered an old 'friend'. More usually a director himself, Pollack's list of credits included *Tootsie* (1982, in which he also acted) and a half dozen or so pictures starring Robert Redford (*Jeremiah Johnson*, *Three Days of the Condor*), as well as *The Firm* (1993) - in which he directed Tom Cruise.

Keitel's exit was, not surprisingly, the subject of much conjecture - inevitably inviting the suggestion that he and Kubrick had clashed artistically, although other evidence pointed to the actor's commitment - after an unexpected six months of shooting - to another production, *The Road to Graceland*, in which he would play Elvis Presley. Nicole Kidman later confirmed to an interviewer that Keitel had 'left amicably amid scheduling problems.'

The literary source of *Eyes Wide Shut* was finally - in December 1997 - revealed as a long out-of-print 1926 novella by Arthur Schnitzler, best known for his book and play *La Ronde*, filmed by Max Ophuls in 1950. The work which had inspired *Eyes Wide Shut* was *Traumnovelle*, published in English as *Rhapsody: A Dream Novel*. Originally set in Vienna during the nineteenth century, the story, in the book, takes place over a single night and concerns a respectable doctor falling into a series of sexual encounters with a sordid underworld. Kubrick had updated the story, which was now set in New York.

Traumnovelle had been mentioned as early as 1971, when Kubrick told Michel Ciment that he was keen to film the story, although he had 'not yet started to work' on it. 'It's a difficult book to describe,' he said, adding 'what good book isn't?' before giving a brief summary of the plot, which 'explores the sexual ambivalence of a happy marriage, and tries to equate the importance of sexual dreams and might-have-beens with reality.' Schnitzler's work, said the director, was 'psychologically brilliant, and greatly admired by Freud,' although he was far from being a household name. The book was again mentioned in press reports - entirely wrongly - a year later as the possible basis of the movie which eventually turned out to *Barry Lyndon*.

Others assumed - wrongly - that Kubrick was in fact acting out the scenario outlined in Terry Southern's novel *Blue Movie*, which had been spurred by his conversations with the director many years before. Some sought parallels with the megalomaniac moviemaker 'Boris' and Stanley Kubrick in the casting of a 'world famous couple' to appear in the film within the book - though whereas *Blue Movie*'s movie was unashamedly no more than a porn flick, *Eyes Wide Shut* promised to be an erotic suspense thriller.

Tom Cruise and Nicole Kidman, it was reported, had been tentatively approached with an offer of working with Stanley Kubrick, with no further details given. According to *The Sunday Times*, Kubrick allowed them to see a script only once before signing a contract, although Kidman later told *Vanity Fair* 'I would have agreed to do it even if he hadn't shown it to me.' While reports made much of the enormous sums of money that the stars were 'losing' by agreeing to an 'open-ended' contract - which meant that they would continue working on the picture until Kubrick agreed to release them, however long that might be - Kidman denied that there was any hardship involved: 'You don't think that way artistically,' she said (and, it has to be said, if Cruise could command $15 - 20 million per film, he could likely afford to spend longer on this movie than usual).

The Cruise family - the stars and their two adopted children - had already been resident in London for the making of *Mission: Impossible*, and stayed on to work with Kubrick, renting a house within walking distance of Pinewood Studios, where *Eyes Wide Shut* was in production. Kidman revealed that there had been a high number of takes involved on occasion, but that 'the thing is that you know you're working with someone who cares. He lives and breathes movies, and he makes so few that he enjoys the process that much more; he wants to explore all the possibilities.' This suggestion that Kubrick actually enjoyed film-making was one which had often been overlooked. He had previously explained his involvement with the hand-held camera shots on *A Clockwork Orange* by saying that it was 'more fun' to do it yourself. How many other directors refer to the job as 'fun'?

As for Kubrick's demands on the stars, it was said that he rarely asked them to work at weekends - the couple were seen at the Westminster Abbey funeral service for Diana, Princess of Wales in September 1997 alongside Steven Spielberg and Tom Hanks - both in England filming *Saving Private Ryan* - and Kidman further explained that she would be 'really sad when it ends, actually. It's been such a period of our lives.' One of the film's many extras described the atmosphere on set where, he said, 'Tom, Nicole and Stanley had an excellent relationship as far as I could see - there was no tension or anything of that sort.' This particular extra spent some six weeks on the movie, working on just one scene. 'Stanley paid very close attention to detail,' he says, 'but he was very fair and spent lots of time helping, coaching and guiding all parties so they were able to give their best... some shoots were until three or four in the morning, and we were getting grumpy,' says the source, 'but Stanley was fine. He never raised his voice or became agitated.'

Shooting continued, with exteriors filmed in central London in and around Hatton Garden and Worship

Street - the locations heavily disguised as New York - as well as specially constructed sets at Pinewood. Insiders offered revelations that Kubrick had hired the toy department of Selfridges in Oxford Street, but then decided to film at Harrods instead - or maybe it was Hamleys in Regent Street. Luton Hoo - an impressive stately home - was the setting for either a party scene, or merely a month of rehearsals, depending on who you believed. A London Soho transvestite bar called Madame JoJo's was transformed into a New York night club, prompting rumours that Tom Cruise's character cross-dresses in the film. Other reports claimed that Nicole Kidman played a heroin addict in the story, and had been coached on-set by a leading clinical psychiatrist in simulating a realistic injection, filmed in 70mm black and white. Kidman would only tell reporters that the director 'deals with me and Tom separately,' adding that 'when you see the film you'll understand why.'

Tales of a huge masked ball featuring 'hundreds of extras' and a smaller 'masked orgy' filtered through as further cast members were named, including Alan Cumming, Vinessa Shaw and Thomas Gibson - who had worked with both Cruise and Kidman on *Far and Away* (1992) - before filming was reported as officially completed on 31 January 1998, after something like four hundred days - the longest official shoot in film history. Despite this, the total cost of the movie was said to still be within the agreed budget - a relatively modest $65 million - partly as a result of Kubrick's traditionally small crew, which prompted Kidman to compare it to 'almost like making a student film.'

Within weeks, however, Kubrick was said to be unhappy with Jennifer Jason Leigh's performance, and calling her back for retakes - although by April it was announced that she was 'currently filming in Canada with David Cronenberg, [and] would be unavailable to do a few days of shooting on the cameo scene she played with Tom Cruise in *Eyes Wide Shut*.' Interestingly, her character was now revealed as a 'cameo' whereas it had previously been thought to be major. 'The role will now be played by Marie Richardson,' the statement continued, describing her as 'one of Ingmar Bergman's leading actresses.' Cruise and Kidman would both also be needed again, as the picture went back into production.

Behind the camera, Douglas Milsome had not joined Kubrick's crew after all, and in the period that *Eyes Wide Shut* continued shooting, completed four other movies - mainly action adventures including

Breakdown (1997), starring Kurt Russell, and *Legionnaire* (1998), with the equally heroic Jean Claude van Damme. No formal announcement was made concerning Milsome's 'replacement', eventually revealed as Larry Smith, whose association with the director stretched back 25 years. Hired as chief electrician on *Barry Lyndon*, Smith's later credits appear to amount to little more than 'driver' on *My Demon Lover* (1987) and *Beastmaster III* (1995). Amazingly, *Eyes Wide Shut* was to be his first major work as cinematographer.

Other crew members remained similarly anonymous, although the music score - said by Warner chairman Terry Semel to be 'principally classical, and Stanley wanted to add a few beats to it' - was again the subject of some conjecture. Producer Goldie was 'in discussion' with Kubrick over his possible contribution, while Jocelyn Pook - founder of eight piece ensemble the Electra Strings - was said to have been 'commissioned' to work on the picture, which would again be edited by Nigel Galt (retained from *Full Metal Jacket*).

If Warners were nervous about the achingly slow progress of the picture - as they probably had every right to be - they were certainly not giving anything away to the press, although gossip columns carried unconfirmed rumours that studio executives were unhappy with the lack of any firm release date and, as a result of Kubrick's agreement with the company, the fact that they were not allowed to see any of the film until it was completed. One of the more fanciful reports claimed that 'industry insiders say it may be too bizarre ever to go on general release.' Meanwhile, the movie's premiere was pushed back, firstly from autumn 1997 to summer 1998 to November to December and, finally confirmed via the first official entry on the Warners *Eyes Wide Shut* web site in October which read simply '*Eyes Wide Shut* 16th July 1999.'

Although Kidman had been interviewed by Vanity Fair - carefully avoiding any comment which might reveal the nature of her role or of the plot itself other than to pronounce various rumours as 'absolutely wrong' - Cruise remained silent throughout the two years he had been involved with Kubrick, allowing those with nothing better to do to surmise that he was unhappy with the movie and with his treatment at the hands of the 'tyrant' director. He finally spoke at the Toronto Film Festival in September, enthusing 'There are some things you don't do for the money. To have a chance to work with Stanley Kubrick, that's worth it for

---

*As if to emphasize the non-financially led nature of their choice of work, Cruise and Kidman remained in the UK several months after completing their work on *Eyes Wide Shut*, with Kidman making a highly publicized and low-paid (£250 per week) West End stage debut (at the Donmar Warehouse - with Kubrick in the audience) in a notably erotic version of Schnitzler's *La Ronde*, under the title of *The Blue Room*, before the play transferred to Broadway.

me.' The star further praised the director's methods by adding 'Suddenly he'll say something to you, or you'll see how he creates a shot, and you realise this man is different, this man is profound. And it seems without effort.' Confirming that he had 'never seen a movie made this way,' Cruise found Kubrick to be 'demanding and surprising, but not unreasonable' - this despite rumours that he had been asked to repeat one scene 93 times. Even with almost 18 months spent on the picture - although he revealed that the shoot itself 'probably took ten months... there were times he gave us time off' - Cruise insisted that Kubrick 'doesn't waste any time, he's not indulgent - he works seven days a week.'

With the film in the can - though Kubrick would not deliver it to Warner Brothers until early 1999 - 16-year old French actress Leelee Sobieski told *Neon* magazine that she had won a place in the movie after sending two video auditions - reportedly scripted for her by 'Quentin Tarantino's writer.' Describing Kubrick as 'an elegant, caring man, so cool,' she confirmed the director's on-set appearance - previously remarked on by several of those who had worked with him - as consisting of a 'black smock with lots of pockets which he wore every day. He didn't smell bad or anything, though, so he must have lots of them.' Sobieski still did not reveal anything concerning the actual film itself, other than that she had been 'only meant to be there for two weeks, but I spent two months filming. I was supposed to do something else in that time, but I wasn't allowed to leave.'

Although the final cut version of *Eyes Wide Shut* would normally have been screened under the director's supervision in London for studio executives, Kubrick was happy to accommodate his now US-based stars (Kidman was still in *The Blue Room* on Broadway - although currently absent through illness - while Cruise was about to fly to Australia for *Mission: Impossible II*) and sent the sole print of the movie with an assistant to New York where, at Warner Brothers' Fifth Avenue headquarters, on Tuesday 2 March, Cruise, Kidman, Warner co-chairmen Terry Semel and Robert Daley formed the entire audience of this long-awaited first screening - even the projectionist, it was reported, was asked to turn away from the screen!

The response to the picture was extraordinary - one Warner source said that 'Nicole and Tom were both weeping - Nicole kept saying "He was like a father figure to me"' - while Semel later said 'the part that blew us was that it's a terrific suspense thriller. It's a wonderful film - really challenging and filled with suspense.'

With the film flown back to Childwickbury immediately, only minor adjustments remained - titles and 'a couple of color corrections, and some technical things,' said Semel. The next day, former Warners production chief John Calley spoke to Kubrick by phone and found him to be 'so excited because Terry and Bob had seen his film and they loved it. Nicole and Tom had seen it and they loved it. I've never heard him as excited about a film.' On Saturday, Kubrick spent an hour talking with Semel about an upcoming ShoWest convention in Las Vegas the following Wednesday, at which a 90-second teaser/trailer would be shown - a specially chosen sequence of Cruise fondling Kidman in front of a mirror, with both stars nude, and accompanied by a surprisingly raucous - but highly appropriate - blues soundtrack.

'We were all on cloud nine,' said Semel. '[Stanley] was thrilled with the collective reaction all four of us had to the film. He called me again an hour later to tell me a joke he had heard.' In the afternoon, Kubrick discussed with Julian Senior the promotion of the film: 'He said, "Get me a list of the top four or five magazines and the best writers. We'll do a few interviews"' - a sign that Kubrick was preparing to go public again as - no doubt encouraged by Tom Cruise's successful recent action - he had even filed a libel suit against *Punch* magazine over an article published in August 1998, and seemed intent on attending the hearing in person.

That aside, however, the initial reaction to *Eyes Wide Shut* had been entirely positive, with Kubrick telling Julian Senior 'It's my best film ever.' Terry Semel would relate afterwards that 'Stanley definitely went to sleep that night with a smile on his face.'

BEYOND THE INFINITE

Early March and, even as parts of the country suffered heavy flooding from burst river banks caused by unusually heavy and persistent rain, the promise of the English Spring seemed daily to be in the air. Buds began to appear on the trees and bushes, and the first prematurely blooming daffodils cautiously opened their bright yellow faces to the light.

Stanley Kubrick did not wake to see the watery sun rise on that Sunday 7 March 1999. A statement released later that day by a family spokesman read simply 'We regret to announce that he died early this morning. There is no further comment.' He was five months short of his 71st birthday.

As in Kubrick's life, immediate details were hard to come by, as Hertfordshire police said only that they had been called to Childwickbury by a local doctor. Other than the police-speak confirmation that 'there were no suspicious circumstances,' nothing further was to be forthcoming until a statement issued a few days later, when an autopsy had revealed the director died of 'natural causes.'

Instantly, tributes were paid to probably the last great director of the studio era - although Kubrick's independence had seen him transcend that same era. Terry Semel and Robert Daley of Warner Brothers were 'deeply saddened by the loss of Stanley Kubrick, a towering figure in the world of film and a deeply loved and respected member of the Warner family for nearly three decades.' Confirming that they had just seen *Eyes Wide Shut*, the co-chairmen described it as 'a fitting close to a tremendous career. We look forward to sharing this movie when it is released as planned this summer and believe that it is a tribute to a remarkable and unforgettable man. We will miss him very much.'

Steven Spielberg called him 'the grand master of film-making. He copied no-one while all of us were scrambling to imitate him,' and again confirmed that Kubrick had been 'terribly misunderstood as a recluse just because he didn't do a lot of press. He actually communicated more than many people I know. When we spoke on the phone, our conversations lasted for hours. He was constantly in contact with hundreds of people all over the world.' Long-time friend and Warner associate Julian Senior reiterated this: 'Stanley didn't want a photo spread about himself in *Hello!* magazine, but he was aware of everything going on and especially what was going on with his beloved New York Yankees. He loved life, he loved chess, he loved

documentaries. He was not reclusive at all.'

Over the next few days, comments appeared from a variety of people - some less qualified than others - about the Stanley Kubrick they 'knew'. Oliver Stone declared for the benefit of the world media that 'He was the single greatest American director of his generation. He influenced me deeply.'

James B. Harris told the *Observer* that he had 'spent a lot of this week reading about a man I don't recognize. I haven't read about the guy I would watch football with, have a beer with, talk about music with, the guy who was my pal. What I most remember is the fun I had speaking to him. Football one minute, then the next he would tell you what was going on in the world of thermo-nuclear development. You were never bored.'

Harris further revealed that Kubrick was 'always watching movies, new movies. They would come to him. He would get prints. He knew what was going on in Los Angeles, and would read the trade press. The beauty, though, as he saw it, was that he didn't have to deal directly with all the people in Hollywood.' Malcolm McDowell had also 'felt lots of disgust since his death. People talking about Stanley Kubrick who are not even qualified to talk about a black pudding.'

McDowell - whose previously reported negative feelings about Kubrick had apparently stemmed largely from an expectation of 'the relationship I had had with Lindsay Anderson. He had needed me for every frame, then didn't need me any more. Later we resumed contact' - had clearly resolved some of his differences with the director by now, and was a further witness to Kubrick's deliberate aloofness toward the centre of the US industry. 'He'd keep in touch all the time,' McDowell noted, but 'he knew that it was easier to control that world from a distance.'

Attention turned now to *Eyes Wide Shut*, especially following the 10 March screening of the 84 second trailer at the Las Vegas ShoWest convention, which went ahead at the insistence of Kubrick's widow Christiane, who said the event had 'meant a great deal' to Kubrick. The trade audience was reported to be 'stunned' by the explicit nature of the clip, although Terry Semel announced that he expected the film to receive an R rating in the US. Earlier reports had suggested that Warner Bros might press Kubrick to avoid the film being classified NC-17 (barring anyone under seventeen), which could seriously affect the profit-

Kubrick behind the camera.

him to recall movies - *2001* and *The Shining* - for further cuts even after their initial public screenings, to be re-released only when he was satisfied with the result. As alarmists claimed that this left the status of *Eyes Wide Shut* as still not officially finished - and that it may yet go unreleased - or that the studio would now impose their own cut on the picture, the Warner chairman confirmed that 'when he showed the movie, it was his final version.' Tom Cruise added that 'anyone trying to cut this movie would have to go through me. It's Stanley's film.'

At the end of a frantic and traumatic week, a small group gathered at Childwickbury on Friday for Stanley Kubrick's private funeral. Among those present were Tom Cruise, Nicole Kidman, Terry Semel, Robert Daley, James B. Harris, Steven Spielberg and Alan Yentob, BBC head of programming who as editor of the *Arena* programme had negotiated the television screening of Vivian Kubrick's *Making of The Shining* documentary almost twenty years before, and now named the director as 'a good friend... incredibly loveable. Contrary to his reputation, he wasn't difficult or stand-offish. He was a great enthusiast who gave freely of his time.'

In contrast to the extravagant public funeral of singer Dusty Springfield - held the same day and which brought her home town to a standstill as the procession made its way through crowd-lined streets to a church relaying her Greatest Hits by loudspeaker to those outside - no details or information concerning Kubrick's service were made public, with only invited and authorized persons allowed through the electronic gates to the estate. A news report later noted that 'after dark, a small firework display lit up the rain-soaked countryside around his home, Childwickbury Manor.'

making potential of the movie. Semel, however, insisted that he and Kubrick had discussed this, and that the aimed-for R rating 'was not only our deal, it was what Stanley wanted - for the film to be available to the masses.'

Kubrick's total control over his work had allowed

A SORT OF CONCLUSION

In June 1998, to mark the centenary of motion pictures, the American Film Institute released its list of the 100 Greatest Films Ever Made, compiled by 'AFI's blue-ribbon panel of more than 1500 leaders of the American movie community' - an enterprise which many other organizations, publications and armchair critics had already attempted with predictably controversial results.

Heading the list was, not surprisingly, *Citizen Kane*, followed by *Casablanca* (1942) and *The Godfather* (1972). The full 100 - although its apparent purpose had been to find the Best American films - put *2001: A Space Odyssey* in 22nd position, with *Dr Strangelove* four places behind it and *A Clockwork Orange* at No. 46.

The result apparently confirmed Stanley Kubrick's continuing relevance to American cinema - despite all three movies being made in the UK (where a British Film Institute 'Treasures from the Archive' inventory had named 360 titles of exceptional merit, including *Paths of Glory*, *Lolita* and *2001*). The AFI selection, however, also indicated that Kubrick's 'golden period' was still to be regarded as running from the 1964 release of *Dr Strangelove* to that of *A Clockwork Orange* seven years later. Those pictures that followed - *Barry Lyndon*, *The Shining* and *Full Metal Jacket* - may have their admirers, but are clearly not held in the same wide regard as his work of the sixties.

With increasingly lengthy periods between his films of the 80s and 90s,the director was running the risk that critical opinion would lean towards disappointment after such prolonged anticipation, though it is difficult to recall any other film-maker who has generated that level of sustained interest over such a period. Kubrick's oft-questioned working methods - can that amount of care and attention be noticeably reflected in the finished picture? - seemed almost at odds with his own comment that 'some of the most spectacular examples of film art are to be found in the best television commercials' which, by their very nature, are often made relatively quickly and inexpensively. (Malcolm McDowell considered 'Kubrick's problem, I suppose, is that he was an obsessive working in the great collaborative medium. When you are making a film, you are often only as strong as the weakest link in the chain. That's why he wanted to do everything himself, and it took so long.')

In the March 1985 edition of *Film Dope*, Richard Chatten even bemoaned the quality of Kubrick's output, claiming that only the two 1950s collaborations with Jim Thompson - *The Killing* and *Paths of Glory* - had been wholly satisfactory, and 'serve as a reminder to his critics of just how succinct the lad could be once upon a time, or as a deeply depressing one to those of us who have gaped helplessly at the recent spectacle of extravagant waste.' Reflecting that Sam Fuller was reportedly sitting on some 300 or so unproduced scripts, Chatten offered the suggestion that 'somebody really ought to give Stanley a swift clip around the ear, thrust one of those scripts into his hands and give him just two weeks in which to shoot it, preferably in black-and-white.'

All superficially very interesting, except that this would have denied us the spectacle of *2001: A Space Odyssey*, the power of *A Clockwork Orange* or the sheer beauty of *Barry Lyndon* and, whatever one feels about *The Shining*, it is a film which has provoked considerable comment, as did *Full Metal Jacket* on its release. The likelihood of Kubrick returning to small-scale 'quickies' at such a point in his career was clearly as remote as the remaining members of The Beatles regrouping to perform at Litherland Town Hall.

For the record, in 1963 Stanley Kubrick named the following as his own personal list of favourite films:
1. *I Vitelloni* (Federico Fellini)
2. *Wild Strawberries* (Ingmar Bergman)
3. *Citizen Kane* (Orson Welles)
4. *Treasure of the Sierra Madre* (John Huston)
5. *City Lights* (Charles Chaplin)
6. *Henry V* (Laurence Olivier)
7. *La Notte* (Michelangelo Antonioni)
8. *The Bank Dick* (W.C. Fields)
9. *Roxie Hart* (William Wellman)
10. *Hell's Angels* (Howard Hughes)

With a further 35 years of moviewatching, who knows what this list might have been in 1999?

When I initially 'finished' this book, the closing paragraphs read as follows:

"Whatever else one might feel about his movies, Kubrick certainly shows no sign of going soft on us: In July 1998, he reached the age of 70 as the cutting of *Eyes Wide Shut* continued, with the promise of *A.I.* to follow. At a similar age, John Huston was preparing to inflict the dreadful and wholly unnecessary *Annie* on the world, Alfred Hitchcock was churning out the least impressive movies of his life (*Torn Curtain*, *Topaz*), Orson Welles was dead, not having made a wholly satisfactory picture since *Chimes at Midnight*, twenty years earlier, and William Wyler, John Ford, Frank Capra, King Vidor and Billy Wilder had all faded quietly into retirement or 'advisory' roles.

Whatever their past glories, few film directors have retained such a cynical and enquiring edge as they grew older. Having made what amounted to definitive science-fiction, anti-war and nightmare-comedy statements, Kubrick's *A.I.* promises to further explore his deep pessimism about humanity. Brian Aldiss reflects that 'Stanley thinks androids may eventually take over - and be an improvement over the human race.' Could this be the picture that tops the lot? As always, he isn't saying - but Stanley Kubrick clearly hasn't finished with us yet..."

A.I. now seems destined to remain unfilmed, while *Eyes Wide Shut* will be, as Terry Semel promises, a 'fitting close to a remarkable career' - pushing cinema further again than it would comfortably prefer to go. Perhaps Stanley Kubrick's legacy is that he indeed has not finished with us yet - what follows will always be influenced by the best of what went before, and 'the best' would be incomplete without Stanley Kubrick.

As a private rumination, it may be worth noting one of the fundamental differences between Kubrick and many of these other directors, most of whom were to be photographed on numerous occasions with absurdly huge cigars stuffed in their mouths, as though this somehow signified the extent of their greatness. Stanley Kubrick, so far as I can tell, never struck such a symbolic pose for the camera. As James B. Harris says, 'he was not insecure.'

✳ ✳ ✳

On the Saturday afternoon two weeks after Kubrick's death, I received a telephone call from someone identifying himself as 'Stanley Kubrick's assistant' - I was able to confirm this later with a technician who had worked with Kubrick and had also had recent contact with the same assistant - who said he was 'clearing up a few loose ends, going through Stanley's correspondence,' and had come across one of the letters I had sent to him a few months earlier (one of which included a first draft of the opening "Stanley Kubrick and Me" chapter to this book).

As I absorbed the fact that my letters had actually reached their target - 'Stanley received everything,' I was told - the assistant related a conversation which took place in January or thereabouts, where 'Stanley asked me if I knew who you were. I told him you'd done a very good book on Micky Powell, which I had a copy of, and he was quite interested in what you were doing.'

More was to come - 'Stanley said he would be in touch with you once he had finished with *Eyes Wide Shut*, although of course he never managed to get around to it, since he was working eighteen hours a day on the film.' Forgive me if I just repeat that - Stanley Kubrick was aware that I was writing this book, had read some of it - and was interested enough in what I was doing to get in touch.

I think back to an Alexander Walker article I read some time ago in which it was said that, if Kubrick wanted to speak to you, he would manage it somehow - even if you were on the other side of the planet. Steven Spielberg had related tales of Kubrick's generosity - 'when he loved someone's movie, he would pick up the phone and call a complete stranger to say how much his or her movie had impressed him. To those of us who were lucky enough to know him, he was a teddy bear - kind and compassionate.'

Despite the horror stories, the rumours, the myths, the difficulties in tracking down people who had worked with him in the past (some, I came to realise, had already spoken with Kubrick's two most recent biographers, so were probably suspicious of how their contribution might be used, or else were simply 'talked out') in the end I think my instincts were right about Kubrick. The more I got to 'know' him, the more I seemed to like him, and if circumstances had been different, then that phone call at three o'clock on that Saturday afternoon could have been Stanley Kubrick himself.

FURTHER READING

I deliberately avoided reading any of the standard biographies on Stanley Kubrick – notably Alexander Walker's *Stanley Kubrick Directs* (1971) and the more recent tomes by John Baxter and Vincent LoBrutto, whose reviews suggested that they had not uncovered anything new about the man. Michel Ciment's *Kubrick* has the advantage over most of us in that it contains three lengthy interviews with the director – extended and corrected by Kubrick himself.

Those publications, articles, journals and books I did consult included the collected reviews and editions of the *New York Times, Monthly Film Bulletin, American Cinematographer, Variety* and *Sight and Sound*, as well as the following:

Beahm, George., *The Stephen King Story*, Little, Brown & Co., 1992

Brosnan, John., *Future Tense*, Macdonald, 1978

Burgess, Anthony., *A Clockwork Orange*, Heinemann, 1971

Cahill, Tim., 'Stanley Kubrick: The Rolling Stone Interview', *Rolling Stone*, 1987

Chase, Chris., 'Now I'll Tell You How to be a Movie Star', *New York Times*, 1971

Ciment, Michel., *Kubrick*, Collins, 1983

Clarke, Arthur C., *2001: A Space Odyssey*, Hutchinson, 1968

Clarke, Arthur C., *The Lost Worlds of 2001*, Macmillan, 1972

Curtis, Tony and Paris, Barry., *Tony Curtis: The Autobiography*, Heinemann, 1994

Douglas, Kirk., *The Ragman's Son*, Simon & Schuster, 1988

Glatt, John., *The Chieftains*, Century Publishing, 1997

Hayden, Sterling., *Wanderer*, Longmans, 1963

Huston, John., *An Open Book*, Macmillan, 1980

King, Stephen., *The Shining*, New English Library, 1977

Lack, Russell., *24 Frames Under – A Buried History of Film Music*, Quartet Books, 1997

Larkin, Patrick., 'The Stanley Kubrick Multimedia Film Guide' internet web site

Levy, Adrian and Scott-Clark, Cathy., 'America's Unknown Soldier', *Sunday Times*, September 1998

Lewis, Roger., *The Life and Death of Peter Sellers*, Century Publishing, 1994

McGilligan, Patrick., *Jack's Life*, Hutchinson, 1995

Manso, Peter., *Brando*, Weidenfeld & Nicolson, 1994

Mason James., *Before I Forget*, Hamish Hamilton, 1981

Millar, Peter., 'The Bomb', *Sunday Times* magazine, July 1995

Nabokov, Vladimir., *Lolita,* Weidenfeld and Nicolson, 1955

Parisi, Paula., 'The Intelligence Behind A.I', *Wired*, January 1997

Parsons, Tony and Black, Johnny., 'A Clockwork Orange', *Empire*, December 1993

Rique., 'Stanley Kubrick, The Master Film-maker' internet web site

Strick, Philip and Houston, Penelope., 'Interview with Stanley Kubrick', *Sight and Sound*, Spring 1972

Thackeray, Willam Makepeace., *Barry Lyndon*, first published in 1884

Ustinov, Peter., *Dear Me*, William Heinemann, 1977

Winters, Shelley., *Shelley II*, Simon & Schuster, 1989

INDEX

E

Ermey, Lee 160, 166, 167
Eyes Wide Shut 17, 18, 21, 22, 24, 175-181, 184

F

Fail Safe 93
Fast, Howard 65, 66, 71
Fear and Desire 15, 33-35, 37, 38, 45, 124, 143
Flippen, Jay C. 48
Flying Padre 31
Flynn, Errol 77, 78
Fried, Gerald 37, 48
Full Metal Jacket 18, 19, 20, 159-170, 175-177, 179, 183

G

George, Peter 91, 93
Griffith, D. W. 19, 23

H

Halliwell, Leslie 60, 132, 142
Harris, James B. 15, 17, 18, 20, 22, 23, 45-50, 55-58, 60-62, 67, 68, 70, 72, 77, 79, 80, 82, 83, 85, 91, 98, 176, 181, 182
Hasford, Gustav 162, 169
Hayden, Sterling 21, 46-48, 50, 94, 97
Herr, Michael, 163
Hitchcock, Alfred 16, 19, 67, 130, 184
House of Unamerican Activities 45, 65, 66
Huston, John 23, 37, 46-48, 50, 55, 83, 184

I

I stole $16 million 22, 72

J

Johnson, Diane 149, 150
Jurassic Park 20, 176, 177

K

Kane, Irene 15, 37, 38
Karlin, Miriam 124, 129
Keitel, Harvey 162, 177, 178
Kidman, Nicole 23, 177-180, 182
Killer's Kiss 15, 29, 34, 36-38, 45-47, 50, 57
Killing, The 15, 21, 29, 43-51, 55, 58, 61, 79
King, Stephen 149, 154-156
Kubrick, Christiane 15, 61, 181
Kubrick, Vivian 15, 111, 152-154, 168, 182

L

Laughton, Charles 68, 79, 151
Lean, David 21, 66, 116, 164
Leigh, Jennifer Jason 177, 179
Ligeti, Gyorgy 111
Lloyd, Danny 150, 151
Lockwood, Gary 106, 109, 110
Lolita 15, 17, 22, 62, 67, 72-85, 149, 168, 183, 185
Look magazine 14, 29, 30, 37
Lucas, George 21, 71, 115, 149
Lyne, Adrian 84, 85
Lyon, Sue 76, 79, 80, 82-84

M

N

O

P

R

S

T

U

W